# SECURE
*in*
# HEART

# SECURE *in* HEART

## OVERCOMING INSECURITY IN A WOMAN'S LIFE

## ROBIN WEIDNER

DPI
DISCIPLESHIP
PUBLICATIONS
INTERNATIONAL

www.dpibooks.org

**Secure in Heart**
© 2006 by Discipleship Publications International
300 Fifth Avenue
Fifth Floor
Waltham, Massachusetts 02451

All Scripture quotations, unless indicated, are taken from
the NEW INTERNATIONAL VERSION.
Copyright ©1973, 1978, 1984 by the International Bible Society.
Used by permission of Zondervan Publishing House.
All rights reserved.

The "NIV" and "New International Version" trademarks
are registered in the United States Patent Trademark Office
by the International Bible Society.
Use of either trademark requires the permission of
the International Bible Society.

Printed in the United States of America

ISBN: 1-57782-207-2

Cover Design: Christine Nye/Canary Design
Front Photo Credit: Robin Weidner
Back Photo Credit: David Barrow/OC Imageworks
Interior Design: Thais Gloor

To my mother,
my sister Jennifer,
and my sister in Christ, Terri

The Spirit of the Sovereign LORD is on me,
    because the LORD has anointed me
    to preach the good news to the poor.
He has sent me to bind up the brokenhearted,
    to proclaim freedom for the captives
    and release from darkness for the prisoners,
To proclaim the year of the LORD's favor
    and the day of vengeance of our God,
to comfort all who mourn,
    and provide for those who grieve in Zion—
to bestow on them a crown of beauty
    instead of ashes,
the oil of gladness
    instead of mourning,
and a garment of praise
    instead of a spirit of despair.
They will be called oaks of righteousness
    a planting of the LORD
    for the display of his splendor.

                    Isaiah 61:1–3

# SECURE IN HEART
*Overcoming Insecurity in a Woman's Life*

Introduction .................................................................9

PART ONE — *The Secure Foundation*
1. The Beginning of Security:
   Mapping Out the Battlefield.............................17
2. Eve's Daughters: The Stronghold of Insecurity .............35
3. All That Glitters: Unmasking False Securities ................53
4. Knowing God: The Key to a Secure Heart ......................73

PART TWO — *Secure in Heart*
5. Am I Enough? God's Goodness .........................................93
6. Who Can I Count On? The Rock.....................................119
7. Will I Be Rescued? The Anchor.......................................143
8. Will I Be Successful? The Guide .....................................169
9. Who Will Protect Me? The Guard ..................................195
10. What Do Others Think of Me? The Advocate..............221
11. Will I Be Alone? The Comforter ..................................247

PART THREE — *Walking Securely*
12. Secure Love: The One True Treasure............................277

A Note from Dave .............................................................300
Starting a Soup and Security Group .................................301

# SOUP AND SECURITY

PAUL SAID IN 1 THESSALONIANS 2:8, "WE LOVED YOU SO MUCH that we were delighted to share with you not only the gospel of God but our lives as well, because you had become so dear to us."

This expresses my heart, and I believe the hearts of the other women who generously opened up their lives within these pages. Although we may not know you yet, I think if all of us could sit down (perhaps for a cup of hot mint tea or even a bowl of soup), we would find that our battles are very similar. I'm convinced we would quickly become endeared to each other.

This is exactly what has happened in my house every Sunday afternoon for the last six months. Around 12:30 PM, a group of friends began arriving to discuss the latest part of the book. I called this time Soup and Security. I would prepare a big bowl of soup, or as the cool days gave way to spring and summer, a big salad. As we sat around the antique oak table in my dining room, we would share a meal, read the latest version of the latest chapter and open up about our personal battles with insecurity.

Our Soup and Security group was made up of women who were far from being alike. We were a mix of college students, singles and young and not-so-young married women. One of us had children in college, and another had preteen grandchildren. We were black and white, married for just six months, married for thirty years, divorced, or even wondering if we'd ever get married. Some of us were raised in insecure homes where alcoholism, abuse and heartache prevailed; others of us were raised from the time we were young to serve God. We were a group who would never have guessed from outward appearances that our battles were much the same.

But as we opened up about our insecurities, we found that we were all very much alike in our spiritual battles. For each of us, insecurity turned out to be something much bigger than whether we were feeling particularly confident on any given day. This battle affected the way we viewed God and ourselves. Together, we began to understand that the way we fight this battle determined much about our walk with God and our view of whatever life sent our way.

On some days, I came to that table just a little afraid. There were many things I had written about that none of them knew about me. Was it possible that I had shared too much? Was I really ready to be open about the things I once was ashamed of, but now believed that God wanted to use for his glory?

What the women at that table didn't always know was the agony that brought those words to life. Often, I wrote out of times of prayer. I would go down on the elliptical trainer in my basement, and begin working out and praying out loud, surrendering my life and circumstances to the Lordship of Christ. Being an emotional person, I would often end up in tears as I dealt with the fears and heartaches of daily living.

But then, the words would begin to come. I would put the machine on pause and run upstairs rummaging for a pencil and paper. Then I would sit and write furiously as the words came. These weren't eloquent Biblical musings, but rather God himself discipling my motives and revealing to me the depth of insecurity that still resided in my heart. Often, I would think, *God, you don't really expect me to share this, do you?* Finally, I started coming to my workouts with paper and pencil in hand.

But in Soup and Security, I not only received valuable input that impacted the content of this book, I also found grace. These women responded to my openness by opening up their hearts in return. They honored the trust I had in them and then encouraged me to keep in the book the stories I might be tempted to remove. They gave me, an insecure soul, the courage to scorn the shame I'd always felt about certain parts of my past or my character, and follow Jesus "the author and perfecter of our faith, who for the joy set before him endured the cross, scorning its shame, and sat down at the right hand of the throne of God" (Hebrews 12:2).

My father, who graciously agreed to let part of his battle be reflected in my story, had some wise words for me about this book. He said, "Remember, Robin, that you may look back one day and wonder, why did I include that? Was that really necessary?" Then he paused, and said, "Honey, only you can decide what to include. You just have to be ready to trust what you do share." So in that spirit, I give you my weakness, trusting that it may lead to your strength.

Because of the length and breadth of what God has brought together in these pages, I'd like to offer a few suggestions on how to approach it. My dream from the very beginning was to create a book that could serve as a resource on insecurity. A book that you could go back to again and again, and find more ideas for what to study and fresh inspiration for your battles.

I've divided the book into three sections. In the first section, we'll talk about the beginnings of insecurity—starting all the way from the Garden of Eden. We'll see how Satan attacks us with false securities and then talk about how knowing God gives us the power to take down Satan's strongholds. These teachings lay the foundation for what follows and introduce you to the seven questions that we'll address later. The study guide for these chapters is purposely short.

The second section is the heart of the book. Each chapter revolves around a question that we ask as women. Each will also highlight a false security that Satan seeks to sell us and will oftentimes take us back to the Garden of Eden to understand ourselves better through Eve. Lastly, the chapter will offer up the answer as found in the knowledge of God.

Infused throughout these chapters are my stories and the

stories of women (and sometimes men) from the Bible. Each chapter ends with (1) an extended story from a woman highlighting her battle with insecurity and (2) a study guide with numerous quiet time suggestions. There are many ways you can approach these chapters. But do remember that the study guide can be left for later, and gone back to again and again.

In this center section, I've also included many charts that contrast and compare Satan's whispers to our hearts with the truth of the Scriptures. I would suggest that you skim through these, and then focus on the ones that most speak to your heart.

In the final section, we'll look at the most-feared (and most-reverential) territory that we find ourselves unwillingly taken to: death itself. In Soup and Security, we literally wept our way through this terrain. You may be tempted to skip ahead and read the end first, but I'd encourage you to let God take you through this journey one step at a time. Save the end for the last.

Right from the beginning, I want you to know that this is a book that calls for a response. At least in part, I hope your response will be to find a woman, or a group of women (perhaps even your own Soup and Security group), with whom you can open up and find strength for the battle. In the material at the end, you'll find some suggestions for starting up a Soup and Security group.

As Paul says in 1 Timothy 4:16, "Watch your life and your doctrine closely. Persevere in them, because if you do, you will save both yourself and your hearers." Although I've sought to carefully hold to the Bible's teaching, my goal isn't for you to agree with everything I share in these pages. Certainly, in my own search for security, I've allowed myself to look at the Scriptures from many different angles. My hope is that you'll simply take this message and apply it to the exact place you are in your spiritual journey.

Before we get going, I'd like to pause to give honor where honor is due. First, I thank my husband of twenty-five years, Dave. All through the process of writing, Dave encouraged me not to hold back anything that would be helpful, even some of the details of his battles. (Be sure to read his letter in the back of the book.) I respect him for his example of courage, and I could never have completed this project without his undying support and sacrificial love. I also want to thank my children, Josh, Bekah and Caleb, who provided editing, encouragement and perspective.

Lastly, I want to honor the women in my Soup and Security group. I hope each of you will count this as your victory as well as mine: Jessica Armato, Nicky Cole, Judy Hastings, Latrease Heath, Crystal Keys, Candace Montgomery, Wonzey Moss, Stephanie Sullivan, Nicole Sykes, Amy Poirier, Rebekah Weidner, Brandy Rito, Shannon Barranca and Meegan Zillman. The quotes at the beginning of each chapter are from some of the women who were in this group.

Are you ready to get started? Once we are in heaven, I look forward to hearing your stories of how God led you through the valleys of insecurity to a secure place where you stand—complete, confident and unashamed in him.

Note: Most of the names and some of the details of the life stories in this book have been changed to protect the identity of people mentioned in the stories.

# PART ONE

## *The Secure Foundation*

He will be the sure foundation for your times,

a rich store of salvation and wisdom and knowledge;

the fear of the Lord is the key to this treasure.

Isaiah 33:6

"To be secure in heart would mean being comfortable with the fact that I'm not perfect. I get very hard on myself when I'm less than I think I should be. Sometimes I wonder if God is looking down on me in my insecurities and thinking, 'Will you ever get over this? You're wasting my time and your time with your self-focus.'

"I'd like to learn how to love myself."

— College student

# THE BEGINNING OF SECURITY

*Mapping Out the Battlefield*

I call as my heart grows faint,
    lead me to the rock that is higher than I.
For you have been my refuge,
    a strong tower against the foe.

Psalm 61:2

...God is so vastly wonderful, so utterly and completely delightful that He can, without anything other than Himself, meet and overflow the deepest demands of our total nature, mysterious and deep as that nature is.

— A. W. Tozer

I PAUSED AT THE FRONT DOOR AND TOOK A DEEP BREATH. THE usually quiet stretch of street in front of the small brick home I grew up in was filled with cars. I pushed open the front door and walked into a living room full of people both young and old. Upon my entrance, everyone seemed to simultaneously breathe in, looking at me solemnly. Some I knew; others were complete strangers to me. The whole scene seemed surreal, like time was playing some sort of cruel trick on me. My mother came rushing over. She flung her arms around my neck and started sobbing into my shoulder as everyone looked on.

"Oh, Robin, thank God you're here… Did your dad tell you everything? I still can't believe it… How are you doing, honey?"

Oddly enough, embarrassment was the only emotion that I

could summon. I mumbled a few awkward expressions of sorrow. Certainly, I had grieved when I first heard the news. My husband, Dave, and I had moved to downtown Indianapolis and were lying on the just-filled waterbed when a phone call came from an old boyfriend, who I hadn't talked to in many years. He immediately told me that my family was frantically trying to contact me.

A phone call to my father yielded the tragic news. My sister Jennifer had been in a freak automobile accident involving freezing rain and a sixteen-year-old who had been driving a truck with a winch on the front. My sister had stopped at a stop sign and rolled down the window trying to see. She ventured out into the intersection just as the truck flew over a hill. The teenager panicked, and the winch on the front of his truck caught my sister in the back of the neck, killing her instantly.

She was just a few weeks shy of turning twenty-one.

After I got off the phone, I lay on the bed crying while my husband tried to comfort me. I had just seen my sister several months earlier when I was home for Christmas. We had promised each other some extended time to talk, but she was spending lots of time with her boyfriend. Before she hurried out the door the last time I saw her, she gave me a big hug, told me she loved me, and assured me that we would find more time later to catch up. Now I knew that time would never come.

I brushed away my tears and pulled myself together. There were arrangements to be made. I had to get to Virginia as soon as possible. And as I closed my suitcase and rode to the airport, something inside of me closed as well. When my family all stood in a circle, wrapped their arms around each other and wept, I couldn't separate what I was feeling from what I thought I should be feeling. I was used to being the pillar of strength in the family—the spiritual one who was supposed to comfort everybody else.

What didn't occur to me, though, was that I needed the funeral for myself—I needed time to grieve the loss I had just suffered. And so I found ways to stay on the perimeter, letting out just enough sorrow to stay engaged but not enough to heal, outwardly giving the illusion of being strong, inwardly feeling weak.

Unknowingly, I had been transported back to a key moment in my childhood. I was lying on the bottom bunk of my bed while listening to my two little sisters crying. My parents were arguing in the other room, screaming words at each other that no child ought to hear and throwing things at each other. I willed myself not to cry, biting my bottom lip. Somebody had to be strong. At least that's what I told myself. In reality I was hiding behind a wall of strength. I was willing myself not to be hurt by what was going on around me. At a tender eleven years old, I was already well trained in my role as the oldest daughter. I had already developed codependent coping mechanisms that I would carry with me into adulthood.

And now, twenty-four years later, I was feeling more than a little disappointed with myself. I yearned to be more like my mother in her grief—vulnerable, courageous and unashamed. But I simply wasn't secure enough to be vulnerable in the most difficult test I had faced yet in life. As a Christian, a committed follower of Christ, I knew that Jesus had wept openly at the death of his friend Lazarus. I wanted to be like him, to grieve with others—my mother, my brothers and sisters, and even the people from my childhood who had gathered to support my family—but I couldn't.

When I returned to Indianapolis, I didn't let anyone else in either—even my brothers and sisters in Christ who sincerely wanted to minister to me. With nowhere else to go, that sorrow got shoved back deep into my heart. I didn't know how to find my way through it, so instead I found my way around it.

## Seeking Security

> Sad, too, is the love that has no communion with those we
> love when they suffer. How miserable it is to have to stand
> in mute sorrow with nothing to say to those we love when
> they are in great pain. It is a terrible confession that our love
> is not big enough to surmount suffering.[1]

It wasn't long after my sister's funeral that I asked God to create something new in me. A new heart. A secure heart. Later, at a missions conference in the Philippines, a women's ministry leader from Russia, inspired by our discussion of insecurity, challenged me to write a book on insecurity. "We all need this," she said in her sketchy English. "God wants you to write this book."

They say you shouldn't ask God for what you really don't want because he might just give it to you. I did so much want to be secure. I wanted to be secure enough to be vulnerable with my heartaches, my fears and especially with my own private suffering. I was inspired by the thought of being able to help other women as well. And, I sensed that all of this would take a bigger love for God. But as much as I desperately yearned to be secure, I had no idea what I was really asking for. As it turns out, before I could move toward security, God had a lot more work to do in my heart. And Satan certainly wasn't ready to let go of the stronghold he had built in my heart.

In the couple of years that followed, Satan unleashed a full-fledged attack on my security. When the church Dave and I were serving full-time came into a time of struggle, I took it on my own shoulders. *Since the church is struggling that must mean that I'm struggling.* My attempts to please everybody were dividing my heart and separating me from my faith. When a well-meaning friend suggested that my pride was at fault, I took it to the nth degree, taking some of the most challenging scriptures and trying to bring myself to repentance. I started questioning whether I was even a Christian at all. I started talking about being "re-baptized."

1. Thomas Merton, *No Man Is an Island* (New York: Barnes & Noble Books, 2003), 86.

One day I had an emotional breakdown at a church leaders meeting. I was cracking. But the more others around me tried to help me, the worse I became. Eventually, out of fear for my mental health, we were asked to step down from the ministry, forcing my husband to give up his lifelong dream. I had hit the bottom.

But now I know that God in his abundant mercy was actually protecting me. He was preparing to do major surgery on my heart. I could no longer put off dealing with the way that I had grown up—with my dad's alcoholism and the accompanying verbal abuse.

Amazingly, just a couple of days after we stepped out of the ministry, my head began to clear. Thanks to my husband's encouragement, I read the book of 1 John and saw with certainty that I was a Christian. My salvation was secure. It was like a dark cloud had started its sojourn off my soul.

My husband and I made a major transition out of the full-time ministry into the secular world and job market. We moved to Chicago to try to transition and nearly went bankrupt. My husband eventually landed a job downstate in Bloomington, Illinois. We were broke and humbled, but ready to turn a new chapter in our lives. And for me, I knew that turning that chapter meant somehow figuring out the causes of the insecurity that seemed to chase me in every corner of my life. And my hope was that if I could figure out why I felt so swallowed up by insecurity, maybe I could help other women as well.

As I began to open up more and more about my insecurity, I didn't find shame. Instead, I found kindred souls. I began to understand more and more that this wasn't my battle to face alone. As I risked letting my insecurities out in all of their unkemptness, I made some of the best friends of my life. With their help, I engaged the battle. Somehow, acknowledging the depth of my insecurities didn't make other women look down on me. Rather, they felt they could trust me with theirs as well. And through that I bonded with another woman who was to become one of my best friends—Andrea. Together, over the last ten years, we've fought together and held up each other's arms in our own individual battles to be secure. Graciously, she's agreed to let you into her battle as well.

Andrea's story highlights an important truth about insecurity. Andrea didn't grow up with physical abuse or some dramatic story of trauma. Yet her father's inability to connect with her emotionally from the time she was a little girl combined with her mother's death at the age of fourteen created emotional deficits that she is still trying to understand. In this part of her story, she shares about how a childhood incident started what eventually grew into a full-fledged insecurity in her heart.

## Andrea's Story—In Her Own Words

A few months ago, I became painfully aware that my reactions to hurt feelings, disappointments and conflict in my relationship with my husband were really unwarranted given the situation at hand. In other words, when my feelings were hurt, I overreacted, and my emotions seemed to skyrocket, fueled by memories from my past.

I remember that as a young girl if I had done something wrong or displayed any type of negative emotion or attitude, I was sent to my room. It didn't seem to me to be a form of discipline for the wrong behavior, but rather a way to remove me and my "unacceptable" emotion from everyone else's view. There was never any follow-up interaction or processing talk about the situation, just an understanding that I was not to come out until I had the right attitude.

Of course my dad never gave me any explanation as to what the right attitude should be. He only used phrases like… *"Don't be that way,"* or *"That is an ugly way to be"* or *"Don't come out until you are ready to be reasonable."* What I felt didn't seem to matter. Therefore, the message I heard was *"You do not matter."*

I would sit in my room, hurt and feeling like no one cared, especially the people who were supposed to care for and love me. This, of course, would make me angry, and the only way that I knew to feel better was to plot some kind of revenge or behavior that would "pay them back" for how they made me feel. Of course, I could never carry out what I so wanted to do.

Once, I did pack my little suitcase and walk out the door. I only got as far as the end of the driveway because I was terrified of the dark. So I turned around and came home, even more angry and hurt because my parents didn't seem at all phased. This was more proof to me that I didn't matter, even though I was obviously crying out for confirmation that I did.

Anyway, those times in my room, alone, left me to process things on my own. And how accurate can a little girl be when trying to deal with all those emotions and trying to make the right conclusions about herself? What I concluded is that there is a right way to be and act, and I was at the mercy of the ones who "loved" me.

So now, as an adult, this has mostly exhibited itself in my relationship with my husband. When my feelings are hurt and then not validated or recognized to be reasonable, my childhood feelings come flooding in.

I start thinking, *"My feelings do not matter, therefore I don't matter and I am not important. I have not met the standard, the right way to think and feel, so I just need to be sent away from this person."* Then I become angry and start thinking of ways to pay back my husband when he hurts me.

I have said things to him like: *"If you don't learn to give me what I need emotionally, I will have to find it from someone else."* By communicating my hurt in the form of a threat, I try to make the problem him and not me. The anger is a defense to protect myself from hurt because being hurt confirms the message that I don't matter. I withdraw and go into hiding. Instead of reaching out (which is what I need), I stay isolated emotionally because of feeling isolated physically as a little girl. It's hard to forgive, hard to trust and hard to give my heart again.

This has impacted me not only in my relationship with my husband, but also in my overall insecurity. I constantly have to fight the idea that I must live up to a standard or expectation that is not spelled out, and consequently, I don't know what to shoot for. So, I live under a cloud of feeling that at any moment I will fail and be exposed and then be embarrassed and isolated.

I think this is why I am quiet in nature. I am always hanging back, searching for the acceptable behavior for a situation—not wanting to risk behaving different than anyone else. Of course, this makes me different and therefore ends up confirming the very thing I fear.

I guess the bottom line is that I have listened to the conclusions that I made as a little girl and have ended up following that blueprint for my life. I feel like I must be "sent away" whenever I feel I am saying or doing the wrong thing. I know I will never really measure up to anyone else, so I just count it as a victory if I don't get exposed.

What other people think about me becomes incredibly controlling, and I learn to show what I think is acceptable to them. Just now at forty-something, I am making progress on who I am and being okay with that.

## Developing a Secure Heart

Like Andrea, each of us has our own unique story. But in my experience, all of our stories have common threads—childhood messages run amok, a fear of exposure and rejection, feeling unacceptable, isolating ourselves from others, willing ourselves to be strong, capable, confident or whatever else it is that we think we *should* be.

Now, Andrea is developing a battle-tested security—a security that comes from fleeing to God as her refuge. I hope you'll agree that her vulnerability is inspiring! And I thank God that he's given me her friendship to help give me courage and strength!

How do we develop the kind of security that allows us to face our weakness head-on and engage it in spiritual warfare? How do we engage our insecurities without losing ourselves in them? I've found three keys that we'll talk about at length. These three keys are the boiled-down conclusion of years of battle to find a secure heart.

## Building a Foundation for Security—Chapters 1–4

To understand security, we'll first take a look at the roots of insecurity—going back all the way to the Garden of Eden. Then we'll talk about how God reveals himself to us in the Bible through many names that show his personal and relational nature. When we know him and experience him in these specific ways, the result will be a growing trust and security.

> The LORD is a refuge for the oppressed,
>     a stronghold in times of trouble.
> Those who know your name will trust in you,
>     for you, LORD, have never forsaken those who seek you.
> (Psalm 9:9–10)

## Renouncing and Replacing Satan's False Securities—Chapters 5–11

Satan comes after us with a vision of secure life that is a flat-out lie, enticing us with false dreams and avenues of comfort that only lead us to a deeper insecurity. By renouncing his false securities, and replacing them with the knowledge of God, we can more clearly see the path to true security.

> The idols speak deceit.
>     Diviners see visions that lie,
> they tell dreams that are false.
>     They give comfort in vain.
> Therefore the people wander like sheep
>     oppressed for lack of a shepherd. (Zechariah 10:2)

## Walking Securely—Chapter 12

A security that comes from God's eternal and unchanging nature thrives even in times of darkness, even when facing death. And most of all, it is a personal security that comes from hearing him call your name and then experiencing his goodness firsthand.

> "I will go before you
>    and will level the mountains;
> I will break down gates of bronze
>    and cut through bars of iron.
> I will give you the treasures of darkness,
>    riches stored in secret places,
> so that you may know that I am the Lord,
>    the God of Israel, who summons you by name."
> (Isaiah 45:2–3)

## Circling Back

Just one year ago, some fifteen years after the death of my sister, I sat at another funeral—the memorial service for my mother. Right after the service ended, my sister Dona spontaneously walked over to Jennifer's grave, wiped off the marker with her hands and turned over the vase recessed into her headstone, tenderly clearing out the cobwebs and dust that had accumulated. She then walked over to my mother's grave and began picking some flowers out of the large silk arrangements. Following her example, the remaining children walked from arrangement to arrangement, carefully picking out flowers as well. We then walked one by one over to Jennifer's grave, knelt and tenderly added to the growing arrangement in the vase. Those who had come to the graveside silently circled around us.

Using Mom's flowers to honor Jennifer only seemed appropriate, since there wasn't a day in my mother's life that she did not mourn losing her next-to-youngest daughter. The only solace Mom found in facing death was her faith that she would be with Jennifer again.

Facing my mother's death had also brought me back to the death of my sister. Knowing the person I was when my sister died, I was more than a little afraid of facing the grieving process all over again. But tragedy can open your heart in unexpected ways, and through the six weeks that passed from my mom's cancer diagnosis to the day when I sat on her bed and watched as she departed this world with a slight smile on her lips, it became obvious that God had built in me a deeper security and trust in him.

As a result, I was able to share my grief with a wide assortment of people—weeping into the shoulders of nurses and social workers, opening my heart wide to those who gathered at my mother's funeral, and even allowing myself to be ministered to by strangers.

What made the difference in the way I handled the deaths of two of the most important people in my life? I now not only *knew* and *intellectually asserted* that God is my rock, I'd also *experienced* him as my fortress; I'd *trusted* him as my guide; I'd *leaned* on him as my anchor; and I'd *surrendered* to him as my refuge.

And this time, God ensured that I would be able to let the funeral meet my needs by sending two angels, two of my best friends, all the way to Virginia to stand by my side and make sure that I took the time necessary to grieve. Even though they barely knew each other and lived in different locales, they each independently decided to come. God flew them in on different airlines, and they arrived within an hour of each other so that they were delivered to my doorstep in one swoop, a giant kiss from God.

Right before the funeral, they took me aside and expressed their concern that I have time to grieve (yep, as you can imagine, as the oldest daughter I was arranging everything). They prayed with me and, quite honestly, changed my focus. In them I saw God as my protector—granting me exactly what I needed.

And so I came to the fiery trial of my mother's illness and death clinging to the only place, the only refuge, the only rock that could hold me steady amidst the roller-coaster ride—my relationship with God. This security of heart gave me the ability to choose to face my fear of vulnerability and weakness, and to be generous with my grief, seeing God in the midst of my pain.

But what had happened in the fifteen years between my sister's death and my mother's death? As you might guess, the growth that came wasn't because everything suddenly got easier—life's difficulties only got more and more challenging. What then, did those fifteen years bring?

**Marital bliss?** My husband's and my intertwined addiction/co-dependency progressed to the near break-up of our marriage. We then went through years of counseling.

**Financial Ease**? Our transition from ministry to "real" jobs (Dave had a degree in Biblical Greek and Hebrew) led to near financial disaster. The pinnacle was our family of five living with Dave's sister and her husband in their basement so we could mend financially.

**Health and Beauty?** An anaphylactic reaction to an allergy shot almost took my life. A severe bout with Grave's Disease changed my appearance and made my eyes severely swollen for more than five years.

**Friends?** Moving to Bloomington brought lonely years as I struggled to create new relationships. A later move to Chicago again brought another period of loneliness.

**Strength?** Getting rear-ended led to a slow-healing shoulder injury for which the other person's insurance refused to pay, leading to a lawsuit that ended in a settlement far below the medical bills amassed.

**Church?** Our church went through a crisis, which led to some dear friends leaving. Some women whom I had labored over and loved suddenly no longer wanted contact. They moved on, leaving me reeling.

**Ministry?** Later on, in a totally unrelated incident, a dear friend that I helped bring to Christ (and who had struggled for years with mental illness) committed suicide. Three different friends went through serious bouts with cancer. And another woman died just months after she stayed at my house.

### God's Faithfulness

Although there have been setbacks in the last fifteen years, as I look at the big picture I see that God has stood beside me (and my husband), leading us from strength to strength. After re-entering the job market killing roaches and throwing newspapers, Dave eventually began a highly successful career in pharmaceutical sales and is now working on a master's degree in organizational psychology.

I also went through several career changes until I found my calling as a full-time writer. I was able to open my own business, and in spite of hardship, have had three highly successful years in business.

Our three children are finding their way into adulthood—our daughter just graduated from college, our oldest son will graduate soon. We were able to help plant a church in Bloomington, Illinois, that has now been in existence for more than ten years. We've seen friends and neighbors give their lives to God. Personally, my relationship with God has only grown richer, and my love and appreciation for my husband has deepened (we just celebrated twenty-five years of marriage). God's goodness has been abundant.

Would I have needed all these things in order to be secure? I hope not. I'm convinced that this security can stand no matter what life throws at me. But I thank God that through much pain, he has refined my faith and proved it to be genuine.

During all of these years, I've kept a single goal. My single-hearted desire has been simple, and it still remains the same: I want to be *secure in heart.* Through the years, I've filled journals with my studies on security/insecurity, reading every book I could find that was even remotely connected to the topic. And even though sometimes I felt like I was barely making any progress at all, a beautiful thing was happening. Bit by bit, I was being transformed. I was getting more and more vulnerable in my relationship with God, and I was learning new ways to connect with him. And I was becoming more firmly committed to my dream that one day I would be able to help others.

*Am I totally free from insecurity?* Far from it. Insecurity is always there, taunting me, asking me to listen to its "wisdom." Although I know I'll see new areas of insecurity as I go along and continue to battle old ones, I feel hope and peace from God. This is what I've learned: Being secure isn't so much about banishing every little bit of insecurity from our lives. It's more about actively engaging in the battle. *By engaging in the battle, you are standing up and defending what has already been given to you—your security in God through Christ.*

Like Andrea, I think many of us are asking the question, "Do I matter?" And the funny thing is, many of us are not even aware that we are asking it. We pose the question unconsciously to the men in our lives—whether father, boyfriend, husband, brothers in Christ, or if we get desperate enough, to men who don't know us at all. We ask it when we get "dolled up," hoping someone might see something beautiful in us. We ask it in our careers and in trying to find our calling. We ask it as Christians to our brothers and sisters in God's church. We ask it in our approach to our roles as wives and mothers. We ask it when we go through hard times that pull the rug of security from under our feet. And most of all, we ask it to God!

Why else would we be so devastated when it seems like God isn't answering? Why else would something like the inability to lose weight, to find a boyfriend, to have good health, to pay the bills, to get pregnant, or to do well in school become a deep-seated spiritual issue that can knock us flat spiritually? I think it's because we're asking, in not so many words, "God, do you see what's going on down here with me? Do you care? Do I really matter? Or do you just want me to retreat to a little room, and only let me come out when my attitude is exactly like what you talk about in the Bible—spiritual enough, good enough?"

The truth is, dear sister, that you do matter! You matter because God says so. And although you may not see or feel the security that he gives you, it is still there. Like the old song goes, "Jesus loves me this I know. For the Bible tells me so." Now God is singing another song over you, telling you through scripture after scripture that you are secure. How can you know this? Because he says so. And because he says so, you can have peace—peace of heart.

Because God wants each of us to be absolutely sure of our heritage as his daughters, he has filled his word with analogies designed to help us understand exactly how he feels about you and me. And some of these seem to me to appeal almost exclusively to the heart of a woman.

> But Zion said, "The LORD has forsaken me,
>    the LORD has forgotten me."
> "Can a mother forget the baby at her breast
>    and have no compassion on the child she has borne?
> Though she may forget,
>    I will not forget you!
> See, I have engraved you on the palms of my hands;
>    your walls are ever before me." (Isaiah 49:14–16)

Ask any nursing mother what that scripture means, and she'll most likely get a little misty-eyed. When each of my three children was nursing, they shared a common characteristic. They would often stroke my face and look directly into my eyes, as if trying to memorize my every feature. I can't even fathom forgetting them, or even worse being totally without feeling at their cries for help. When my child would cry out in hunger, I would feel the milk surge in my breast. My body, my heart—everything within me—moved toward that child. I can't even imagine having no compassion. (Nursing so impacted me that I still have dreams that I'm nursing a child—and my youngest is twenty-one!)

How does this apply to you? The truth is that it's more likely for you to forget an infant nursing at your breast than for God to forget you. It's more likely for you to have absolutely no compassion for the baby stroking your face, than it is for God to forget to have compassion for you. Even more than that, having compassion for you is such a part of his nature that it's like you're engraved on his hands. Every time he reaches a palm out, he sees you. And his heart is moved with love. Do you matter to him? Absolutely!

Security in heart is our most precious gift from God—the ultimate overflowing of his goodness to us. But because of its extreme value, it's a gift that must be battled for and protected. And knowing that, should it surprise us that security is the gift that Satan most wants to steal from us?

# The Beginning of Security: Mapping Out the Battlefield

*Personal Study Guide & Life Application*

Security usually doesn't come from everything in life going well, but instead through trials and suffering. In Romans 8:10, Paul reminds us, "Our present sufferings are not worth comparing to the glory that will be revealed in us."

> *What challenges in your life tend to make you insecure? To map out your own personal battlefield, make a beginning list of areas in your life that have caused you insecurity in the past and present. Then read Romans 8:10. What does this scripture mean to you?*

"You would think that since I view God as my Father, and had a great relationship with my dad, that I wouldn't struggle with keeping my relationship with God in perspective. But that's not quite true. I don't struggle so much with feeling forgiven, I struggle more with excusing everything I do. I think God won't blame me...it's really not that big of a deal. I forget that I'm in a battle."

— Mother of two

# EVE'S DAUGHTERS
## *The Stronghold of Insecurity*

> And there is a far worse anxiety, a far worse insecurity, which
> comes from being afraid to ask the right questions—because
> they might turn out to have no answer.
> —Thomas Merton, *No Man Is an Island*

IN BOTH MY CALLING AS A CHRISTIAN AND MY CAREER AS A COPY-
writer and consultant, I talk to other women all the time.
Because I am self-employed, I participate in many networking
groups and associations where I talk with women who have made
the gutsy move of opening their own businesses. Likewise,
through twenty-some years of ministry experience, I've coun-
seled with women from all sorts of backgrounds. But whether
entrepreneur or stay-at-home mom, deeply committed to their
faith or not sure what they believe, I've found women everywhere to have a common thread: Nearly all of them relate to
insecurity on some level.

When I've mentioned that I'm writing a book about insecurity, many groan. Then they usually ask how they can get the
book! The word itself strikes a deep chord within most of us. It's
a struggle that most of us don't readily admit to, even if someone
else admits it first! But when they do, we're naturally relieved.
*Maybe I'm not alone. Perhaps I can talk about it.*

Then there are other friends of mine who have a different
reaction to the word "insecurity." To them, insecurity is a negative trait—a sign of weakness that they don't want to seem to
relate to. They simply have never seen themselves as insecure.

As a friend who owns a very successful business told me recently:

> Robin, when you first mentioned that you'd like me to read
> something on insecurity, I was thinking...well, I guess I
> could read it so that I could help someone else. I've never
> seen myself as an insecure person. But although I don't feel
> insecure (at least from the perspective of how I define inse-
> curity), I do feel the intense desire for my husband's
> approval and attention, almost like the measure of my wom-
> anhood is directly attached. The intensity of it blows me
> away. Perhaps I need this security message more than I
> think!

Where then, does this tendency toward insecurity come
from? The answer is simple: Satan has sought from the very
beginning to attack woman in her security, and then to make it
even worse, he turns around and shames her for being insecure.
Insecurity coupled with shame is the one-two punch Satan uses
to try to take us away from our Creator and from the secure status that he has gifted to us.

**Why Insecurity?**

Through my studies and experiences, I've found what I
believe to be an important corollary. It seems obvious that Satan
has singled out man to attack him through his purity because of
his unique nature. Why is that? Men are hardwired differently
than women. They are programmed to respond to sight. Man's
sexual make-up then helps to move him toward relationship. His
nature is the handiwork of God, created to mesh beautifully with
woman's nature. But it's also a door that Satan has used to bring
shame and devastation into many lives.

Likewise, Satan has singled out woman by attacking her
security. Woman is generally more sensitive, more intuitive,
more in touch with her emotional side. Perfectly wired to complement man's nature, she finds her need for relationship moves
her toward sexual expression. Should we be surprised that this is

the very spot Satan chooses to set up camp? His goal is to take woman's sensitivity, emotional strength and nurturing nature and turn it into the vast array of emotions that make up what we call insecurity. Insecurity is the path Satan uses to try to distract, discourage and disparage us in our true destiny as God's daughters. And through insecurity, Satan seeks to impose a self-consciousness that causes us to look to others to try to find our worth.

MAN'S BATTLE: PURITY—PUTTING SEX IN ITS GOD-ORDAINED PLACE
WOMAN'S BATTLE: SECURITY—PUTTING RELATIONSHIP IN ITS GOD-ORDAINED PLACE

But what about women who struggle with purity, and men who struggle with security? It's the same struggle, usually coming from completely different motives. Women are usually propelled into purity struggles because of their quest for romantic love. Simply said, woman goes where she thinks she can find man, even if it means compromising her desire to put relationship first.

Men are propelled into security struggles because of their God-ordained desire to initiate, to lead, to pursue. They struggle with security when those attempts are frustrated, and their manhood is brought into question.

**Why Now?**
Why are we just now coming around to talking openly about insecurity? Let's just take a very brief glance at man's battle with impurity for insight. For years, in the place that should be the safest of all—God's church—men haven't felt free to come forward with their battles with lust. It's encouraging to see that bit by bit, in small pockets, in the church and outside of it, we are making it safer for men to admit and battle their purity issues.

My husband and I have spent a lot of time with couples ensnared by sexual addiction. We've come out of the closet in our marriage and have been willing to admit years of struggle, of codependency, and of sexual and love addiction[1] stemming from both of our childhoods. We are no longer ashamed. We are both recovering through God's grace and are willing to be the poster children in our church, and in our community, for hope.

But where is there help for women battling insecurity? If you search the bookshelves, you won't find much help. When you do find insecurity talked about, chances are that it will be shrouded in shame. And along with that some authors suggest what many of us in Christian circles have been told for years—get over it! Repent!

## Unbelieving? I Don't Think So!

It's no wonder then, that women aren't always quick to admit the depth of their insecurities! As an insecure soul and an avid reader, I've noticed that it is hard to define "insecurity" without finger-pointing. Some of the words I've run into that are linked with "insecurity" are "unbelieving," "ignorance," "wickedness" and "mental instability." Can insecurity end up there? Sure it can. But honestly, many of the women I know who are fellow-battlers with insecurity aren't characterized by any of those things. They are God-fearing women who possess many unique gifts and are committed to following Christ. Among them are some of the women that I respect most in the world. Do they struggle? Absolutely! Is their struggle because they are mentally unstable? I don't think so!

My standard response to the question as to why there are so few books on insecurity is that insecure souls like me are too insecure to write them! Satan has made us insecure about our insecurities. Somewhere in our hearts we believe that if we push our insecurity back far enough (much like Christian men have

---

1. Copendency expert, Pia Mellody, describes three major behavioral symptoms of Love Addiction, including that of assigning "a disproportionate amount of time, attention and 'value above themselves' to the person to whom they are addicted," having "unrealistic expectations for unconditional positive regard from the other person in the relationship," and neglecting "to care for or value themselves while they're in the relationship." From *Facing Love Addiction*, (San Francisco: Harper, 2003), 10.

done for years with their struggles with purity), it will go away. Perhaps, if we act confidently and faithfully, the insecurities that stalk us in the darkness will shrink back.

Personally, I think it's time to admit the depth of our struggles and stand up to claim our true legacy as God's daughters. There is a better way—a secure path promised us by our Father. To find that path we need to go back to the beginning.

## Daughters of Eve

Where did all this start? Those of you who wonder whether your insecurity is something you should be ashamed of may be surprised to find out that insecurity has existed from the very beginning of humanity. Insecurity came in Satan's initial attack on God's first precious children—Adam and Eve.

> Then the LORD GOD made a woman from the rib he had taken out of the man and he brought her to the man.
> The man said,
>
> > "This is now bone of my bones
> > and flesh of my flesh;
> > she shall be called 'woman,'
> > for she was taken out of man."
>
> For this reason a man will leave his father and mother and be united to his wife, and they will become one flesh.
> The man and his wife were both naked, and they felt no shame. (Genesis 2:22–25)

Before Satan entered the picture in the Garden of Eden, Adam and Eve were together in a joyous union. They were totally naked, but their nakedness ran deeper than just their lack of clothing. They had absolutely nothing to hide—spiritually, emotionally or physically. They were totally transparent with God and with each other. The result? The Bible tells us that "they felt no shame." Shame and hiding were both foreign concepts to them because they had nothing to pretend about, and certainly nothing to try to deceive each other or God about.

Then, Satan arrives on the scene in the form of the serpent. And he has one single agenda—to take away the perfect security and peace with God that Adam and Eve had.

> He said to the woman, "Did God really say, 'You must not eat from any tree in the garden'?"
>
> The woman said to the serpent, "We may eat fruit from the trees in the garden, but God did say, 'You must not eat fruit from the tree that is in the middle of the garden, and you must not touch it, or you will die.'"
>
> "You will not surely die," the serpent said to the woman. "For God knows that when you eat of it, your eyes will be opened, and you will be like God, knowing good and evil." (Genesis 3:1b–5)

How does Satan go after Eve? He questions her knowledge of God. And although he doesn't use these exact words, here's what he insinuates:

*Eve, do you really know God as well as you think you do?*
*Do you understand why he set that rule?*
*What were God's motives exactly?*
*Do you think perhaps you're being a little naive?*

And we all know what happens from there. Satan convinces the woman to partake; she then passes it along to Adam. Their eyes are opened to the knowledge of good and evil, and they run and hide. Before they disobeyed, they had nothing to hide. But now they realize that they are naked—and not just physically.

> Then the eyes of both of them were opened, and they realized they were naked; so they sewed fig leaves together and made covering for themselves.
>
> Then the man and his wife heard the sound of the Lord God as he was walking in the garden in the cool of the day, and they hid from the Lord God among the trees of the garden." (Genesis 3:7–8)

**Going into Hiding**

With the knowledge of good and evil that comes bundled with the forbidden fruit, Adam and Eve receive a crash course entitled "Vulnerability 101." Now they understand the full potential of evil that God had protected them from in his goodness. All of a sudden, they know they are at risk in relationship with each other and in relationship with God. Shame is no longer absent. Adam and Eve now see the potential of humanity to be evil as well as good.

- **Eve's fear**—Eve now knows that her vulnerability can and will be abused. So she devises a new use for her creative nature—constructing barriers (made of fig leaves) that keep her vulnerable parts hidden.

- **Adam's inadequacy**—Adam's failure to protect Eve has shown him firsthand that his ability to lead and provide will be tested and that he will fail.

- **Adam and Eve's guilt**—For the first time Adam and Eve experience the guilt of betraying the Father who has freely given to them out of his goodness. But instead of taking them back to God, their guilt leads them down the path to shame.

So they hide from the Father—from the true source of life, wisdom and spiritual protection.

For some of us, hiding is a theme that resonates deep within our childhood memories. When I was around eight or nine, my mother was frequently frazzled with the five children she was home with all day. Although she yelled a lot, she never disciplined us. She would keep us in line by threatening what Dad would do when he got home. I learned at a young age to crawl under the covers and pretend I was asleep. At other times, I hid in the closet when he came home. Sometimes (but not always) hiding would save me from the stripes on my legs that his belt would leave.

It was far into my marriage before I realized that in my

relationship with my husband I was using this same coping mechanism of hiding. If I had unresolved issues with him, I would simply pull the covers over my head and pretend to be asleep. Or I would hide behind a headache that was hardly there.

Then the next day, I would seek to make up for my "small" deceit and bridge the emotional gap I felt with my husband by extra kindness. The reality is that hiding not only reveals our insecurity, it also increases it.

With the knowledge of good and evil, also came responsibility. Adam and Eve had to accept the consequences of choosing disobedience over obedience. They could no longer function in that same secure setting. So God cast them out to find their own way.

> To the woman he said,
>
>> "I will greatly increase your pains in childbearing;
>>> with pain you will give birth to children.
>> Your desire will be for your husband,
>>> and he will rule over you."
>
> To Adam he said...
>
>> "Cursed is the ground because of you;
>>> through painful toil you will eat of it
>>> all the days of your life.
>> It will produce thorns and thistles for you
>>> and you will eat the plants of the field.
>> By the sweat of your brow
>>> you will eat your food...." (Genesis 3:16–19a)

## Looking to Man for Security

I used to think that God somehow increased Eve's dependence on her husband, just as he increased her pain in childbearing. But now I see it differently. God told Eve that her desire would be for her husband, and he would rule over her. In other words: *"Eve, here are the consequences of your decision. Here's where you'll end up. You will start looking to Adam for security, and your desire to please him and satisfy him will rule over you."* Once Eve gave up the perfect spiritual security that she had in the garden, it was only natural for her to open her eyes to other sources of security, including Adam. So with a note of Fatherly sadness, God tells Eve exactly where she'll end up.

For Adam, God predicts the futility that he will feel in providing for his family. Now he gets to look forward to painful labor, thorns and thistles, and sweat. Again, this predicts much more than Adam's struggle with his gardening skills. Man's very manhood will be questioned. And just as woman turns to man, man will turn to woman to try to answer the question of whether he has what it takes. Of course, from after the garden until this very day, Satan has been more than happy to provide a false place of refuge for man—impurity. In the brazen stare of women totally disrobed before him, whether in a magazine, video or on the Internet, Satan whispers: "Man, look at all these women who want you! You do have what it takes!"

|  | Curse | Question | Temptation |
|---|---|---|---|
| Man | Earn a living by sweat of his brow | Do I have what it takes to lead? | Look to woman for validation—impurity |
| Woman | Your desire will be for your husband | Do I have what it takes to love? | Look to man for approval—insecurity |

## Enslaved to Romantic Love

Since the Garden of Eden, women have been looking to men to fill up their insecure parts. All the evidence proclaims loud and clear that we have let that desire rule over us. Why would a woman, who is built for relationship and emotional intimacy, throw herself at a man she barely knows? Why would she have sex before there is commitment? Why would she become enslaved to romantic love, let it dictate who she is and how she conducts herself? Why would she stay with a man who is physically or verbally abusing her most vulnerable parts? And, why else would a woman go as far as posing nude for magazines or dancing in a strip club? All of these are so much against her nature.

It's because in the garden Satan tricked woman out of her security and then shamed her for losing it. In her God-created desire for relationship, she has translated her need for security into her relationship with man, and later into all kinds of other places.

And Satan hasn't changed his agenda one bit.

## Unprotected Life

Why does Satan attack us in our security? Remember that Satan tricked Eve out of the most secure parts of her existence: the Garden of Eden and the pure vulnerability and unfettered trust in her relationship with Adam. Likewise, I'm convinced that Satan uses our insecurity to take away our protection of the most vulnerable spiritual parts of our existence. Just as with Eve, Satan's goal is to get us to trade in our security with God for the false security that he offers.

But we have a distinct advantage over Eve. We've been trained by Christ how to defend our feminine hearts against what Paul calls "the powers of this dark world and the spiritual forces of evil in the heavenly realms" and stand even more secure (Ephesians 6:12). Think of it this way. With the advent of the sexual revolution, a term was coined called "unprotected sex." With the increase of sexual promiscuity, STDs, unwanted pregnancies and AIDS, we sent out the message that if you are going to have sex, have the good sense to use protection.

But what Satan wants for you is far worse. He wants you to go into your day-to-day activities with an *unprotected life*! And without a dynamic relationship with God that allows you to arm yourself for battle, that's exactly what you are doing. Satan is still at war, but you're not! One of Satan's best tools for encouraging you to have an unprotected life is nudging you toward insecurity in your relationship with God and your view of yourself. In that insecurity, he's hoping that you'll take yourself outside of the spiritual protection that God gives you—what the Bible calls the armor of God.

Understanding what exactly Satan is trying to undermine in your heart—your legacy as a daughter of God—is the start of standing up and saying, "No more!"

> Put on the full armor of God so that you can take your stand against the devil's schemes.... Stand firm then, with the belt of truth buckled around your waist, with the breastplate of righteousness in place and with your feet fitted with the readiness that comes from the gospel of peace. In addition to all this, take up the shield of faith, with which you can extinguish all the flaming arrows of the evil one. Take the helmet of salvation and the sword of the Spirit, which is the word of God. And pray in the Spirit on all occasions with all kinds of prayers and requests. With this in mind, be alert and always keep on praying for all the saints. (Ephesians 6:11, 14–18)

How does insecurity tamper with the armor that Paul so eloquently describes? Let's look a little deeper.

**Our Heads**—Satan wants to make us insecure about our salvation so that our helmet gets loose and wobbly, or even worse, lies unused in our spiritual closet. A few years back a bike helmet saved my husband's life the very first time he used it. He was riding a brand new red mountain bike when a car suddenly shot out of an alley right in front of him and sent him tumbling over the hood. He escaped with just a broken arm and a cracked helmet. That crack could have been a fatal blow to his head. Satan wants to deal a fatal blow to our security by echoing the same kind of sentiments he voiced to Eve in the garden: "Did God really say that you are completely saved? Is there any possibility you've somehow misunderstood?"

**Our Hearts**—When the righteousness of Christ isn't firmly fastened in front of our hearts, Satan offers cheap substitutes. Just like Satan offered Eve a fig leaf and a clump of bushes, he offers us false securities that in reality don't protect our hearts one bit! When we aren't secure in the righteousness of Christ, things like PMS, perimenopause, health issues, relationship issues, school, work, kids, fertility issues and how men treat us become our measure of how we see ourselves, rather than how God sees us.

**The Truth**—From her daily walks in the garden with God, Eve undoubtedly knew that God loved and cherished her. How did Satan slither in to her thinking? He got her to question her knowledge of God. Like Eve, when our grasp on the truth about who we are and who God is gets tentative, we become vulnerable to believe a lie instead—that we are deficient and that God is withholding good from us. The Bible tells us we need to buckle this truth—who God is and who we are—around our waist every single day so that it goes with us everywhere.

**Our Sword**—Why has God given each of us what he describes as a sword in the form of his word? Because we have a battle to fight! You can be sure that Satan picked a time to attack Eve when she least expected it. Perhaps he chose to approach her after a high time, when she had just shared some great time with Adam. Or perhaps it was at a low time, when Eve's hormones were pulling her off balance. In the same way Satan has a way of coming at me when I least expect it. And just as in battle, if I drop my sword, the word of God, Satan picks it up and pursues me with it, making me afraid of the very Scriptures that give me life.

**Our Armor**—I've heard the shield described as the armor that protects the armor. The shield kept a soldier from taking a blow to the armor that was dangerously close to the vulnerable parts of his body. Likewise, our faith is the armor for our armor. Insecurity makes us feel like it's hopeless for us to trust in God's armor. Instead of having the shield of faith out in front of us, we start putting other types of protective barriers around our feminine hearts—ones that keep others and God at bay. Faith enables us to trust in the helmet of salvation, put on the belt of truth, and to use the sword of God's word whenever Satan attacks.

**Our Purpose**—The Bible encourages us to have our feet "fitted with the readiness that comes from the gospel of peace." Satan, on the other hand, wants to convince us that our place is cowering in the bushes, rather than carrying his word to others. "How can I share with others when I'm so...?" (You fill in the blank!) Insecurity takes us away from the truth that God's gospel of peace equips us perfectly to carry out our role in the world as his ambassadors.

**Our Petitions**—Although Ephesians doesn't identify prayer as a specific piece of armor, it's interesting that the description of the armor of God is wrapped in prayer. I'm convinced that one of Satan's goals was to get Eve to question God, so that she would not feel comfortable crying out to him for guidance and help in the face of temptation. Prayer is where we'll find the deepest kind of security—the kind that comes from surrender and entrusting our anxious hearts to God and his care.

### Praying Your Way to Security

There is no true spiritual security without talking with God. In fact, Satan's whole plan for Eve was to divide her from her Creator by making her too ashamed to talk with him. Perhaps that's why Satan works so diligently to keep us from praying. Prayer takes us before the very throne of God, enlisting his power to work within us. Even beyond that, it is my personal belief that, as a woman, I have a very special prayer role to play. I have been chosen as an intercessor for my husband, my children and my other family members. If I don't pray for them, who will?

To be perfectly honest though, there was a period of several years when I didn't pray faithfully or even consistently for my kids. I would pray for them here and there, and usually guiltily because I knew I had yet again let time lapse without praying for them. The problem wasn't that I didn't love or deeply desire for them to know God. So why wasn't I carrying out my role? It was because I had listened to the accusing voice of Satan telling me that I wasn't what I needed to be as a mother. He had made me an insecure parent. And my insecure parenting made me less (rather than more) inclined to pray.

To take my stand against that satanic scheme, I've learned to push past my fears and rely on God through prayer. Now, instead of sitting back in my insecurity and rehearsing my weaknesses while Satan works behind my back fortifying his strongholds, I'm trusting day by day in God's mighty power by lifting my family before his throne in prayer.

I've found that without the armor of God, it's hard to engage prayer. The helmet of salvation gives me confidence that as a daughter of God he hears and answers my prayers. The belt of truth leads me to surrender control of all the ins and outs of my life to the Lordship of Christ and the authority of the word of God. The breastplate of righteousness teaches me that I can come sinful, weak and struggling and stand firm in his righteousness alone. The shield of faith allows me to confidently approach the throne of grace and to know that I can find mercy in my time of need.

Likewise, without prayer, putting on the armor of God is next to impossible. Prayer allows me to trust in my salvation, honor God's truth and lay claim to the righteousness of Christ as a free and undeserved gift. Prayer allows me to take up the sword of the Spirit in spiritual warfare. Prayer grows and nurtures my faith into a strong shield able to resist the flaming arrows that Satan throws at me.

How are you doing on putting on your daily armor? *Are you going through day after day with an unprotected life?* If so, you can bet that Satan has come in while you were sleeping and has set up insecurities in your thoughts, in your view of God and in your view of yourself. But wherever you've been in your walk with God, it's never too late to begin to pursue the secure heart that God desires for you.

## Engaging the Battle

Although we are all Eve's daughters, there is a sense in which we have a distinct advantage over her. Although she had the privilege of having walked with God in person, of knowing his voice intimately and of experiencing a security untarnished by shame, the Bible tells us we have a better way in Christ. The whole book of Hebrews is devoted to this topic, so it seems appropriate that it ends with a supreme declaration of the better way:

> May the God of peace, who through the blood of the eternal covenant brought back from the dead our Lord Jesus, that great Shepherd of the sheep, equip you with everything good for doing his will, and may he work in us what is pleasing to him, through Jesus Christ, to whom be glory for ever and ever. Amen. (Hebrews 13:20–21)

What does it mean for a woman to be secure in heart? Bottom line, it means knowing that through the resurrection of Jesus, your own personal great Shepherd, that you have been equipped with everything you need to do his will. It's a confidence that he will work in you everything that is pleasing to him. It's believing that your life will bring him glory for ever and ever. It's trusting that the covenant between you and God is eternal. And it's looking to him as your only true source of security.

But sisters, this security we were created for won't come easily. It won't come as an "aha!" moment at the end of a sermon or as the result of a particularly great quiet time with God. It won't come because someone exhorted you to "Be secure!" And it certainly won't come because you've willed yourself to be secure. *Security will come because with God and Christ at your side, you've battled for it.*

> For though we live in the world, we do not wage war as the world does. The weapons we fight with are not the weapons of the world. On the contrary, they have divine power to demolish strongholds. We demolish arguments and every pretension that sets itself up against the knowledge of God, and we take captive every thought to make it obedient to Christ. (2 Corinthians 10:3–5)

To engage in spiritual warfare, we need to identify the strongholds and fortresses that Satan has set up in the form of false securities. Only as we remove the false securities and expose Satan's strongholds, will we grow more secure in heart.

Are you ready to go to battle?

# EVE'S DAUGHTERS:
# THE STRONGHOLD OF INSECURITY

*Personal Study Guide & Life Application*

In order to fight for a secure heart, it is important to identify how Satan is scheming to take away our security. One of his evil schemes, as demonstrated in Eve's story, is to trick us out of our security and then make us feel ashamed and shrink back from our relationship with God.

> *Make a list of some of the things Satan whispers to you on a day-to-day basis to make you feel ashamed about your battles. Read Ephesians 6:11–18. What part of God's armor do you most need to focus on to protect yourself from Satan's attacks?*

"When I arrived, she asked me the simple question, 'How are you?' In a matter of minutes I was weeping, telling her everything. She listened and then came over, put her arms around me and held me for a moment while I cried. Then she made me a cup of mint tea and we sat and talked for several hours.

"It turned out we both needed that time together in a big way. My vulnerability gave her the faith she needed to press into areas she had been afraid of sharing. Her support diffused my over-emotionality and helped me think clearly about what was really bothering me."

— Learning to share my insecurities

# ALL THAT GLITTERS
## *Unmasking False Securities*

> But I am afraid that just as Eve was deceived by the serpent's cunning, your minds may somehow be led astray from your sincere and pure devotion to Christ... And no wonder, for Satan himself masquerades as an angel of light. It is not surprising, then, if his servants masquerade as servants of righteousness.
>
> 2 Corinthians 11:3, 14–15

FROM EVE UNTIL NOW, SATAN HAS SOUGHT TO ALLURE US WITH glitz and glam that looks and sounds good, but in the end delivers a deadly punch. Think of it as a giant masquerade ball where Satan, adorned with the deceptions of the ages, rolls out his red carpet. His choice of costume? He disguises himself as an angel of light who understands and relates to the yearnings of our feminine hearts—love, acceptance, control, independence, beauty, adventure and romance. And Satan is more than happy to show a way—*his way*—to satisfy these yearnings outside of God.

Following close behind him is a whole entourage of evil servants carrying out his every whim. They have been well prepared to show us that the only way we can have our yearnings fulfilled is to venture out onto *his* dance floor. Wanting to drown out the whisper of God in our hearts, they beckon us through magazines, television, radio, billboards and literature. And when none of these things work, they have been trained by Satan himself how to masquerade as servants of righteousness. They worm their way into our faith, into our religious cultures and into our spirituality, seeking to corrupt our view of ourselves, our view of God and our connection to the life-transforming power in his word—the Bible. In our culture, we are bombarded with the voices of these angels of delusion at every corner.

> *"Excuse me, but are you looking for a way to be loved...important...valued...independent...secure? Right this way, my dear. And oh, my, but aren't you beautiful tonight?"*

I'm convinced that these satanic servants are each specially handpicked to cater to our individual weaknesses. Their goal? To seek out the crevices in our hearts where the evil one might find a small foothold that can be cultivated into a full-blown stronghold.

As we discussed in the previous chapter, Satan wasted no time picking out his very first target for attack—the beautiful and pure-hearted woman that God so delighted in. Satan obviously had been studying Eve, looking for just the right place to tempt her. Eve was glorious in every way. She was everything good that God created in woman—vulnerable, unashamed, passionate about her relationship with God and with Adam, intelligent and emotional. Although Eve walked with God in the garden, in a sense her knowledge of him was just beginning. There was so much more she had to learn about God. She was yet to have her knowledge of God tested.

Eve was completely secure, but it was a security largely based on her circumstances. She had a husband who adored her and a God who walked with her daily. She was surrounded by complete beauty. She had never known hardship, sin, rejection, disease or disappointment. Although she may have caught a glimpse of herself in a pool of water, there were no other women to use as a standard for comparison. She saw herself only through her walks in the garden with God and through the eyes of Adam.

In fact, I imagine that part of the glorious freedom she experienced in the garden was a complete lack of self-consciousness. Who wouldn't feel secure under these circumstances? There was a deeper security she knew nothing of that would only come through tests, suffering and sorrow.

No doubt Satan thought carefully about the illusion he would offer Eve. As she stood in the glow of the life-sustaining garden God had given her as her home, Satan offered a shortcut. He convinced Eve that there was actually a quicker way for her to find wisdom and knowledge—offering her a whole different brand of security that could be obtained at a moment's notice.

> *"God's plan to make you complete and secure…well…it is going to be excruciatingly slow. The truth is that you can forge your own path into security, knowledge and wisdom. I'm sad to say it, Eve, but it looks like God is holding you back from your destiny."*

And Satan stood cheerfully by, ready to point out another path to what appeared to be the same destination, only in her timing instead of her Father's.

Satan made himself seem like Eve's advocate, her confidant, an angel of light committed to helping her find *her own* equality and independence, *her own* right to know good and evil. And Eve might have reasoned, "It's just a small bite of one small piece of fruit. How could that hurt anything?"

Unfortunately what Eve didn't know was as soon as Satan enticed her to make this disastrous decision, he would be standing by, ready to turn the blissful security she had enjoyed before she sinned into an overwhelming insecurity.

> *"Why didn't Adam protect you? Why didn't he speak up? You trusted him and he let you down. Can you ever really trust man?*
>
> *"How will God feel about you now that you've let him*

*down? You couldn't even carry out the one thing he asked of
you. Quick, run and hide; otherwise he will see you for what
you really are.*

*"You will never be able to change this mistake. Never.
You've lost everything. You'll be marked forever by this decision."*

## Just Short of True

As I think about Eve, what strikes me is that in our battle to
be secure in heart, Satan comes at us with the exact same ploys.
His dance floor hasn't changed one bit! Satan stands by with lies
that fit perfectly with our fears and misconceptions of God. He
comes to us in areas where our convictions about God are weak,
unsteady, secondhand or perhaps even untested. His goal? To get
us to believe and then act upon a lie, accepting and then integrat-
ing false securities into our feminine hearts to such a degree that
we don't even realize we're trusting in an illusion crafted by the
father of all lies.

In the book of Revelation, the Bible tells us that the mark of
the father of lies, or the beast, is 666.[1] Have you ever wondered
why? Many scholars interpret the use of the number "666" as
representing a kind of counterfeit seven, in appearance brushing
up close to seven, but in reality falling drastically short.[2] This is
significant, because in the Bible seven is the number of Biblical
perfection representing:

- **Creativity**—The Bible starts with seven days of creation.

- **Celebration**—All of the Jewish feasts were related to sevens.
  Pentecost was celebrated on the day after seven weeks passed—
  on the 50th day after Passover. The Feast of Tabernacles was celebrated in the seventh month for seven days. In fact, there were
  exactly seven different feast days that the Jews celebrated.

- **Cleansing**—Naaman dipped in the Jordan seven times and was
  cured of his leprosy.[3]

1. Revelation 13:18
2. Thomas F. Torrance says, "This evil trinity 666 apes the Holy Trinity 777,
but always falls short and fails." *The Apocalypse Today* (Grand Rapids: Eerdmans,
1959), 86.
3. 2 Kings 5:13–14

- **Confirmation**—In his Gospel, John confirms the deity of Jesus by highlighting seven "signs" or miracles that he performed and by recording the seven "I am" statements of Jesus, e.g., "I am the bread of life."

- **Completeness**—The Bible ends with the "book of sevens"—Revelation—where we find seven churches, seals, candlesticks, stars, trumpets, thunders, vials, plagues and seven angels to carry out the plagues.

And these are just a small drop in the bucket of Bible "sevens." Remember Pharaoh's dream? There were seven years of plenty and seven years of famine.[4] How many days did the Israelites march around Jericho? You guessed it, seven, and on the seventh day they marched around Jericho seven times.[5] And the list goes on and on.

Contrast the perfection and completion that the number "seven" represents with what the Bible says the mark of the beast, 666, represents. In Revelation 13, the Bible paints a frightening picture of the evil intentions of the beast, telling us that he will

- Utter proud words and blasphemies

- Slander God's name, his dwelling place and those who live in heaven

- Make war against the saints with the goal of conquering us

- Seek to get us to worship him by deceiving us with false miracles and signs

## 666 Security

Be self-controlled and alert. Your enemy the devil prowls around like a roaring lion looking for someone to devour. Resist him, standing firm in your faith... (1 Peter 5:8–9a)

The number "666" highlights Satan's identity as an imposter

---

4. See Genesis 41.
5. Joshua 6:1–5

and liar, totally committed to making war against God and us. Satan's goal is to brush up as close to the truth ("seven" or Biblical truth) as possible without ever telling the truth. And by doing that, he creates the worst lies possible—lies that deceive and devour us. He stalks us with glittering illusions. His forte is to make something that has no substance at all to appear real or true. But 666 also represents an insidious brand of security that he offers—a false security that appears to meet the needs of our feminine hearts but that leaves us deeply insecure instead.

Real security versus 666 is much like the difference between real gold and pyrite (fool's gold). Real gold shines, but doesn't twinkle or sparkle like pyrite. Real gold is moldable and rare—one of the most valuable elements on the earth. Pyrite is common, brittle (easy to break) and has little value. The security that God gives us through our faith in him is the true gold. This real gold flourishes and shines even though it is refined by fire. In contrast, Satan's false security literally glitters and sparkles with potential, alluring us into a fantasy world where we're in control of how other people see us and where we receive the love and respect we desire. But in reality false security is brittle, meaning that when life's hardships come flooding in, we'll be broken as well.

Satan's false securities look good at first glance, but are designed to eat us alive, leading us to a place where we do the following:

- Shortcut God's plans and seek life outside of the knowledge of God

- Become rebellious toward God, without realizing that we're in rebellion

- Accept Satan's answers to the buried questions that lie dormant and unanswered in our souls

- Change the way we think about ourselves and others, defining ourselves by his standards instead of God's

The Bible says that the key to resisting Satan is standing firm in our faith, or perhaps, as we discussed in the last chapter, putting on the armor of God. That brings up the logical question: *Where is your faith?* Do you just know about God in your head, or is your knowledge of him based on daily experience? We'll talk more about the knowledge of God in the next chapter, but rest assured, Satan's expertise is finding places where your knowledge of God is weak.

## Unmasking Satan's Schemes

To resist Satan and stand firm in our faith, we need to first identify the false securities that he wants to sell us. As we start talking about how to battle for a secure heart, let's take a few minutes to introduce the questions we ask and the places other than God that Satan would tell us to turn for security.

| Question | Satan's 666 Security |
| --- | --- |
| Am I enough? | Perfectionism |
| Who can I count on? | Self-Reliance |
| Will I be rescued? | Dependence |
| Will I be successful? | Worldliness |
| Who will protect me? | Self-Protection |
| What do others think of me? | Approval |
| Will I be alone? | Romantic Love |

First, notice that these questions are all issues of the heart—having to do with what we think, how we feel, what motivates us—what the Bible calls the motives of our heart (1 Corinthians 4:5).

Second, these questions are nothing new—they have been asked throughout the ages. Esther, no doubt, asked, "Am I enough?" before she risked her life to stand in front of the king to plead for the safety of her nation.[6] After her husband died, Ruth must have wondered, "Will I be alone?" as she chose her commitment to her mother-in-law (and her God) over what appeared a quicker road to remarriage.[7] We know David asked

6. Esther 4:10–17

God repeatedly, "Will you rescue me?" In fact, we learn from David that moving toward God through our honest and heart-wrenching questions can be a direct path to his heart!

You will also notice that all of these qualities listed in the second column can be positive in the right context. Learning to be independent and self-sufficient is an important part of functioning in a relationship without being swallowed by it. Depending on others helps us maintain emotional and spiritual health. Romantic love can be thrilling and can mature into the kind of unconditional love and acceptance that is the hallmark of a great relationship. But none of these qualities, apart from God, will bring us security. When we use any of these to replace the security that God offers, they become false securities that make us insecure instead of secure.

Just as idolatry keeps us from the true worship of God, so false securities take us away from the true security God holds out to us. Think of it as a four-step process:

- First, Satan offers us a path to security outside of the knowledge of God through false securities specially designed for our feminine hearts. *In distrust and disobedience Eve stepped away from God to find her own path to security, fulfillment and wisdom.*

- Second, Satan wants to direct toward God the resulting insecurity we feel. *Eve suddenly realized she was naked and vulnerable. She hid from God, ashamed and afraid of his reaction to her sin.*

- Next, Satan convinces us that we must blame our newfound insecurities on others. *After Adam told God that Eve had offered him the fruit, Eve quickly pointed out that the snake had given her the fruit. Insecurity leads toward taking less responsibility for our actions instead of more.*

- Finally Satan hopes we'll define God through our insecurities, changing the way we view him. *In Eve's insecurity she feared God couldn't accept her because of her weakness and sin. She no longer felt worthy to walk with him openly in the garden, so she hid in the bushes.*

7. Ruth 1:8–22

What kind of response do you think Eve would have received if she had come openly to God, owning and confessing her sin and seeking to restore her relationship with him? I believe it could have been a much different one. Some conjecture that God's response to Adam and Eve's sin came as much from the way they dealt with their sin—hiding, finger pointing, distrust and shame—as from the actual sin.

It must have wounded God deeply that now Eve was treating him like he was an entirely different being than the one she had walked with the day before. She had gone from baring her heart and confiding in the one who loved her most, to pushing God away, treating him like he could no longer be trusted, and then refusing to take responsibility for her actions.

Think of your own knowledge of God as the glasses through which you see everything that happens in your life. When we bite into and then accept Satan's counterfeit 666 securities, just like Eve, we start living in line with an image of God that has nothing to do with who he really is. Do you think God is any less hurt by our sin than he was by Eve's?

Let's take a closer look at the questions we ask and the false securities that Satan would pose in response. Although these questions overlap and feed into each other, they give us a starting place for unmasking the false securities that Satan seeks to deceive us with. For now, I'd suggest quickly reading through these and asking God to begin opening up the areas you'll want to focus on as you move through the book. Later on, we'll look in much more detail at each of these false securities and learn how God's divine nature can help us battle these satanic onslaughts.

## 1) Am I enough?— The False Security of Perfectionism

The United States has blossomed into a "measure up" society that flashes makeover shows before us day and night. I enjoy makeover shows, but the problem is the fantasy that if my home looked like that, or if I had that $5,000 wardrobe or if I lost that weight or had that surgery, I would be secure. But the pressure on women to be perfect goes far beyond our clothing, looks and homes. We're expected to be smart, educated and career-savvy, while still being a great mother and keeper at home. In the church, we seek to lead women's ministries, teach Sunday school, head up benevolent projects and counsel other women. And in many households, women find themselves raising children alone with no support from a mate or partner. Is it any wonder that women are prone to chronic fatigue?

Satan wants to entrench perfectionism in our hearts toward every part of our lives—especially toward God. He wants us either to throw ourselves into the pursuit of our own goodness or give up on being good altogether, while forgetting the most important fact in the universe—that God is good.

> **The impact of Perfectionism on our view of God**—God's affection for me comes and goes in direct proportion to my ability to meet his standards. His goodness is based on my goodness— therefore I can only trust his goodness as much as I trust my own.

> **The truth?**—True security isn't found in perfectionism, performance or in my own goodness. Knowing God in his goodness allows me to let go of the false illusion of perfectionism and accept my weakness, confident that his strength and grace are enough to make me truly perfect in his eyes.

## 2) Who can I count on?—The False Security of Self-Reliance

"What's wrong with self-reliance?" you might ask. "Isn't being self-sufficient an admirable trait for a woman?" Let's look at the definition to answer that question. The word "sufficient" means "adequate, having everything we need." "Self-sufficiency," therefore, tells you that you can find everything you need in yourself. In contrast, the Bible tells us that we're given everything we need through our *knowledge of him*.

His divine power has given us everything we need for life and godliness through our knowledge of him who called us to his own glory and goodness. (2 Peter 1:3)

Through his false security of self-reliance, Satan proposes that I do it all in order to make sure it gets done right. He suggests that I can go without daily Bible study and prayer and still expect to somehow live out my Christianity and have spiritual strength for trials and hardships. He whispers that I can't possibly trust someone else without being hurt, let down or disappointed. In contrast, trusting in God's divine power and his provision allows me to be vulnerable with God and with others.

**The impact of Self-Reliance on our view of God**—Since God isn't coming through for me the way I see him coming through for others, I have to come through for myself.

**The truth?**—There is only one place that I really stand—in God's presence. Knowing God as my Rock enables me to continue to give my heart even when life hurts.

## 3) Will I be rescued?—The False Security of Dependence

Sometimes the false security that Satan holds out to us is our own strength. Other times he tempts us to be totally dependent upon the strength of others or even hope for a rescue—our own custom-fitted fairy tale. Just watch any of the popular reality shows on television where a large group of women compete to win the heart of one bachelor. In the beginning episode, you'll hear woman after woman saying, "I'm here for the fairy tale, to find my Prince Charming." In other words, they want to be rescued.

We aren't just tempted to depend on men for security. We can look to a ministry leader or even to a church to provide us with everything we need. Some of us become overly dependent on our children for our self-esteem, insisting that they come through for us in ways that our mates won't. In the company we work for, we can seek validation and acknowledgment for our work performance.

The funny thing is that although dependence appears to be all about others, it really is all about us. "How are you going to fix me?" we ask those around us. "And when are you going to come through and meet my needs?" In doing so, we unknowingly give in to Satan's plot to get us to give up responsibility for our own emotions, our own needs, even our own spirituality.

> **The impact of Dependence on our view of God**—God has let me down. The reason I'm bitter, unhappy or dissatisfied is because God doesn't care about my heart's desire and doesn't send anyone to meet my needs.

> **The truth?**—No person or organization can anchor my life or anyone else's. Knowing God as my Anchor gives me assurance that when the storms come or when others let me down, he is holding me steady.

## 4) Will I be successful?—The False Security of Worldliness

What exactly is "worldliness"? The book of 1 John tells us that when we love the world, God's love is not in us (1 John 2:15). Since the Bible uses *he* generically, let's change the pronouns here and read the rest of the scripture:

> For everything in the world—the cravings of sinful woman, the lust of her eyes and the boasting of what she has and does—comes not from the Father but from the world. The world and its desires pass away, but the woman who does the will of God lives forever. (1 John 2:16–17)

What "worldliness" means is the temptation to let good desires such as love, marriage, children, career and home turn into lustful cravings that in our hearts we insist on having. Then when we have them, we boast as if we achieved them by our own worthiness. The problem is that the world, along with all of its standards of womanly success, only gives a temporary and fleeting satisfaction that evaporates and leaves us spiritually even more thirsty.

Satan wants to convince us that the only way we can find the happiness and self-worth that we desire, is through his measures of success.

**The impact of Worldliness on our view of God**—God uses the standards of the world to judge my worth. He only rewards those who do everything well and everything right.

**The truth?**—Interpreting my life through worldly wisdom only leads to pride or deep despair. Knowing God as my Guide will lead me to life and to godly confidence and acceptance.

## 5) Who will protect me?—The False Security of Self-Protection

From my own experiences, and from the experiences of other women I talk with, I find that self-protection is a huge issue for us. And self-protection brings with it the desire to control. Why? Because we hope to buffer ourselves from hardship, disappointment and grief. And with the news constantly giving us images of the insecure world we live in—terrorism, violence, disease and war—our desire to protect ourselves becomes even greater.

One big reason we try to find security in self-protection is the heartache of having our hopes deferred (Proverbs 13:12). Just as he did with Eve, Satan seeks to convince us that God may never meet us at our heartfelt desires. Therefore we must reach over and grab the wheel, taking the timing of our heart's desires into our own hands.

Satan proposes self-protection knowing that control may momentarily give a sensation of relief: "There, at least someone is taking this situation under hand."

**The impact of Self-Protection on our view of God**—God is only concerned with his own agenda or bigger things in the world—

my problems seem insignificant to him. He has forgotten about me.

**The truth?**—Knowing God as my Guard means that I trust his protection even when it appears that he is nowhere to be found.

## 6) What do others think of me—The False Security of Approval

Perhaps more than any of these other false securities, seeking approval has been a huge issue throughout my life. Through childhood experiences I came to believe that the best way to ensure my good standing with others was through performance and lots of it. When I came to God in my teen years, I quickly transferred my performance mentality into the realm of spirituality, thinking that I needed to perform for God in order for him and others to love me. I turned to spiritual role models in the church to give me the approval that I craved.

Satan wants to give us a false, conditional approval that makes us feel like we swing in and out of good standing with God, depending on the day and the amount of sin that we're struggling with. He delights in making us double-minded—asking God and then not believing that we'll receive anything in return.

**The impact of Approval on our view of God**—God's love is conditional, inconsistent and based on my performance. I can never count on how God feels about me.

**The truth?**—Having God as my Advocate means that I walk confidently, knowing he gave me Jesus as my defense attorney to protect me from the accusing voice of Satan.

## 7) Will I be alone?—The False Security of Romantic Love

As mentioned earlier, women are created to be relational. In our desire for connectedness, we long for intimacy—emotionally, spiritually and even sexually. Here's where Satan steps into the arena as a master illusionist. He knows that we long for relationship so much that we might be willing to trade the pain inherent in real intimacy, for a false intimacy, "a self-created illusion to help a person avoid the pain inherent in real intimacy," that is more easily available.[8]

In real intimacy there are imperfect relationships, disappointments, the fear of being abandoned and/or the loss of control. Real intimacy isn't something that comes easily. And for some of us, finding a partner for life may be a long process that involves patience, perseverance and even suffering.

Satan would like to take us to a place where we so fear being left alone that we're willing to accept a counterfeit.

**The impact of Romantic Love on our view of God**—God practices favoritism, giving freely to others, yet withholding from me.

**The truth?**—Knowing God through his Holy Spirit, the Comforter, takes away my fear of being alone. In fact, I am filled with assurance that I am never really alone.

## Morgan's Story

Years ago I studied the Bible with a vibrant young woman named Morgan. She was a student, working hard to make her way through school. With blue eyes, long wavy blonde hair, and a naturally curvaceous figure and all-American looks, she was an aspiring writer who had always felt a nagging spiritual interest. She had a small child with her fiancé. Although she professed a desire to know God, she couldn't seem to make any kind of emotional connection with the Bible.

I couldn't put my finger on it, but it seemed like there was something that was numbing her. The spiritual feelings were still there but she couldn't find any oomph to act on those feelings. She wanted to read the Bible, but she never picked it up. Prayer intrigued her, but it also evaded her. The spiritual part of her heart was buried, and no matter how many scriptures we talked about together, she couldn't budge it any closer to the surface.

8. Harry W. Schaumburg, *False Intimacy* (Colorado Springs: Navpress, 1993), 18.

Finally Morgan opened up. For years, she had engaged in a lucrative career on the side as an "exotic dancer." Why would a bright and beautiful girl like Morgan decide to work for a strip club? She started as a short-term solution to a financial crunch. But the hundreds of dollars she could make in a single evening (and the attention she was receiving) was addictive. In fact, the money was so good, when she first moved in with her fiancé, he encouraged her to keep it up until they could get their feet on the ground financially.

Since she was pregnant, she wasn't currently working at the strip club. Although she could clearly see that God did not approve of the profession, she was reluctant to disown it. It was her financial fallback. And as much as she hated to admit it, part of her liked who she was when she was working in the club. She felt powerful, alive, tantalizing—in a way she never felt outside of that arena.

Revealing her body and having men practically throw money at her in response gave her a security, a false security sold to her by the prince of lies, but a security all the same that was difficult to disown. This false security rescued her when she was financially destitute. It encouraged her when she felt like she wasn't beautiful. When things were challenging at home, it gave her an escape into a fantasy world where the women were sexy and the men were powerful.

Finally, after many studies and conversations, Morgan decided that she just wasn't ready to have a relationship with God yet. I had become good friends with her and wanted to hold on to our friendship. But finally she stopped returning my phone calls and became unavailable. I'm guessing contact with me was a reminder of everything she wanted, yet didn't quite have the conviction to go to battle for. Like the rich, young ruler, she meant well, but walked away sad.[9]

## Guarding Our Hearts

Before we are too quick to judge Morgan, we all need to remember that we're not so unlike her in the battles we wage in our hearts. Like her, we've all been tempted with and at times have given ourselves over to glittering false securities built on counterfeit miracles, illusions and downright lies. We also see in Morgan's story how our hearts can be led astray when we don't have an active and committed relationship with God and his word. It takes an aggressive battle to keep the word of God in its rightful place in our hearts. Why is it so important to know the Bible? Because it is through the Bible that God reveals himself to us.

Real gold, the "seven" security we all long for doesn't come easy. Having a secure heart is something we need to fight and struggle for. Just as Satan has been working throughout time to undo man's purity, he is equally if not more determined to undermine woman's security. It is time to see insecurity not as something to carry with deep shame, but as something to engage in spiritual warfare.

What is the beginning of real security? An active relationship with God. It comes from knowing him—not just knowing about him, but walking with him. It also comes from believing, trusting and applying that knowledge. Are you ready to disown false securities and embrace the true security that God offers? Are you ready to get off Satan's dance floor and let yourself be led by the lover of your soul into a secure place? Let's start by looking at the foundation of security—the knowledge of God.

---

9. Mark 10:17–23

## ALL THAT GLITTERS:
## UNMASKING FALSE SECURITIES

*Personal Study Guide & Life Application*

Satan, as the master illusionist, seeks to sell us a 666 security that takes us away from God. His ultimate hope is to get us to short-cut God's good plans for us, hoping ultimately to get us to either blame others or even begin to see God through our insecurities.

> *Which of the false securities do you most relate to? How has that false security affected your view of God? Read Psalm 139. Write a prayer similar to David's asking God to walk with you on your journey through the book—revealing any offensive way in you and leading you in the way everlasting.*

"Oftentimes, I find myself feeling all these things about God, and I won't realize that it's because my relationship with God is so superficial. I'll be telling him, 'I love you, thank you, thank you,' without really sharing what I'm feeling or thinking about getting my needs met by him. And then I wonder why I'm not feeling secure."

— Newly married

# KNOWING GOD
## *The Key to a Secure Heart*

This is what the LORD says,

"Let not the wise man boast of his wisdom
   or the strong man boast of his strength
   or the rich man boast of his riches,
but let him who boasts boast about this;
   that he understands and knows me,
that I am the LORD, who exercises kindness,
   justice and righteousness on earth,
   for in these I delight."

Jeremiah 9:23–24

HAVE YOU EVER SPENT TIME WITH A COUPLE THAT HAS BEEN MAR-
ried for fifty years? They are so in sync that sometimes it seems
as if their tissues and ligaments have become intertwined. There
is a beautiful security evident in their knowledge of each other.

Marriage is an analogy that God uses often to describe his
desire to know us. In fact, in the Old Testament, one of the
Hebrew words for "know" is *yada*, a word also used to describe
sexual intimacy.[1] In the book of Hosea, Israel is called the bride
of God.[2] In the New Testament, Jesus told more than one para-
ble describing himself as a bridegroom waiting for his bride.[3] In
Ephesians 5, Paul explains that marriage is parallel to the relationship Christ has with his church.

In fact, the Bible from beginning to end could be described
as a set of divine nuptials, ending with the wedding of the Lamb

---

1. *Yada* is used in Genesis 4:1 to refer to sexual intercourse between Adam
and Eve.
2. Hosea 2:16–20
3. For example, Matthew 25:1–13.

(Christ) to the church in the last chapters of Revelation.[4] Perhaps we can take some cues from the marriage relationship to understand knowing God.

Marriage expert, Gary Smalley, has written many books about how couples achieve intimacy. In *Secrets to Lasting Love: Uncovering the Keys to Life-Long Intimacy*, Smalley shares the five levels of intimacy that couples go through in marriage:

1) Speaking in clichés
2) Sharing facts
3) Sharing opinions
4) Sharing feelings
5) Sharing needs

Smalley explains that many young marriages start off at levels one and two (clichés and facts). Whenever a couple moves into sharing opinions, concerns and expectations, there will be conflict. This conflict either bounces them back into the lower levels of only sharing clichés and facts, or gives them a doorway into deeper intimacy achieved through sharing feelings and needs. Smalley has found that if a couple doesn't successfully transition into communication in levels four and five by the fifth year of marriage, they will most likely separate.[5]

It strikes me how closely Smalley's levels of intimacy in marriage parallel the levels of intimacy we can choose to have with God. Some of us have a cliché-based knowledge—we know all the Christian sayings and consider this as having a relationship with God. *I can talk about things such as sermons, quiet times, devotionals and fellowship with the best of them.*

Some of us take a step further into facts—*I can tell Bible stories and perhaps even quote a few scriptures.* We think knowing information about God is the same as knowing God. Or it could even be a Christian-book relationship with God—*I've learned everything I need to know about God through Christian books.*

The third level would be an opinion-based relationship with

4. See Revelation 19:6–8, 21:1–4.

5. Reprinted with the permission of Simon & Schuster Adult Publishing Group from *Secrets to Lasting Love: Uncovering the Keys to Life-Long Intimacy* by Gary Smalley. Copyright © 2000 by Gary and Norma Smalley Trust.

God, where we take security in doctrinal correctness—*As long as I believe the "correct" thing, I'll go to heaven.*

The truth is, in and of themselves, none of these first three levels of communication will give us intimacy with God. None of these teach us how God feels about us when we fall flat on our faces. None of these teach us to trust enough to be vulnerable. And none of these will keep us faithful to God through the long haul. There's got to be a point where we go deeper—past facts, opinions and a "head knowledge" of God to the point that our walk with God engages our feelings, our needs, our desires and our passions.

Going back to Smalley, if conflict is what determines whether a marriage goes deeper or becomes shallower, what is the parallel in our relationship with God? What is the doorway through which we can experience God on a much deeper level? I've found that trials and struggles act as the doorway to intimacy with God. Hardship either causes us to shut the door and flee back into safe levels of Christian existence where we don't have to answer hard questions, or it will cause us to go toward intimacy with God, where we begin to engage God on a much deeper level.

The good news is that God doesn't sit back and wait for us to find a way to somehow know him. In fact when we come to the door of decision, God is standing there patiently knocking. And the truth is that behind the scenes, he was the one who brought us to the door in the first place. Simply said, God pursues us with wild abandon.

## God's Abandon

In his classic Christian book, *Knowing God*, J. I. Packer points out that the more complex a person and their position, the more challenge involved in getting to know them. He says that it is easier to know a house, a book or a language than to know a person. Similarly, it is far easier to know another person, than it is to know God.[6]

---

6. J. I. Packer, *Knowing God* (Downer's Grove, Illinois: Intervarsity Press, 1973), 30–32.

Likewise, when we consider the complexity of God reflected in all the "omni's"—his omnipresence (he is everywhere), his omniscience (he knows everything), his omnipotence (he's all powerful) or even his omnibenevolence (he is all good)—it's understandable why someone might think trying to know God intimately is a worthy goal, but, well…kind of ambitious or even super-spiritual. We think, *Maybe this is something that should be left to people who can devote themselves to it full time, like the saints, priests and preachers.*

Because God understands the challenges we face in knowing him (including Satan's ploy to distract, dishearten and disillusion us), he takes it upon himself to take all the risk. God is willing to put his heart on the line first, taking a gamble that we'll want to know him just as he wants to know us.

In Psalm 139, David marvels at all the ways that God pursues him. Using the words of the psalmist, imagine God speaking to you in the most personal of terms, expressing his desire to know you:

*Dear* _____ *(insert your name),*

*From the very beginning of your life to now, I have searched you thoroughly and I've known you. I know when you sit down, and when you rise up. I understand your thoughts from far off. In fact, there is not an unuttered word on your tongue that I don't hear; I know it altogether. I am in front of you and behind you. I have laid my hand upon you.*

*There is nowhere you can flee away from my Spirit, nowhere you run from my presence. If you ascend up to heaven, I am there. If you go to the depths of the grave, I am there. If you were to flee on the wings of the morning to the uttermost parts of the sea, even there my hand will guide you, and my right hand will hold you.*

*If you say, "Surely the darkness is covering me," that darkness is like light to me. For I formed your inward parts. I knit you together in your mother's womb. Your frame was not hidden from me, when you were formed in secret in the depths of the earth. My eyes saw your unformed substance, and all the days of your life were written in my book long before they ever took shape. Your inner self knows my wonderful works.*

*How vast is the sum of my thoughts about you. If you could count them, they would be as many as all the grains of sand, and when you finished counting, I would still be there. Let me search you and thoroughly know you. Let me know your thoughts. Let me help you if there is any hurtful or wicked way in you. And I will lead you in the way everlasting.[7]*

*Your Maker and Husband,*
*God*

Whether you've walked with God for years or you are just now considering the possibilities, God wants to know you better. In fact, God has shown his commitment to helping you know him through a variety of ways—including making himself vulnerable, accessible and personal.

## God Makes Himself Vulnerable

In the Bible, God reveals himself through hundreds of different names, titles and analogies, letting us see numerous facets of his personality.[8] With a tender vulnerability, God reveals his heart of love and desire for us to know him. I think we've got it all wrong if we think that it is easy for God to be vulnerable. (From a human perspective, I understand what an investment of heart it takes to be gut-wrenchingly transparent!) His vulnerability is compelling evidence that God wants me to know him.

Much like us, when God communicates his heart of love and

---

7. Paraphrased from Psalm 139, *Amplified Bible.*
8. For an extended list see "Names, Titles and Descriptions of God" in *Experiencing God,* Henry T. Blackaby & Claude V. King, (Nashville: Broadman & Holman Publishers, 1988), 281–288.

then ends up being rejected or misunderstood, it hurts. And he doesn't just open up to those who invite him in for a cup of mint tea. He doesn't wait for us to be vulnerable first, showing him that it's safe. He opens up to those who reject him, to those who would turn his words against him; he even opens up to his enemies.

Because God wants every nation to seek him and find him, his risk of being hurt is exponentially greater. Love always carries with it the risk of rejection. In fact, if it doesn't hurt when someone rejects you, you can hardly say that you love them. Even with the likelihood of rejection, in scripture after scripture, the vulnerability of God comes shining through: *I love you. I delight in you. I want to walk with you. I care about you.* If we really understand his vulnerability, I think we can find the courage to come to God. Even though our steps toward humility and transparency may be halting, they'll still take us toward the goal of knowing God and knowing Christ.

## God Makes Himself Accessible

An important part in being secure in a relationship is knowing that you are a priority. God doesn't tell us to get in touch *only if it's really important.* Like the president of a country who pauses in the middle of a world crisis to take a call from his child, God gives us total accessibility. In fact, he demonstrates his desire to know us by orchestrating the details of our lives so that we will be in the best position to seek him and find him.

> "From one man he made every nation of men, that they should inhabit the whole earth; and he determined the times set for them and the exact places where they should live. God did this so that men would seek him and perhaps reach out for him and find him, though he is not far from each one of us." (Acts 17:26–27)

*Why are you in the exact place where you live?* The Bible gives a simple explanation. It is because it is meant to be a stepping-stone in your path toward knowing God. *Who do you have in your life that is encouraging you to know God?* God also shows his desire to know you by the people he brings into your life at just the time when you need them. *What circumstances in your life have turned your attention toward God?* Even the tiny details of our day-to-day life are overseen by a loving God who wants to know us. In fact, one day when you sit in heaven with God, you can anticipate learning all the ways he worked to show his heart of love to you, starting from the time you were a little girl.

But God doesn't treat us like he's doing us some big favor—letting us squeak into his kingdom and stay there, just barely hanging on by our fingernails. Rather he wants us to come boldly, assured that he'll give us exactly what we need in our time of weakness.

> For we do not have a high priest who is unable to sympathize with our weaknesses, but we have one who has been tempted in every way, just as we are—yet was without sin. Let us then approach the throne of grace with confidence, so that we may receive mercy and find grace to help us in our time of need. (Hebrews 4:15–16)

God is not bothered or inconvenienced by us coming to his throne. In fact, he encourages us to come boldly with confidence, and pledges to meet us there with mercy and grace.

But to really appreciate God's accessibility, I think we've got to ask ourselves an important question—*what would it be like if God weren't so accessible?* To answer that question, let's look at the story of Esther.

Esther was a Jewess who became queen to King Xerxes in a year-long beauty contest. To make a long story short, Xerxes was a pagan king who put aside his first wife after she disobeyed him. Through a beauty pageant of sorts (where the participants didn't have a choice of whether to participate and were "worked on" for a year to make them their most attractive), he chose Esther, a Jew, as his new queen.

After she became queen, Esther knew King Xerxes' intimately. But even as his wife, the law severely restricted her accessibility to him. If fact, if she ventured into his throne room unbidden, the penalty was death. (The only way she would be spared was if the king extended his scepter, waiving the death penalty.) It seems pretty obvious to me that any queen in her right mind wouldn't dare come into the king's throne room unless she was summoned. It simply wasn't worth the risk.

But when Haaman hatched a plot to have all of the Jews destroyed, Esther was the only hope of her nation. Her uncle, Mordecai, urged her to make a plea to the king even though she hadn't been summoned in over thirty days. In case you haven't read the story, Esther did courageously decide to approach the king. But before she made her request, which could have cost her life, she went through an amazing array of preparations.

First, Esther, her maidens and all the Jews fasted and prayed for three days for God's intervention. In preparation, her staff of beauty experts made sure she looked exquisite. She put on the royal robes and all the finery of her queenly position. Trusting in God as her protector, she went into the king's throne room unbidden.

When he granted her permission to speak, she invited him to a banquet she had prepared for him and Haaman. I'm picturing gold dishes, the finest crystal, the king's favorite foods, talented musicians and world-class entertainment.

After the banquet, she invited both the king and Haaman to a second, similar banquet, where she finally revealed Haaman as the enemy who wanted to destroy her and her people.

And lastly, she came before the king unbidden a second time to ask him to allow the Jews to take up arms to protect themselves. Her courageous actions led to the redemption of her people, celebrated in the Jewish holiday of Purim.

If we compare Xerxes to God, all of Xerxes' wealth, power and influence are a mere blip on the screen of eternity. Xerxes ruled over a staggering 127 provinces, no doubt thousands of miles of territory, yet God rules over the span of the entire universe measured in light years. Xerxes had untold wealth and seemingly unlimited resources, but God, as the true owner and creator of every source of wealth, could have taken it all away if he chose in one swift move. Xerxes had great power that men everywhere feared, but God rules over every nation, every tongue, and every king on the earth. God makes Xerxes look like a pauper!

Yet God does the unthinkable. He bids us come into his throne room any time, without any special procedures or permission. He invites us to come as we are without beauty treatments and expensive and elaborate dress. He bids us to come without stained glass windows and confessionals, and even unaccompanied by a preacher or a priest. He bids us come in all our weakness, bringing our tangle of feelings, wants, fears and desires before him, promising us grace and mercy in our time of need. As a daughter and a bride of the Creator of the universe, we have complete access to the presence and heart of our king.

But here's my question. Do you ever treat God like he's Xerxes? Is coming to God with your hurts, heartaches and concerns something that you're only comfortable doing if you think you deserve his help? Do you think you have to be perfect to come into his presence? Are you secretly afraid that God would give you the thumbs down if you dared to come close? Do you only venture into God's presence if you have an escort—someone you think is spiritual enough to get you in?

Unlike Xerxes, God doesn't have a complex system that requires you to jump through hoops to make a request. There is only God, the lover of your soul, who invites you to bring your needs confidently before his very throne. Beside him is Jesus, your great high priest, waiting to advocate for you, and the Holy Spirit, who takes the deep longings of your heart that you struggle to express and brings them straight to the heart of God. God's accessibility is amazing!

## God Makes Himself Personal

Just as God paves the way for us to know him through his vulnerability and his accessibility, he also reveals himself by being personal with us. God so wanted us to know him that he intervened in human history, entering our world as a tiny baby, birthed, nurtured and raised by imperfect human parents. Jesus came so that we could see God in the flesh and know him in a personal way.

Through Jesus we see God bouncing a child on his knee, embracing a leper, eating with "sinners and tax collectors" and assuring those that the religious leaders of the time had judged as "sinners" that they were forgiven. Some of the very last words of Jesus, in his longest recorded prayer in the Bible, let us know without a doubt what God's goal was in coming to us in such personal ways:

> "Now this is eternal life: that they may know you, the only true God and Jesus Christ, who you have sent... I have made you known to them, and will continue to make you known in order that the love you have for me may be in them and that I myself may be in them." (John 17:3, 26)

What did Jesus see as his highest calling from his Father? Miracles? Teaching? Training his apostles to carry out his mission? Dying on the cross? All of these, including his death, were a means to the bigger goal of helping us to know God. Miracles gave us the faith for knowing God. Teaching and training gave us the foundation of knowing God. The cross paid the cost of our knowing God. In fact, in his prayer Jesus says that "this is eternal life": to know God and to know Jesus, his Son. Knowing God is of enormous value—eternal value.

> What makes life worthwhile is having a big enough objective, something which catches our imagination and lays hold of our allegiance; and this the Christian has, in a way that no other man has. For what higher, more exalted, and more compelling goal can there be than to know God?[9]

Is it any wonder then that the Bible compares knowing God to finding a treasure hidden in a field, and then selling everything you have to buy that field?[10]

So the question is, in light of God's vulnerability, accessibility and the personal way he comes to us, why do we find it so difficult to know God beyond cliché and fact? Why do we battle to have the kind of deep, intimate friendship with him that is the true need of our heart?

## Satan's Plot

Satan wants us to join him in the unrelenting insecurity he's felt ever since he turned his back on God and was cast out of heaven. If Satan can pervert, twist or even fade out the truth about who God is, then he can frustrate God's desire for us to know him.

In the last chapter we talked about some of the questions that we ask in our hearts as women: Am I enough? Who can I count on? Will I be rescued? Will I be successful? Who will protect me? What do others think of me? Will I be alone? With each of these questions, we have a decision to make: Will I use my own experiences to answer this question, or I will answer it with an intimate knowledge of God? When we replace the true knowledge of God with a view filtered through our own shame and disappointment, we're left with a deep insecurity. Here are just a few of the ways this might work.

1) We take a faulty, sketchy or even an untrue childhood notion of

9. Packer, *Knowing God*, 30.
10. Matthew 13:44

God and apply it to ourselves. *I was taught to follow God through guilt-trips, fear and manipulation, so God must be oppressive.*

2) We evaluate God through things that happened to us or didn't happen to us. *I lost my mother at a time I really needed her, so God must be uncaring. When I finally received the "Christian" mate I prayed for, he turned out to have a devastating addiction. God must not understand the true needs of my heart.*

3) We judge God by our own perceived worthiness instead of by his own goodness. *Others receive the blessings I yearn for, so I must not be worthy of his attention.*

4) Instead of trying to see ourselves through God, we try to interpret him through our own roller coaster of emotions. *I'm feeling sad and unloved, so God must not love me. I'm feeling depressed, so God must be distant and angry.*

5) We use our misunderstanding of God to distance ourselves from him, rather than to come closer to him. *God may be good, but I'm bad. Coming closer to him will only make me feel worse about myself.*

6) We blame God (or our own "badness") for situations we create. *God, why did you let this situation get so messed up? Why didn't you stop me from making that mistake? Or...I'm in this situation because I'm bad and unworthy of God.*

These "interpretations" of the knowledge of God are downright dangerous. They serve as footholds, places in our thinking where Satan can hoist himself in.[11] And if he can get into our thoughts, he knows he can set up strongholds in our hearts—a place where he moves in and takes a *strong hold* of our thinking.

Strongholds are downright oppressive, but most of all they have the potential to destroy what's most precious to us—our knowledge of God. As we will see later, the Bible describes these strongholds as consisting of any argument or pretension that "sets itself up against the knowledge of God."

After Satan scopes out the possibilities, he gets right to work entrenching himself. He wants to shut the windows, clamp the

---

11. "Do not let the sun go down while you are still angry, and do not give the devil a foothold." (Ephesians 4:26–27)

doors, turn out the lights and ensnare us in spiritual bondage. What does this mean for us as women?

First of all, we need to get very good at identifying Satan's messages and exposing the lies they are built on. I asked my daughter, who just graduated with a degree in advertising from the University of Illinois, what she thought Satan's advertisements might look like. She suggested a few:

THERE'S ALWAYS ROOM FOR SELF-DOUBT.

BE ALL *THEY* WANT YOU TO BE!

GOTTA HAVE THE NICEST HOUSE, CAR AND CLOTHES.

NOT GONE ANYWHERE FOR QUITE AWHILE? STOP TRUSTING GOD.

IF YOU'RE NOT BORN WITH IT, GOD DOESN'T LOVE YOU AS MUCH.

SEE WHAT A BOYFRIEND CAN DO FOR YOU!

Second, we need to get these satanic messages cleaned out regularly through prayer, forgiveness and by taking our thoughts captive and making them obedient to Christ. Believe me, this takes more than a half-hearted attempt to will ourselves to think differently. In fact, the Bible says we've got to *demolish* these strongholds. We've got to tear them down completely, raze them, with the goal of completely ridding ourselves of them:

> The weapons we fight with are not the weapons of the world. On the contrary, they have divine power to demolish strongholds. We demolish arguments and every pretension that sets itself up against the knowledge of God, and we take captive every thought to make it obedient to Christ.
> (2 Corinthians 10:4–5)

Remember that above all, Satan wants to keep us from an intimate knowledge of God. (Honestly, I don't think he's too intimidated by clichés or facts!) The best way to defeat him is to embrace the knowledge of God and then use that knowledge to cast Satan out of our thinking. But to do this, we will need to get to know God better and then translate that knowledge into trust and surrender.

## Knowing God Intimately

> Through these he has given us his very great and precious promises, so that through them you may participate in the divine nature and escape the corruption in the world caused by evil desires. (2 Peter 1:4)

God not only helps us to know his divine nature, but he also gives us the opportunity to participate in it. How do we do this? Consider the following analogy: I'm a member of NAWBO—the National Association of Women Business Owners. As a result I participate in the privileges, status, benefits, knowledge and even power of the organization. But if I don't get involved in committees, learn the benefits, figure out how they apply to my business, and take advantage of the experience and knowledge of other members, my "participation" will be worth little to me. I hardly can blame NAWBO for letting me down if I don't take advantage of the many ways they pledge to stand by my side and help me as a small-business owner.

In the same way, God's eternal nature and all the beautiful and heart-moving ways that he describes himself will only help us to the extent that we participate in his divine nature. We need to learn to live as if God is who he says he is—applying his divine nature to whatever we're going through. And in doing so, we'll find a security that doesn't depend on ourselves, but instead depends on God. So how do we apply the attributes of God to our day-to-day life? Perhaps a small example from my own battle to rely on God's nature might help.

Just recently, I woke up one morning brimming with anxiety. Even though I knew I had much to be thankful for, the reality was that I felt unhappy and discontent with another day of work.

There were a lot of things bothering me. We were facing some situations with our college-aged children that I had no idea how to handle. I had hit a wall in dealing with my codependency that I just didn't want to deal with.

As is my practice, I went down to the basement to work out on my elliptical trainer and pray. I felt so depressed and clogged up with emotion that it was difficult to know where to start. So I started praising God for his different attributes. When the words, "God, thank you for your wisdom," came out of my mouth, I stopped praying for a moment. God suddenly had my attention.

> *Do you believe that I am wise?* God whispered in my heart.
> "Yes, I do, Lord." I ventured.
> *What does my wisdom mean for all of those situations you are fretting about?*
> "Your wisdom means that if I listen to you, then you will lead me."
> *Is there any reason for you to be so anxious if you trust in my wisdom?*

At that point, tears started spilling down my cheeks. Before I knew it, a torrent of emotion came pouring out. (It must be quite a sight to see a woman bouncing up and down on an elliptical trainer sobbing.)

It occurred to me that if I let God cast the anxiety out of my heart, that I would be able to hear the whisper of the Spirit leading me. And, although I didn't know what to do, God certainly did. The rest of my prayer time was a time of surrender, as I surrendered one by one the areas in my life that I was unsure of.

When I stepped off the elliptical, nearly an hour after I started, I felt secure and at peace in God's wisdom. But God's wisdom is just one of his eternal attributes, just one facet of his nature. Just imagine the wealth of security that is available to us as we get to know God better and take who he says he is more seriously. When we find security through understanding God's attributes and applying them to our lives, we become participants in God's divine nature.

In the last chapter, we talked in depth about the questions that are behind much of what we struggle with as women. We also unmasked the 666 securities that Satan wants us to use to answer those questions. Now it's time to apply the missing ingredient. This ingredient will help us demolish the strongholds that Satan has set in our thinking. It will give us the belt of truth to put around our waist and the shield of faith to extinguish the flaming arrows of the evil one. It will help us battle the false securities that we've unknowingly bought into. This ingredient is what we have been talking about: God's unchanging, eternal nature.

Here are the questions we'll be addressing in the rest of the book and the attributes of God that we'll learn to lean on, rejoice in and participate in.

| Chapter | Question | False Security | Knowledge of God |
|---------|----------|----------------|------------------|
| 5 | Am I enough? | Perfectionism | God's Goodness |
| 6 | Who can I count on? | Self-Reliance | The Rock |
| 7 | Will I be rescued? | Dependence | The Anchor |
| 8 | Will I be successful? | Worldliness | The Guide |
| 9 | Who will protect me? | Self-Protection | The Guard |
| 10 | What do others think of me? | Approval | The Advocate |
| 11 | Will I be alone? | Romance | The Comforter |

As we look at these questions, we'll also hear the stories of women who have battled intensely to find answers. These won't be women who consider themselves to be towers of strength, but instead women who are bringing their weakness to God's strength. I think their stories will inspire you and perhaps even help you to see yourself and your battles in a new light.

## Back to the Beginning

Since I first identified insecurity as the root of many of my battles as a woman, I've hoped that by finding answers for myself, I could also help others. For a long time I had a vision that God would have me share only when all of the hardships I was going through had come to a successful and even spectacular fulfillment. Sure, at that point I might still have some difficulties, but I would have numerous victory stories to share about my marriage, my kids, my career and my general well being. *When I was ready to be painfully honest with myself, I realized that all of these goals were fed by insecurity.* And so, God gently said, "Not yet, Robin. You're not ready." And, sure enough, the last five years have not only contained some of the toughest trials I've faced yet, but also some of the most precious lessons I've learned about true security of heart. God didn't want me to write from a place of strength, but rather from a place of weakness.

But how about you? When and where will you meet God? How will you battle insecurity in the unique ways it manifests itself in your life? How will you defend yourself when Satan whispers, "Did God really say?" Before we change gears, let's go back to Eve just one more time.

> Then the LORD God said to the woman, "What is this you have done?"
> The woman said, "The serpent deceived me, and I ate."
> So the LORD God said to the serpent, "Because you have done this,
>
>> Cursed are you above all the livestock....
>> And I will put enmity
>>> between you and the woman,
>>> and between your offspring and hers;
>> he will crush your head,
>>> and you will strike his heel." (Genesis 3:13–15)

Ultimately this scripture points to Jesus. As the offspring of woman, Jesus had his heel struck on the cross, but ultimately crushed the head of Satan through his resurrection. But I think we can also apply this to us. Each of us has an Achilles' heel in the form of insecurity. Satan takes advantage of our weakness and attacks us in it—he strikes our heel of insecurity. He may even give us a spiritual limp. But the good news is that as we claim our heritage to true security in heart, we join Jesus in crushing the head of Satan.

When it comes to security, the story is only really beginning. I invite you to come along with me as we build on the foundation we've laid. Let's take the hard questions head on, believing that the knowledge of God will give us everything we need for life and godliness. Where should we start? God's goal from creation has been to fill the earth with his goodness. Understanding the goodness of God is the first, and I believe the most important, step toward security of heart.

# KNOWING GOD:
# UNMASKING FALSE SECURITIES
*Personal Study Guide & Life Application*

In order to develop a secure heart, our knowledge of God needs to go far beyond clichés, facts and opinions. We need to learn to relate to God on a feeling and need level. Knowing all of the effort that God has gone to by making himself vulnerable, personal and accessible helps us to learn to trust his heart toward us.

> *It's been said that the best way to find out how someone wants to be loved, is to watch how he or she expresses love to others. Read Jeremiah 31:33–35. Then write down three ways you can make yourself more vulnerable, personal and accessible to God.*

# PART TWO

## *Secure in Heart*

"Yet if you devote your heart to him
and stretch out your hands to him,
if you put away the sin that is in your hand
and allow no evil to dwell in your tent,
then you will lift up your face without shame;
you will stand firm and without fear."

Job 11:13–15

"Even though I was a 'good girl' who remained a virgin until I was married, I wanted my fiancé to struggle over me sexually. It gave me a feeling of power over him that fed my feelings of being loved."

— Married for 40 years

# AM I ENOUGH?
## *God's Goodness*

How great is your goodness,
    which you have stored up for those who fear you,
which you bestow in the sight of men
    on those who take refuge in you.

Psalm 31:19

Give me a sign of your goodness,
    that my enemies may see it and be put to shame,
for you, O LORD, have helped me and comforted me.

Psalm 86:17

AS WOMEN, GOD HAS GIVEN US QUALITIES OF THE HEART AS OUR biological make-up. He created us with a deep well of emotionality that makes connecting with God and others an intuitive part of our nature. The language of love is our native language.

God saw Adam's desire for relationship and thrilled his heart by giving him the perfect complement and partner in Eve. Likewise, each of us has been uniquely gifted with the ability to love a man. Our soft curves, deep wells of emotion and nurturing capacity all complement man's drive to conquer the world around him.

Although God taught Eve her first lessons in human love through Adam, she was gifted with so much more. As women, we don't have to be taught to love the child we bear. We may need help learning *how* to love, but unless something was terribly broken in the way we were raised, we find loving a child the most natural thing in the world to do. Our bodies were intricately and perfectly designed to carry, birth, nurse and nurture children.

Even if we aren't married or don't have children, we still have the innate gift of love. We are equipped to love our friends and family, and bring our relational gifts to those around us. Whether single, married, single mother, divorced, bereaved, in our golden years, or in whatever life situation, we are well equipped to carry out our powerful relational role in creation.

What's more, as daughters of God, disciples of Jesus, we have even more reason to feel totally equipped. In 2 Peter 1:3–4, the Bible tells us that we've been given everything we need for life and godliness through the one who called us. And, no matter what deficits we bring to life, God wants each of us to know that his grace is sufficient for us, since his power is made perfect in weakness (2 Corinthians 12:9).

So why are we still asking the question, "Am I enough?" Certainly, one reason is our rapidly evolving world and the increased pressures on women. We not only are required to break the glass ceiling, but to have a pristine home and well-balanced children. We're supposed to look beautiful, work smart and play hard, while still keeping the laundry up and the dust down.

In fact, "Am I enough?" can take us in a hundred different directions! Am I smart, sexy, beautiful, spiritual, nurturing, ambitious, talented (and the list goes on and on) enough? If we aren't able to answer this question through our understanding of the goodness of God, we leave ourselves vulnerable to spiritual attack.

Satan is standing by with his answer as well: *Here, take security from how good* you *are.* And then when we bite, he seeks to build this lie into a full-blown stronghold that takes our hearts captive: *You must decide that you can never, ever, do anything other than the very, very best you are capable of.* Satan wants you to believe that you must be beyond good. In fact, perfectly good.

## My Roots of Perfectionism

Since my mother died, I've had a lot of time to reflect about my relationship with her. I've been surprised at some of the things that were right in front of me that I was blind to. First of all, I'm realizing that my mother was a writer. We found some notebooks after her death that contained some of her writings, and I've been struck by the sheer eloquence of her prose. I remember when I was a preteen, Mom wrote and illustrated a children's book and circulated it to several publishers. I sat with her at our grey, speckled Formica kitchen table while she shed a few tears over a rejection letter she had received.

My mother was a talented artist. She went through a period when I was younger where she brought in extra money by doing oil paintings—mainly commissioned portraits.

She was also a prolific seamstress. When I went through my baton, dance and pageant phase, my mother made me flowing gowns and rhinestone-studded costumes, and soon started making them for other girls as well to fund my lessons. My mother loved fashion—she could take two Vogue patterns and custom-design a stylish creation to wear out to a Moose Club function with my father. I think she easily could have been a fashion designer.

But my mother also had a clamoring inside of herself for something more than what my father's income could support. She filled that desire by spending money—investing loads of money on us kids in lessons of various sorts, an expensive membership at an area swim club (where most of us swam on the swim team), and eventually pushing for the purchase of a lakeside trailer where the family could retreat. Money became a huge source of contention between her and my dad. She felt justified, since Dad spent money on his Moose Club membership and was gone much of the time due to his work and club obligations.

As time went on and my father continued his downward

plunge into alcoholism, my mom became increasingly depressed. Perhaps part of it was fueled by the death of Matthew, the child my mom carried who died shortly before he was due. But for whatever reason, she buried herself in romance novels and soap operas. Understandably, our cramped little three-bedroom, one-bath house, filled to the brim with five children, often looked like a tornado had torn through it. (And not too long after Matthew's death, my mother was pregnant with her sixth child, my youngest sister.) Embarrassed for my friends to come over and see our house, I went through phases when I would clean it up myself, and other phases when I would just stay away as much as possible.

When I was sixteen, I got involved with a church in our community and came to the conviction that I should serve my parents more. One weekend, when they took off with all of the other children for a getaway, I crafted a plan to surprise them. While they were gone, I decided I would clean the house from top to bottom. I did all of the laundry and even re-papered the peeling shelves in our bathroom. I spent hours working. I was eager for them to come home and see what I had done.

When they arrived, I was waiting at the door. I toured my mother through the house. All she could find to say was "Humph" after each new area was revealed. Finally, she walked in the bathroom, looked at the toilet and proclaimed, "You missed a spot." No "thank you." No praise. Nothing.

You can imagine the damage that did to my teenaged heart. It was like someone had pulled me aside and confirmed my worst fear, telling me, "Your best simply isn't good enough." What didn't occur to me until I began facing the perfectionism in my own life, is how my mother must have felt. Although I wanted to encourage her, what I did surely only highlighted her feelings of inadequacy. What did my gesture say about her as a housekeeper? As a mother? I think I unknowingly touched a deep sadness inside my mother. She valued beauty above all things. To feel so out of control of her own household must have been a deep burden.

I'm also realizing that as a creative soul, she was a frustrated perfectionist. Mom couldn't measure up to her own standards, nor did she want to face the depth of despair she had about her marriage, so she had largely retreated, and ended up feeling much guilt:

> I've mentally tortured myself over and over for being a stupid, dumb, lazy wife, who neglected my husband and children spiritually. I've had to deal with these feelings over and over again and I'm in the process of asking every member of my family to forgive me for any wrong I have done.
> —*From my mother's journal, after joining a codependency group*

My mother, like so many of us, tried to find the route to happiness through her own goodness and found it wanting. She was struggling with what women have battled ever since Eve—that in and of ourselves, we can never be enough.

## Back to the Garden

As Eve walked in the early morning mist that watered the Garden of Eden, she was surrounded by God's goodness. As she partook of the food growing freely around her, she saw God's good gifts. Her relationship with Adam was no exception. God's goodness was reflected in the intimacy that they achieved, unhampered by sin or selfish ambition. And most of all she could see God's goodness through God himself and his obvious love for her. Eve wasn't on the fringes of God's goodness; she was immersed in it. Because she had never experienced anything different, her temptation was to take God's goodness for granted. After all, Eve had never needed to dig deep in her faith to understand God's goodness through heartache, suffering or sickness. It was in this untested place that Satan chose to set up camp. *Is God really good? Or do you need something more?* Satan challenged God's goodness by inferring that God was holding out on her:

> "For God knows that when you eat of it, your eyes will be opened, and you will be like God, knowing good and evil." (Genesis 3:5)

Satan told Eve that eating the fruit would not only open her eyes, but it would also enable her to know good and evil. What was Satan inferring here? He basically was telling Eve that God was withholding part of the good that was due her. In fact, there was some good (and some evil) that God hadn't even bothered to tell her about! In that sense, Eve was the consummate sheltered daughter. (Talk about being a preacher's kid—Eve was the Creator's kid!) The truth was that God's withholding of information and experiences she wasn't ready for was part of his goodness to her. Satan made it seem like God was withholding the fruit, not for her good, but for his own purposes. *God knows that if you eat this you will be equal to him.*

But there's more here. Satan was telling Eve, in not so many words, that she must go out and get her own goodness. In fact, she had to become like God in his perfect knowledge. *Absolutely perfect.* And the only way she could get it was to step outside of God's control of her life. Sound familiar to our battles? We start to wonder why we're not getting the good we think is surely due us. *God, why are you holding out on me? Where is the good that you promised me?* Satan's goal for us is similar to the one he had for Eve: to lead us astray where we miss the most fundamental fact of the universe—God is good.

### The False Security of Perfectionism

Just as with Eve, Satan wants to take us one step further into a performance mentality. Satan knows that if we come to depend on our own performance and perfection, we will cease to depend on the goodness of God. How does this work? He first gives you the question: *Are you enough?* He then proposes an answer: *If you can be perfect enough, then the world will be in its rightful place.* Satan then waits for you to fall flat on your face, exhausted from performing. And once you do fall, you can bet that he is standing by ready to heap on the shame. *See…you'll never be good enough.*

But Satan doesn't only point out the good we're missing out on. He also is glad to point out the knowledge of evil we're missing as well. *Why should those out in the world get to have more fun than you? Since you can never measure up as a good girl, why don't you try being a bad girl for awhile?*

## Good Girl, Bad Girl

Last summer, I had the opportunity to travel to Barbados with my sister Meredith. After mom's death, we both missed being able to travel with her and thought a trip together might be good medicine for our hearts. One day we decided to navigate the bus system to try to make our way around to the other side of the island, while saving a $60 to $75 cab ride. To do this we had to change buses in Bridgetown and navigate our way on foot from one bus stop to another through alleyways and across bridges, following a little elderly woman who was rapidly telling us things in Bajan (Barbadian slang) that we couldn't understand a word of.

When we finally hopped on the bus we thought (and hoped) was the right one, we were greeted by rap music booming out of the speakers. Our driver and his assistant were both grooving in time to the beat. At the front of the bus, there was a huge picture of a famous rapper, holding a massive gun pointed out toward the riders. On one side of the bus, painted above the windows, was the word "Gangstas." On the other side, were the words, "Gangsta Girlz." It turned out that there are public bus lines and private bus lines in Barbados, and we happened upon a private line with a hip-hop spin on transportation. (Thankfully an elderly woman on the bus took us under her wing and made sure we got off at the right spot!)

What is the meaning of Gangsta Girlz? I think that it's the idea that a truly *bad* man needs a *bad* girl. Sometimes we can reason that if we can't measure up as good girls, why not embrace our badness? The bad girl outwardly gives up on the illusion that she can be enough and usually behaves and sometimes dresses in a way that makes it clear to everyone—back off. *Don't you even try to get me to be enough.* But just like good girls, most bad girls are simply trying to measure up in someone's eyes. So, they seek entrance into men's hearts by loosening their morals, giving themselves over to sexual promiscuity, or even by becoming their own version of a nonconformist (maybe even a gangsta girl!).

The good girl keeps fighting for the illusion that she can be good enough. Good girls do everything right: look right, weigh right, eat right, accomplish right. Good girls make good grades in school and marry good men when they get older. But deep within, the good girl always knows that her goodness is in doubt. Therefore, she has to exalt it and build it up as a wall of protection. From there, it's easy for her to start worshipping her own goodness. But growing up as a good girl myself, I know that trusting in my own goodness actually betrays my own inadequacy and insecurity. Some of us good girls even try to work out a split life, living as the good girl at home or church but switching into the bad girl when we venture out at night, testing out our womanly powers through drinking alcohol, going to bars and being with men.

For women my age, unresolved issues with goodness and badness can emerge as a midlife crisis. Some of us slide into the good wife, bad wife mentality. The good wife works hard to measure up, whereas the bad wife gives up. And this is a legacy we can all too easily pass on to our own children. In our denial of our own "badness," we can inadvertently lay charges against our children that they'll fight for their entire lives: *You're an embar-*

*rassment. You're too shy. You're too moody. Go to your room until you can be a good girl.*

But even more so, when we trust in our own goodness (or badness) we are missing out on the beauty and power of knowing God in his goodness. Trusting in our own goodness—the root of perfectionism—drives us to look to places other than God for validation. We start asking an unspoken question: "Is what I have to give good enough?"

Here's what I've found. When we are not focused on God's goodness, Satan has a point of entry into our thinking that can take us as far as even questioning our status as daughters of God. And just as he did with Eve, he's standing by to take the secure status that God has promised us and send us running for the bushes. Satan's desire is to get us to do any or all of the following:

- **Compare ourselves to other women**—Satan knows that using comparisons to try to find our self-worth only leads to a deep insecurity and feelings of inadequacy.[1]

- **Give in to envy and jealousy**—Satan wants to stir up the "disorder and every evil practice" that comes when bitter envy and selfish ambition take residence in our hearts.[2] This insecurity can cause us to be relieved when other people fall off the pedestal that we placed them on, and then quickly be ashamed for feeling that way.

- **Put up walls of protection**—Satan knows that the very walls we put up to protect ourselves from the fear of failure and rejection, also keep us from seeing God's goodness all around us. He prods us to insist on our own agendas, instead of facing the disappointment of life and still glorifying God.

- **Trust in our own goodness**—Satan's goal is to incite us to trust in and worship our own goodness instead of God's. Then we not only take credit for our strengths and gifts (the very ones we were given by God), but we also seek validation from others of our goodness.

---

1. "If anyone thinks he is something when he is nothing, he deceives himself. Each one should test his own actions. Then he can take pride in himself, without comparing himself to somebody else, for each one should carry his own load." (Galatians 6:3–5)

2. James 3:14–16

- **Throw away our confidence**—Satan seeks to put us on a treadmill where we live out of performance and perfectionism, and then shame us when we can't keep up the pace. His goal? To get us to wonder, "Why should I even try?" and to shrink back from living out our faith.[3]

We can become so tuned in to other voices, as Eve did, that we miss the resounding voice of God saying, "I've got you covered with my goodness."

## Am I Enough?

My personal battle with perfectionism came into full bloom during my husband's and my years in the full-time ministry. Ministry became another arena that I could gain self-esteem in by finding new levels of performance. It wasn't that I was unaware of my tendency to get my self-esteem from what I do. After I gave my life to God at sixteen, I had a big transition to make: learning to live through God's grace, rather than through my own performance. During my first experiences with serving God, seeking approval played a much larger role than I was aware of for years afterward (more about that later).

After Dave and I married, in our early years of teen ministry in New Mexico, dealing with performance issues wasn't quite as much of a challenge. After all, I was busy having babies and going back to school to try to finish a degree in social work. (I had quit a year short of my degree to marry Dave.) Beyond that, the church we were involved with didn't consider me a part of their staff. They were grateful for anything I could do to help, but only considered Dave to be on the payroll.

That all changed five years later when we made a decision to retrain for the ministry in an evangelistic church in Chicago. Now, I suddenly was a part of the full-time staff and considered a women's ministry leader. Although I had three small children, I was now balancing staff meetings and Bible studies, as well as being held accountable for my contribution to the ministry.

3. Hebrews 10:35–39

At first, being in the ministry helped me strip a layer of performance mentality out of my Christianity. I realized how Christianity had fed my need for approval from the time I was sixteen years old. I saw very clearly the idolatry of approval from men, and asked God to create a new heart in me with a pure motivation.

During the early years of my full-time work for the church, I thrived. I loved all of it: studying the Bible with other women, teaching lessons and reaching out to others. I felt like I had rediscovered and renewed my first love. And I loved the freedom it gave me to balance a career with taking care of our children.

Eventually, we did so well in the ministry in Chicago that we were asked to move to another city. It was there that I experienced my first difficulties. My problem wasn't that we weren't doing well. Rather, I didn't know how to interpret success without feeling like I'd somehow earned it. The more praise I received, the more praise hungry I became. When I did something well (like heading up a Women's Day, or speaking at a large women's event), I would replay the moment and the resulting praise for days. Honestly, it was almost as if I was experiencing a high that came from my performance. Without realizing it, I had begun to use old wineskins (success through overachieving and perfectionism) to serve in the new wineskin ministry of the Spirit. I was heading toward what Jesus predicted—a point where the wineskins would burst.[4]

Since I felt responsible for the success of the ministry (that truly came from the gracious goodness of God), when things started getting more challenging, I also felt responsible for the defeats. The security that I had felt in coming to Christ was slowly being supplanted by a growing insecurity. When the ministry we were leading stopped growing and started to struggle, I internalized the struggles and felt like any mention of the struggles meant that I was bad. I looked at others' ministries that were

---

4. Matthew 9:16–17

doing well, and somewhere in my heart, I believed that it was due to their goodness. I became insecure in God's ministry, as God in his mercy surfaced the parts of my soul that were still bound up by performance and perfectionism.

Eventually, my perfectionism began to lead toward defensiveness. When I was corrected on my defensive, prideful attitude, I turned in on myself, using the hardest scriptures in the Bible to try to bring myself to repentance. Little did I understand that I was only compounding my insecurity. Since I was being so hard on myself, well-meaning Christians got on board with me, trying to correct me and even rebuke me out of my self-focus. It seemed the more I tried not to be self-focused, the more self-focused I became. I thought I was losing my mind. While attending a large women's retreat, I had multiple emotional meltdowns.

Finally, after studying through Jesus' condemnation of the Pharisees in Matthew 23, I decided I must not even be a Christian. Thanks to wise advice from an older brother and my husband's encouragement to read the book of 1 John, I understood that my salvation was secure. But my crisis still was not over. At the next staff meeting, after I broke down weeping hysterically, we were asked to step out of the ministry for the sake of my mental health.

Where was God in his goodness while I was trying to figure out if I was enough? Now I understand that he was working in my life to begin the next phase of my healing, where I would finally deal with long-buried issues such as my dad's alcoholism and my own codependency. Although getting out of the ministry was painful, it gave me the most valuable gift of my Christianity. Getting out of the ministry didn't decrease my zeal for God or my love for others. With time and healing, I finally understood that I loved God *not* for whatever benefits, praise or victories that Christianity gave me. I loved God for himself. Through getting out of the ministry, God has literally showered me with his goodness and taught me one of the most valuable lessons of my life:

*My daughter, you are surrounded by my infinite goodness and nothing in all creation can change that.*

## Surrounded by God's Goodness

> "My eyes will watch over them for their good, and I will bring them back to this land. I will build them up and not tear them down; I will plant them and not uproot them." (Jeremiah 24:6)

I love the idea that God's eyes are always watching out for me for one purpose and only one purpose—my good! Just to make sure I understand, he clarifies that everything he does on my behalf is to either (a) build me up or (b) plant me. (Take a look at Psalm 1 for a beautiful description of what it means to be planted.) I can also be sure that whatever God allows in my life, his purpose is *not* to tear me down or uproot me. Why is God so committed to my good? What is *his* heart's desire? The scripture goes on to tell us:

> "I will give them a heart to know me, that I am the LORD. They will be my people, and I will be their God, for they will return to me with all their heart." (Jeremiah 24:7)

God watches over us for our good, to give us a heart to know him. Primarily, his purpose isn't that life go exactly how we want; it isn't even that we avoid hardship or suffering. Rather it's that we know who we are and whom we belong to. He wants our hearts. And as we give our hearts to him, he looks for ways to strengthen us.[5]

So the question is, why would a daughter of God go through her day-to-day life feeling like she is barely covered by God's goodness? Shouldn't she feel absolutely surrounded by it? If we picture God's goodness as a circle of loving protection that he

---

5. "For the eyes of the LORD range throughout the earth to strengthen those whose hearts are fully committed to him." (2 Chronicles 16:9a)

wraps around us, I think most of us think that only a few Christians get to sit in the middle. We measure who's in the center of the circle by all the trappings of Christian success—loving Christian husband, fiancé or boyfriend, faithful children, spiritual leadership, even including things such as financial success and health. And certainly, these are all great blessings—gifts of God that we should be grateful for and should even ask God for.

The problem is, we think that to be in the center of the circle, you've got to have it all. And where exactly does that put you if you have none of these things? So then, Satan enters in his role as an angel of light ready to turn our thinking from a starting point that only appears to be slightly off-track to a full 180 degrees away from the truth.

We start to see the different aspects of our spirituality—doing good works, obeying God, being mentored—as a means to get us into the center of that circle, namely the outpouring of God's goodness. Our churches can unintentionally further this misconception if they only point to those who appear to have it all (in our human estimation) as our role models of Christianity. We get the idea that we're supposed to be like them, and then we'll get into the center of God's goodness too!

If we picture the goodness of God as being an immense ocean, we see these people as being so far in the middle of God's goodness that they can't even see the shore. On the other hand, we see ourselves hanging out near the shore, getting battered by the waves. We feel like we are trying to paddle out deeper into our spiritual life to get to where they are, but the currents keep sweeping us back toward the shore.

So how can we rejoice with others in their blessings (as we are commanded to do),[6] when their good gifts only seem to highlight our own disappointments? How can we change from just acknowledging God's goodness in our heads to translating it to our hearts? How can we overcome the insecurity that Satan wants

---

6. 1 Corinthians 12:26

to give us in the form of the false security of perfectionism?

Just as Satan was underhandedly undermining Eve's faith in God's goodness, he looks for every opportunity to attack our faith in much the same way. By standing on the word of God, we need to put up our guard against Satan's message that is designed to get us to lose faith in God's goodness.

| Satan's Whisper | The Bible on God's Goodness |
| --- | --- |
| God treats other people better than you, so you must not be worthy of God's goodness. | God does not show favoritism. (Romans 2:10–12) |
| If God was good, you'd have a great marriage, children, success or whatever else you long for. | God is our shield and our very great reward. (Genesis 15:1–3) |
| God is just setting you up for another disappointment. | God knows the plans he has for you...plans to prosper you and give you a future. (Jeremiah 29:11) |
| Nothing good can possibly come from the persecution, hardship and trials you're experiencing. | God takes every situation in our lives and brings good out of it, including persecution, hardship and trials. (Romans 8:28) |
| Your goal should be to perform well enough to get into the center of God's favor. | God's favor doesn't depend on your desire or efforts, but on God's mercy. (Romans 9:16) |
| The reason you don't have what you long for is because you aren't good enough. | Your boundary lines are in exactly the right places; In fact, you have a delightful inheritance. (Psalm 16:6) |
| God is withholding the good gifts that you need. | Since God didn't even hold back from giving his own Son, he'll also graciously give you all things. (Romans 8:32) |
| You are being deprived of the good you need to be happy. | God has given you everything you need for life and godliness through his goodness. (2 Peter 1:3) |

The key is learning to live and even revel in God's goodness. It is learning to picture ourselves so far in the middle of God's goodness that we can't even see the shore. We do this when we surrender to his goodness, trust in his good plans for us, and then glorify him for the unseen good that is yet to be revealed.

## Reveling in God's Goodness

> "They captured fortified cities and fertile land; they took pos-
> session of houses filled with all kinds of good things, wells
> already dug, vineyards, olive groves and fruit trees in abun-
> dance. They ate to the full and were well-nourished; they
> *reveled* in your great goodness." (Nehemiah 9:25, italics
> added)

In this passage, Nehemiah is speaking to God about the powerful way he had brought his people, the Israelites, into the
Promised Land and had met all of their needs. In fact, he says
that they "reveled" in God's "great goodness." I love the word
"revel." In fact if you look the word up in your thesaurus, you'll
get a profound glimpse of how God's goodness can revolutionize
your spiritual life and help you successfully battle insecurity.
God wants us to bask, luxuriate, savor, indulge, cut loose and
thrive spiritually in his goodness!

How can you see your battles through God's great goodness?
What thoughts do you need to battle the stronghold of perfectionism? The Bible tells us that faith is being "sure of what we
hope for and certain of what we do not see."[7] The truth is that in
our limited vision, we won't always see the good. Trusting God's
goodness means trusting the unseen.[8] Perfectionism causes us to
try to shortcut God's good plans for our lives, whereas the goodness of God moves us to rejoice in his promises long before we
get a glimpse of their fulfillment.[9]

God's goodness gives us the freedom to make mistakes,
knowing that God will teach us through them. It gives us the
freedom to say "No" to the perfectionism that Satan thrusts in
our view at every corner. It gives us the freedom to walk securely with God, even in our weakness, and to hold our head high,

---

7. Hebrews 11:1
8. "Therefore we do not lose heart. Though outwardly we are wasting away,
yet inwardly we are being renewed day by day. For our light and momentary
troubles are achieving for us an eternal glory that far outweighs them all. So we
fix our eyes not on what is seen, but what is unseen. For what is seen is temporary, but what is unseen is eternal." (2 Corinthians 4:16–18)
9. See Psalm 119:162, Romans 4:18–21, Hebrews 11:13.

even when our life doesn't quite seem to fit the mold of Christian success. We have the freedom to find inner joy even in the face of hardship, difficulty and suffering. Understanding and accepting God's goodness is the first and most important step to true security of heart.

# IN HER OWN WORDS

*Jan's Story*

I like to be funny and have fun. Sometimes though, it's to keep from feeling the pain and discomfort of my past. There were the four of us: Dad, Mom, my sister and me. My dad was a graphic designer, and much of his work was designing packaging for foods. He told my sister and me that it is good to be exposed to as much of life as possible in order to find out what we liked and what we would excel in. So, we learned how to ice skate, ride a horse, swim, water ski and snow ski.

He was interested in how we did in school and would help in our studies. He built our bedroom set and painted it. He made a staircase to the roof through our porch ceiling so Mom could sunbathe. We traveled and visited family often. And Dad not only exposed us to it all, he did it with us. It was always fun to be with him.

Mom was beautiful. She was gentle and very patient. She would explain the answers to many questions that I had about life that I didn't feel comfortable asking Dad. And Mom was very creative with the home. She kept an amazing home. She was a great cook and seamstress too! She would sew, and even knit, my Barbie doll clothes. She would tell us funny stories of our baby days. And Mom was right there next to Dad in all that we did. We did everything as a family. And I wanted to be just like them.

Remembering when things began to change is hard for me. Mom began to act differently. She stopped going with Dad when he took us places. She was angry a lot of the time. She started to yell at my sister often. Then Mom started to get physical. She would grab my sister and push her and shove her, telling her she was no good. But nothing was done to me. I didn't know why. The way I saw it, my sister was always bad. I decided to make sure to do everything I could not to be bad. So I was careful not to do the things that my sister did to get punished. I figured my sister deserved it since Mom had never treated her or us that way before.

Then one day in seventh grade, I got a bad report card. My sister and I were sitting at the breakfast nook in the kitchen eating lunch, while Mom was looking at our report cards. While I was eating lunch, Mom struck me in the back of the head. And then she hit my sister. She grabbed her by the hair and pulled her off the stool and dragged her across the floor screaming at her. My sister was terrified. But I sat there thinking she must have deserved it. I was afraid that I would be getting it next, but didn't. So I figured that I was just a little bit bad, because I didn't get beaten like my sister did.

We began to run from Mom whenever she would come near us. She began to look terrible. Her hair was rarely combed and she didn't clean the house very much. She slept a lot and we were left to ourselves often.

Then we moved. The days became violent and the nights full of terror. Mom became a violent alcoholic; she beat my sister and tried to kill her twice. She was taken away by the police and institutionalized. While she was being taken care of, my father took us and moved away, never to go back to her. But there came a day when divorce was the only recourse, and we children had to make a choice in front of them in court who we wanted to live with. We chose my father, of course. He protected us.

Because our mother had been so violent, my sister hated her. And I had tried to be a good girl so I wouldn't get beaten like my sister. Although my mother never treated me the way she treated her, I was later to find out through nightmares and memories that my father had molested me when I didn't understand what he was doing.

My sister and I fought most of the time. One day our father told us to stop fighting or he would take us to our aunt's house and never come back. We kept fighting and he took us away, never to come back. Before we parted I tried to hug my father goodbye. He told me not to touch him because I was making sexual advances toward him. I didn't understand until the memories came back later in life. My sister was thirteen and I was fourteen when our aunt and grandmother took us into their arms.

My sister ran away so many times that she became a ward of the state. I devoted myself to studies and activities so much that I didn't have time to think about what had happened and tucked it all away to a place in my heart where no one could touch it. I had stopped praying because God wasn't a God who rescued; he was a God of pain. He was punishing me for what I had done wrong to make my parents leave. I was unable to trust love from anyone. When I would steadily see a boy, I would always break it off when I felt loved the most, so he wouldn't hurt me.

Later I met a man who took me away. We married and had five beautiful children. I wanted to be loved, but didn't receive any so I sought companionship elsewhere. I took drugs and left the children with him while I was out. Our marriage didn't last, but I was determined that the children would stay with me. I didn't want them to go through what I had been through. Nevertheless, one of my children received all of my anger. One day I couldn't stop spanking him. Once I realized what I was doing, I never laid a hand on him again.

I became a woman who could love no man, who could

not trust anyone but myself. I couldn't make mistakes because I might get beaten or deserted. And yet I wanted to be loved so badly that I would do just about anything to get it. I gave myself to men who I didn't know—I don't even remember any of their names. And I thought I was a good girl because my parents said that sex was a good thing. My life was full of fear and doubt, but I was determined that my children would be protected and never abandoned.

So, much of me became just like my parents. The anger, the violence, the sex. But I still thought I was good because I didn't drink like my mother. I only got drunk twice. And I didn't have sex with my children. I had sex with as many men as I could, because that was an acceptable thing in this day and age. And yet there was something wrong because I didn't like myself afterward. I felt shame.

Then at one point in my life, something really scary happened: I had a grand mal seizure in our living room in front of my daughter. A year went by before I would accept that I had epilepsy. I was afraid and thought I was dying. So I called on God, asking him if he were still there and if he were real; where was he? There was emptiness in my heart that couldn't be filled. Something was missing and I could not figure out what it was. I knew that I was "bad" and wanted to ask for forgiveness before I was punished. I had been punished and abandoned, so why wouldn't God treat me the same way? That seizure was the turning point of my life that led to me finally surrender everything to God. Soon afterwards, I began studying the Bible and started a new life as a Christian. Through our church, I met Dean, who I ended up marrying.

I'm thankful for Dean, the man God has blessed me with—a man who has been blind since the age of twenty-eight. He was shot in the face by a spray of pellets from a

sawed-off shotgun. The lights went out that night. But a
new light has gone on in him. God encourages me every day
as I watch him strive to have a loving heart and strength
from God. I watch him leave for work every day, and come
home every night. For the first four years of our marriage,
he needed to tell me often that he wasn't going anywhere.
Now I wonder how I could not have known that there is a
God who picks us up when we are at our lowest.

Most of the time, I don't think of Dean as blind. And
then there are times I'm overwhelmed with the fact that he
IS blind! He has never seen my face. What trust that is! He
has to rely on what I tell him. I tell him that I am gorgeous!
He says, "Let me see." And he puts his hands on my face.
I told him the other day that I was still in my pajamas, had
not washed my face, my hair wasn't combed, and I needed
to drive him to where he meets his coworker to get a ride to
work. Dean said, "You didn't have to tell me that, Jan. You
look beautiful to me all the time." He has sung to me, "I
only have eyes for you!" (He's a pretty good singer!)

It's frightening to not know when your next seizure is
going to happen and most of mine have been at night.
Somewhere in between being fully awake and fully asleep
the seizures come. The real fear is that it will never stop.
Pacing the floor at night not able to sleep is a common
occurrence. I plead with God to stop it. Then I ask God to
wrap his arms around me. I cry when I feel his calming presence. And when I am angry and jealous of my husband
because he can sleep, I look to God's word, and he changes
my focus. I can smile and laugh because of the immense
encouragement he gives. Then I can accept my sleepless-
ness until I fall asleep again.

Between menopause and epilepsy there has been little
time to think of much else. I have to work on eating the

right foods and taking the right medicine in hopes that my brain will settle down enough for me to even think about God. But I see God's goodness in my epilepsy. It is because of epilepsy that I have a relationship with him. I think of Jeremiah 29:11, *"For I know the plans I have for you. To prosper you and not to harm you."* And I realize that I have everything. I have an amazing God, who has blessed me with a husband with a great memory! God has shown me these things so I will not feel sorry for myself, because he cares about my life. This has taken time to believe, and I am always still battling for my faith. God has blessed us with seven children together from other marriages. The marriages didn't last, but the lasting effects have made us re-examine our hearts and look to God for answers.

It is different for me now. My heart is no longer empty; it's full of God's Spirit. It is good to be overwhelmed with joy knowing that there is a Father who will never leave and will never harm. There is a constant overflow of love. It is so good to be a child again—God's child.

Eighteen years ago, someone said to me, "When you read this Bible, read it as though God is talking to you." And I did. I now know God. He's real, he's alive and he's right here talking to me. I hear God telling me what to do, how to live, how to raise my children. I see God's goodness in that I finally know that there is one way to live and I know which way that is. He is showing me how to be the wife and mother, and now the grandmother, he wants me to be.

I no longer have to figure everything out for myself. I have a Father to guide me and show me how to live. A Father who loves me and will never leave me.

# AM I ENOUGH? GOD'S GOODNESS
*Personal Study Guide & Life Application*

How can understanding God's goodness help you walk more securely? Here are a few suggestions.

**1) Believe that God works all things to the good for you—**
God is working, planning and scheming for our ultimate good whether we see the good or not. It means trusting something in our spirit that we couldn't possibly conceive of in our flesh.

> *By faith, picture yourself surrounded by God's goodness, not because of who you are, but because of who he is. Thank him for the unseen ways he is working on your behalf.*

**2) Trust that the truest revelation of God's goodness is yet to happen—**As women we long to bring perfect beauty, order and relationship to this life. But that longing is supposed to remind us of what God has in store for us in heaven, rather than push us to try to attain it all here and now. God's goodness reminds me that I was created for something higher.

> *Trust that God's goodness wraps itself around you in all the ways you fall short. Lay your quest for perfection at the altar of God, thanking him that he is preparing you for an eternal glory that far outweighs them all.*

**3) Glorify God in his goodness—**When we cease to glorify God, we are vulnerable to all sorts of temptation. Trusting God's goodness allows us to be patient, trusting that "suffering produces perseverance; perseverance, character; and character, hope. And hope does not disappoint us, because God has poured out his love into our hearts..." (Romans 5:3–5).

> *Take a few moments every morning and night to glorify God for his goodness to you and for the good plans for your life that he is in the process of fulfilling.*

**4) Let God's goodness lead you to surrender and repentance**—Perfectionism is rooted in a fear of judgment. When we are motivated by judgment, we just find bigger and bigger performance treadmills to put ourselves on. But when we are motivated by God's goodness, we feel safe to surrender who we are to him and his purposes. God's goodness is liberating!

*List the situations in your life that are less than you hope for, and surrender them to God's goodness. Thank God that he will bring you exactly what you need in his perfect timing.*

**5) Revel in God's goodness!**—Are you ready to cut loose a little in your faith? Trusting God's goodness gives us a glorious freedom in our walk with God.

*Plan a special time with you and God where you celebrate his goodness to you. Pick up or buy a special memento (something from nature or a piece of jewelry) that you keep as a reminder of God's goodness to you.*

**6) Learn from others' battles**—In her story, Jan talks about how epilepsy opened her heart to God and resulted in her becoming a Christian. She now understands that she has everything she needs through the goodness of God.

*Read Jeremiah 29:1–14. What was it that first opened your heart to God? Write a story of your journey to God, focusing on the role God's goodness has played in turning your heart toward him.*

"There have been times where I felt so over-whelmed by my sin that I multiplied it a thousand times in my mind. When I felt this way I couldn't read the Bible. I was tempted to tell God, 'I can't be what you want. This will just have to be my weakness.' Then I tried to make up for it by doing good in other areas.

"By going back to the Bible and letting others help me, I finally began to understand God's unconditional love shown to me through the cross."

—22 years old

# WHO CAN I COUNT ON?
## *The Rock*

He lifted me out of the slimy pit,
 out of the mud and mire;
he set my feet upon a rock
 and gave me a firm place to stand.
He put a new song in my mouth,
 a hymn of praise to our God.
Many will see and fear
 and put their trust in the LORD.
                                        Psalm 40:2–3

HAVE YOU EVER CONSIDERED HOW HARD IT MUST HAVE BEEN FOR God to put the tree of the knowledge of good and evil right in the middle of the Garden of Eden where it could tempt his treasured children Adam and Eve? To adequately ponder that question, we first need to go back to the very nature of God. We talked earlier about how God describes himself as a lover or a husband. But there is another even more pervasive theme throughout the Bible—God as our Father.

Throughout the Old Testament and New, God demonstrates his heart's desire to parent us. Just as a child looks to her parents for approval and affection, God wants us to count on him for everything. He gathers us close to his heart and carries us in his arms (Isaiah 40:11); he has high hopes for our future (Jeremiah 29:11); he wants to teach us great and unsearchable things (Jeremiah 33:3); he wants to provide for us (Matthew 6:25-34) and to pull us close when we're brokenhearted (Psalm 34:18).

And he wants to give us good gifts (Matthew 7:11).

One of the most beautiful parables in the Bible is the Prodigal Son. We see God as a parent in anguish over his son who runs away to squander his inheritance in wild living, and then we see his unfettered joy and all-out celebration when the son returns home again, deeply repentant. For me, the most touching picture of God as a parent is him singing over me before I was even born, joyfully anticipating seeing my story and his story intertwine.

## God Rejoices Over You

> "The LORD your God is with you,
>     he is mighty to save.
> He will take great delight in you,
>     he will quiet you with his love,
>     he will rejoice over you with singing." (Zephaniah 3:17)

When I was pregnant with Rebekah, my husband, Dave, made it his practice from the very beginning to talk to her. Eventually that turned into singing her little songs. When I would lie in bed at night, Dave would curl up next to me and my swollen belly, and sing Rebekah songs about God. He would then talk to her about his dreams for her future.

Rebekah was born around 3 AM in the birthing room of a hospital in Las Cruces, New Mexico. After she had finished nursing for the first time, the nurse hoisted her over to a bassinet to clean her up a little. Rebekah was quite displeased about being uprooted from my arms. As a matter of fact, she started crying frantically as if her little life were ending, her face bright red, her arms and legs waving in protest. Dave walked over to the bassinet and spoke gently, "Rebekah, it's your daddy." Rebekah immediately opened her eyes wide, with a clear look of recognition and surprise. Dave then began to sing her a little song that he had sung to her before she was born: "God is so good, God is so good, God is so good, he's so good to you." Bekah laid quietly in the bassinet as the nurse fussed over her, calmly listening to her father singing over her with joy—quieted by her father's love.

Even as Bekah grew a little older, song was still a healing balm to her. She inherited my anxious nature, so when Bekah was five or six, there were times she would get panicked at night and wouldn't be able to stop crying. She had a little *Psalty Bible*[1] that was peppered with children's songs. (Psalty was a Christian cartoon character that loved to praise God in psalms and song.) When she couldn't calm herself, I would read to her and sing to her from the *Psalty Bible* (often with improvised tunes), and then she would be able to sleep peacefully.

When she was in her teens, Bekah knew she wanted to become a Christian fairly early on, but found it difficult to make the commitment. She watched year after year as friend after friend gave their lives to God. Through those years she studied the Bible often. But there was something missing that she could not put her finger on, and she was determined to wait until it was there.

When Bekah was sixteen, she decided to make a special place for just God and her. She would take her journal, a pillow and a blanket, and would climb out through her brother's window onto the flat roof over our screened porch where she could escape all else to hear God's voice. Soon after that she was baptized (on my birthday) and gave her life totally to God. To this day—Bekah is now twenty-two and a new college grad—she loves to curl up with a worship CD to spend time with God and hear his voice.

Just like Bekah, I think we all are listening for a familiar voice. Not the voice of our earthly father, although Dave's gift of singing about God to Bekah before she was born undoubtedly left an imprint and offered comfort. I believe we are each listening for God's voice rejoicing over us with singing.

---

1. *Psalty's Kids Bible*, (Grand Rapids: Zondervan Publishing, 1991).

In Psalms, David beautifully describes this knowledge:

> You made me trust in you
> even at my mother's breast.
> From birth I was cast upon you;
> from my mother's womb you have been my God.
>
> From birth I have relied on you...
> I will ever praise you. (Psalms 22:9–10, 71:6)

If you are a mother, do you remember when you first started delighting in your child? Do you remember being thrilled at the first sound of your child's heartbeat or the first butterfly-like flutters inside your womb? Just like earthly parents joyfully anticipating the birth of a child, God's delight in us starts from the womb. *He rejoices over us with singing.* And his voice leaves a mark in our souls.

It doesn't matter whether you were born in the middle of a South American rainforest or in an igloo on the North Pole, whether your parents were devout Christians or whether they practiced voodoo or witchcraft, God's voice gives us a longing for him. No matter how far down that longing is buried in your heart, it will only be satisfied when you hear his voice, give him your heart and rely on him as his daughter. In fact, no matter how loud the turmoil, fear and anxiety in your soul are screaming for you to rely on yourself, the only voice that can quiet and fill your soul with rest is the voice of God.

## Back to the Garden

As a mother, my understanding of God as a parent has shifted radically. When you first give birth to an innocent child, his or her ability to rebel is the furthest thing from your mind. But as children begin to grow, you see a sure drive toward independence. When they are around two years old, they learn to assert themselves by saying "No." And the older they get, the more apparent it becomes that you cannot impose your will on the life of another. Most likely, by the time they are in their teens and moving into their college years, they have made it absolutely clear that even though they may appreciate your input (at least some of the time!), it is their own life. We've also had years to grow along with our children and let them have their independence a little bit at a time.

God was in an entirely different situation. Before God "birthed" Adam and Eve and set them on the earth that he had created largely for them, he also had to set into place a way for them to choose to live independently of him. In fact, the Bible tells us that the tree was placed in the garden before Adam and Eve stepped a foot there (Genesis 2:9). After rejoicing over Adam and Eve with singing as they opened their eyes for the first time to behold his creation, it must have caused God sadness to tell them about this tree—the tree of the knowledge of good and evil that he had placed smack in the middle of the garden—with a clear commandment that if they partook of the fruit they would die. In fact, I'm convinced it must have been one of the hardest things God ever did. Remember all the plans and dreams God had for them? How much he longed to keep them in the very closest position possible to his heart? Unlike us, God didn't have eighteen years to prepare to let go of his son and daughter. In a sense, he had to let go of them from square one.

The tree had big implications. By placing the tree right where they couldn't possibly miss it, God let Adam and Eve know that he was withholding information from them that they weren't ready for yet. The tree was a daily reminder that God wanted them to trust him and honor his wisdom and judgment. But their free will meant they could choose otherwise. They could choose self-reliance, self-trust and self-exaltation, rather than trusting in their Father's perfect wisdom. Eve's choice of relying on herself, her own wisdom and instincts, and even her own eye for beauty (the fruit looked pleasing and appeared to be good for food) was just a prediction of what would become one of our biggest temptations as women—self-reliance.

## The False Security of Self-Reliance

So why do we as women, who were created to instinctively move toward relationship, sometimes stubbornly and resolutely determine to rely on ourselves? In my heart, the answer is simple. I so long for my feminine heart to be protected, cherished and nurtured that when I'm disappointed or just afraid, I instinctively look for a way to gain control. Self-reliance is my own answer to the unpredictability of life. The logic is simple. I think the only person I can control is me. Therefore, if I rely on me, I'll have control. And if I have control, I won't be nearly as likely to get hurt.

One of my favorite Christian allegories is *Hinds' Feet on High Places*. In many ways, I identify with one of the characters named Much Afraid, an insecure and timid soul with a twisted mouth and a limp who longed to overcome her fears and follow her Great Shepherd to the High Places. Much Afraid eventually did learn to trust and surrender, receiving the security and healing she desired, but first her faith had to be refined through a painful journey that called her to do, again and again, what she thought was utterly impossible for her. In this excerpt, we see the insecurity Much Afraid had to overcome to complete her journey:

> "Oh, no! No!" Much Afraid almost shrieked. "That path is utterly impossible. The deer may be able to manage it, but no human being could. I could never get up there. I would fall headlong and be broke in pieces on those awful rocks." She burst into hysterical sobbing. "It's an impossibility, an absolute impossibility. I cannot get to the High Places that way, and so can never get there at all." Her two guides tried to say something more, but she put her hands over her ears and broke into another clamor of terrified sobs.[2]

I especially related to Much Afraid a few years ago when my

2. Hannah Hurnard, *Hinds' Feet on High Places*, (Weaton, Illinois: Tyndale House Publishers Inc., 1975), 121.

husband and I traveled to Washington Island (at the far end of Door County Wisconsin) to ride bikes and retreat. From Washington Island, a little ferry goes to a small, uninhabited island where you can hike. We decided to take the day to hike on that island. It was a beautiful sunny day, and since I'm a self-proclaimed water-lover, we wanted to hike on the beach as long as possible. The trail didn't really run on the beach, but a man who worked at the tiny campground there told us we could hike on the beach for a little bit and then cut up onto the real trail. "You can't miss the cutoff," were his last words.

Because the beach was made up of thousands of limestones, it was a fun challenge to hike from stone to stone. The sun was dancing on the water, and I was in total bliss. After a while it occurred to me that we had never seen the cutoff. I glanced at my watch, and was surprised to see that we had already hiked an hour. My legs were getting tired, and I was anxious to get on the real trail, since we hadn't seen another soul on our entire beach hike. The control mechanism in my psyche started bleeping—*turn back, you are venturing into the unknown.*

I suggested to my husband that we go back, since we didn't know when and if there would be access to the trail. Plus, it was just two hours until the last boat of the day left from the island. By this point, the cliffs beside us had long been much too steep to climb to try to find the trail. He pointed out that it would probably be another thirty minutes back to where we could access the trail, and asked that we continue just up to the bend that we could see in the distance. I reluctantly agreed and we forged forward.

As we kept walking, we noticed that the beach was getting more and more narrow. When we finally got close enough to the bend of the island, it was painfully obvious that there was no more beach. The water was slapping up against the edge of a cliff. And we couldn't see what was beyond the cliff. But my husband seemed determined to press on. "Dave," I urged him.

"How will we get around? I don't think it's safe." In fact, I was ready to stand my ground—*I wasn't going any farther.*

Dave asked me to wait while he went ahead and checked it out. I stood firm, not wanting to give him an inch. When he got there, he waved excitedly for me to come. Reluctantly I picked my way across the rocks to where he was. When I got there, I could see what he was excited about. There was a narrow little ledge going around the edge of the cliff. It ranged from one to two feet across, and was wet from the small waves slapping up against it.

"Dave, you've got to be kidding," I said, half panicking. "It's too dangerous! We might slip and get hurt, and no one even knows we're here. No one would ever find us." Dave said, "Honey, let's just give it a try," so I took off my shoes, rolled up my pants and moved up to the edge.

"I'm scared," I said, my eyes begging him not to ask me to do it. "I don't know if I can do it."

I'll never forget what happened next. Dave held out his hand, looked me straight in the eyes, and said, "Robin, trust me." When I hesitated, he said it again, kindly but firmly, "Robin, please trust me. I won't let you fall. In fact, if at some point, if seems obvious that we can't do it, we'll turn back." Dave's eyes weren't full of impatience or even fear. In fact, they were full of love and confidence. I could turn back, take control and march off, forcing my husband to sadly follow me back, or I could trust him and move forward.

I took my husband's hand and stepped onto the ledge. Together, we carefully stepped ourselves around the edge of that cliff, getting soaked by the waves, not sure what was around the bend. And once I was up there, it didn't seem nearly as unsafe as I had imagined. From on the ledge I could see that the water four feet below wasn't as deep as I had thought. There were rocks jutting out of the cliff face that we could hold to steady ourselves, and my husband was guiding me across. There was some danger, but it was definitely doable.

Because I was so excited to make it around that first ledge, I almost started crying when I saw what was ahead. I could see at least four more identical curves, with small swatches of beach in between, leading up to another big curve in the island made entirely of cliff. But with a little reassurance from my husband, we made it around each of the curves until we found another long stretch of beach. In another thirty minutes, we had found a place where it was possible to climb up the side of the cliff, and we found the trail. Honestly, it was beautiful. And following my husband's lead around the edge of that island I felt alive and fully engaged in the adventure of life.

Once we reached the trail, my first impulse was to kiss the ground (which I did!). But more importantly I saw a small glimpse of my relationship with God. To follow Dave, I had to largely trust his heart of love and protection for me. And although I know Dave would give up his life for me, he has limited foresight (he didn't know exactly *how* we could get around that island!) and limited power. But God offers me his *heart of love*, his *perfect foresight* (he knows what is around every bend) and his *mighty power* to save.

As my Father, God looks at me with eyes full of love, hand extended and says, "Trust me, Robin." *But God, I have no idea what's around the next corner. How can I trust you? I feel safer doing it my own way.* If I listen closely, I can hear God, his face full of light, and his gentle voice saying, "Robin, I am your Rock. I am your firm footing. Trust me and follow me to the places I want to take you. I'll keep you safe from the waves. I'll keep you from falling.[3] And I won't lead you anywhere that's beyond what you can handle." And then God waits, hand extended, for me to decide whether I'll rely on him or on myself.

---

3. "To him who is able to keep you from falling and to present you before his glorious presence without fault and with great joy—to the only God our Savior be glory, majesty, power and authority, through Jesus Christ our Lord, before all ages, now and forevermore! Amen." (Jude 24)

## God's Extended Arm

> That night all the people of the community raised their voic-
> es and wept aloud. All the Israelites grumbled against Moses
> and Aaron, and the whole assembly said to them, "If only we
> had died in Egypt! Or in this desert! Why is the Lord bringing
> us to this land only to let us fall by the sword? Our wives and
> children will be taken as plunder. Wouldn't it be better for us
> to go back to Egypt?" And they said to each other, "We
> should choose a leader and go back to Egypt." (Numbers
> 14:1–4)

This passage lets me know I am not the first one to struggle
with trusting where I am being led. We've all heard the story of
how God led Israel out of Egypt with an outstretched arm, parting the Red Sea before them and then destroying the army following close behind. Afterwards Israel was standing on the
boundary of the land God has promised. In obedience to God,
twelve leaders of Israel were sent into Canaan to explore and
bring back a report. When they came back, they carried a cluster
of grapes so large that two men were carrying it on a pole
between them. All twelve of the spies agreed that the land was
everything God said it would be. Two of the spies, Joshua and
Caleb, were full of faith that God would give them the victory.
But the other ten were overwhelmed by the strength and stature
of the people living there, as well as the heavily fortified cities.

Instead of throwing themselves before God and asking for
courage and faith to follow God's clear instructions, or even lean-
ing on the faith of Joshua and Caleb, these ten unfaithful leaders
began to circulate rumors among the people. "We can't attack
those people; they are stronger than we are." "The land we
explored devours those living in it." (Talk about drama!) "We
saw the Nephilim there. We seemed like grasshoppers in our
own eyes, and we looked the same to them."[4] But, if we go back
a little earlier in the story, we see that nothing that had happened
thus far had come from the Israelites' own strength.

---

4. Numbers 13:31–33

When the Israelites were slaves in Egypt, they had prayed and groaned for deliverance with loud cries to the only one who could help them, and *God's heart* was moved with compassion.[5] They had stood by helplessly as their people's newborn sons had been tossed into the Nile River to die,[6] but it was *God in his foresight* who had long before planned to rescue Moses from a tar-pitched basket floating in the Nile, lead him into the desert for intensive preparation and then perform the miraculous signs that would enable Moses to lead them out. They had experienced bitter, hard labor and ruthless oppression under the Egyptians, but *God's power* enabled each of them to first walk out of Egypt carrying the Egyptians' silver and gold, and then walk on dry ground through the Red Sea as their enemies, who were hot on their heels, were washed away.

Now forgetful of God's heart, his perfect foresight and his mighty power, these ten leaders had given in to fear. They grumbled against God by telling the people just the opposite of what God had already personally assured them. And prompted by their instigation, the people came up with a "solution" based on their self-reliance. They decided they would rather return to Egypt and subject themselves again to slavery rather than trust God's leadership into the unknown. They would rather watch their children grow up in bitter bondage, than rely on God. In fact, the Israelites were so set on not "going out on the ledge" with God that they were ready to stone Caleb and Joshua, the two faithful spies who had honored and trusted God, along with Moses and Aaron, the leaders of Israel. Is it any wonder that God was hurt and angered?[7]

God was holding out his hand and saying, "Trust me. I'll take you into this new land," and they stubbornly refused. What the Israelites didn't understand was that God's plan to conquer Canaan had little to do with them or their strength. Forty years later, the walls of the most heavily fortified city, Jericho, would

---

5. Exodus 2:23

6. Exodus 1:22

7. "Don't raise your fist against High God. Don't raise your voice against the Rock of Ages." (Psalm 75:5, *The Message*)

come down by the Israelites doing little more than marching around it.[8]

Just like the Israelites, we can allow self-reliance to cause us to go backwards to places we really don't want to go, even into slavery. Satan seeks to get us to embrace his false security of self-reliance by tempting us to

- **Forget past deliverance in the face of present tests**—Like the Israelites, we can forget God's foresight in arranging the circumstances in our lives. We can lose sight of the power he has shown in answering our prayers. We can forget the ways he has shown us his heart of love. We then feel justified to forge our own paths based on our own understanding, rather than trusting in the Lord and allowing him to direct our paths.[9]

- **Exchange true security for slavery**—The Israelites wanted safety, comfort and freedom from fear so badly that they turned away from the very one who offered them all three. In fact, they began to mistake their past slavery for security. *When we were in Egypt, at least we had food!* Like them, we are sometimes so afraid that we won't receive the blessings we long for, that we are tempted to go back to the insecure situations, lifestyles or people that enslave us. *When I was living that way, at least I could have a man!*

- **Make decisions based on our own strengths and weaknesses**—Ultimately the spies said they felt like grasshoppers and appeared the same way to their enemies.[10] The Israelites were making life-changing decisions based on how they saw themselves rather than how they saw God. The truth is that if we don't put our hand firmly in God's, our insecurities will take the lead instead.

- **Raise our voice in anxiety, instead of raising our voice in prayer**—All night long after hearing the spies' report, the Israelites wept aloud, with tears of self-pity instead of tears of petition. Instead of letting their fear lead them to prayer, they let their fears take charge and fill them with anxiety. The only real way out of our fears is through surrendering to God with thanksgiving and prayer, and then walking with him, our hand in his, straight through our fears.

8. Joshua 6:1–20
9. Proverbs 3:5–7
10. Numbers 13:33

- **Refuse to listen to godly leadership**—God provided a way out through the voices of Joshua, Caleb, Aaron and Moses urging them to trust God. But rather than trusting, the Israelites turned on their leadership. They did not take responsibility for their own distrust and rebellion. Ultimately Satan wants to divide us from the godly voices that urge us to surrender to God's good plans for us.

- **Take control when we don't see how it will work out**—The Israelites had no idea how God was going to give them their promised land. In their human thinking, God was leading them straight into the hands of their enemies! Each decision they made out of their desire to control only had more disastrous effects. Like the Israelites, by taking control and embracing the false security of self-reliance, we learn lessons the hard way.

Self-reliance puts us into bondage—we are taken captive by our fear, our desire to control and our unwillingness to trust. The very things we ask for we don't receive because we're unwilling to take God's hand and follow. And the strongholds and insecurities that Satan sets up in our lives will only come down when we rely on our Father, our Lover, our spiritual Rock—God.

## Relying on God As Your Rock

"You have forgotten God your Savior;
    you have not remembered the Rock, your fortress.
Therefore, though you set out the finest plants
    and plant imported vines,
though on the day you set them out, you make them grow,
    and on the morning when you plant them, you bring
        them to bud,
yet the harvest will be as nothing
    in the day of disease and incurable pain."
(Isaiah 17:10–11)

I love the picture of God as our Rock and our fortress. If you look up the word "fortress" in your thesaurus, you'll get a picture of the immense strength and security we can draw from God as

our Rock. God wants us to trust in him as our protection, stronghold, support, citadel, defense, barrier, safeguard and security.
He wants us to count on him as the Father who knows us intimately, and rejoices over us with singing. He wants to take our
hand and lead us to green pastures and quiet waters.[11] He wants
to take us out of our ashes, mourning and despair, and clothe us
in garments of praise, raising us up as oaks of righteousness,
women of faith.[12]

Yet this scripture paints a vivid picture of what happens when
we forget God as our Rock and then rely on ourselves instead.
We may set out with what appear to be the finest plants in our
spiritual garden, even bringing in fancy imported vines from
other countries. As we tend them, they may initially grow and
even bud. But the real test is the day of disease and incurable
pain. If we've planted and sown self-reliance—choosing our own
ways and then carefully controlling the outcomes—we won't
make it through the tests, pain, disease and hardship. These tests
will expose how far we've wandered off of the path that God has
planned for us. In contrast, look at how God describes the
woman who relies upon him (pronouns changed for emphasis):

> Blessed is the woman
>     who does not walk in the counsel of the wicked
> or stand in the way of sinners
>     or sit in the seat of mockers.
> But her delight is in the law of the LORD,
>     and on his law she meditates day and night.
> She is like a tree planted by streams of water,
>     which yields its fruit in season
> and whose leaf does not wither.
>     Whatever she does prospers. (Psalm 1:1–3)

There is no true security outside of a relationship with God
and his law. But if you build everything you are on God your
Rock, you can be confident that when the day of trouble comes,
by his power, you will stand. When tears come, you will harvest

11. Psalm 23
12. Isaiah 61:3

with shouts of joy. When weakness comes, God will show his strength. Most of all, you'll have the Rock of Ages to count on to take you through whatever life may throw your way.

How does self-reliance stack up against God-reliance? Let's take a look...

| Self-Reliance | God-Reliance |
| --- | --- |
| Forgets God and his works of the past and concentrates on the here and now. *Where is God today when I need him? I must see him right now to believe him.* | Interprets the here and now through how God has already shown his heart of love, his perfect foresight and his mighty power. *God was here then and he's here now, even if I don't see him.* |
| Focuses on following my own understanding and arranging my life as I see best | Focuses on following Christ and delighting in God's law to find the right path |
| May initially seem to be successful | May initially seem to bring more hardship |
| Comes to nothing in the day of disease or pain | Thrives in spite of disease and pain and continues to yield good fruit |
| Causes me to build my house on the sand—when the storms come, my house falls (Matthew 7:24–25) | Causes me to build my house on the rock—when the storms come, my house stands (Matthew 7:26–27) |

I really don't think any of us set out to build our spiritual house on the sand, where we can be washed away by the trials and tests that come our way. But what we need to remember is that we can't have it both ways. Self-reliance and God-reliance can't coexist. Either I'm following God on the path that he's marked out for me, trusting his heart of love, his purpose and his power, or I'm walking independently in my own direction away from God (who by the way, doesn't tag along behind).

When it comes down to it, counting on God is an issue of surrender and trust. But when we do put our hand in his and follow him across what appear to be impassable ledges, God enables us to count on him as our mighty Rock and fortress, walking us step by step toward security of heart.

# IN HER OWN WORDS
## *Leanne's Story*

Even before I was born, my life was marked by a deep instability. I was born in Florida because my dad was in trouble with the law in New York. We moved back and forth—New York to Florida and then Florida to New York. When he got in trouble in one place, we would move to the other.

Some of my first memories are of fierce fighting between my mom and dad. I remember watching my dad beat my mom in fits of rage, over practically anything. Although I was only three years old, I remember my dad bringing drugs into the house, and my mom, furious, flushing them down the toilet. He beat her badly that day.

Although I have no memories of my dad hurting me, much later in life, my mom told me that he had beaten me too. She would come home from nursing school and find bruises on me. When I was four years old, Dad left. It really hurt because as a daddy's girl, I felt he was my whole world. I remember feeling first like it was my fault he left, and then getting even angrier when I decided that it was really my mom's fault—she didn't make him happy enough.

After Dad left, it was just Mom and I. However, she always had a boyfriend. Since none of them were my real dad, I hated them all. I remember walking up to one guy in particular and kicking him in the shins. I would stay with my relatives while Mom was going to school during the day and working at a bar or gas station at night.

When I was six, she started dating a man she met on a bus. He promised to treat her like a queen. I went on their first date with them, sat in between them and made it known that he was not welcome. They dated for a year, and we moved in with him when I was seven. He never hit me or treated me badly. When I was eight, they got married. I was excited because my mom was happy again instead of depressed and crying all the time.

When my brother was born, as far as my step-dad was concerned, I ceased to exist. I had always wanted a dad—someone that cared for me, that would be a real dad to me. Once he had his own son, I guess it emphasized the fact that I wasn't his child. As my brother got older, he got more and more positive attention from my dad, while I seemed to get all of the negative attention. I was a precocious child, who at the age of ten started developing into a woman. My stepfather started doing things to me that weren't natural. He would try to fondle me or climb into bed with me. He never was able to get very far because I would start screaming, hitting and punching. I tried telling my mom that I did not understand certain things he was doing. She would say, "That's just his way of telling you he loves you." I thought, *I guess this is just the way dads act.*

When I started having sleepovers with my girlfriends, my stepfather acted weird toward them too. My best friend wanted me to come to her house because she didn't feel comfortable around him. Things were just getting worse—he would tell me, "You're so beautiful. I wish you were older. I would have married you instead of your mother." He also teased me mercilessly about getting breasts. When he would do the laundry, he would wave my bras around and make me feel dirty that I was getting breasts at such an early age.

I started eating more—I thought if I gained a lot of weight, maybe he would stop trying to jump into bed with me or touch me. Although I did gain a lot of weight, that didn't stop my stepfather's interest, but it did cause me grief at school. Because I was bigger, I was called fat, ugly and stupid.

When I was thirteen, things were still getting worse

with my stepfather. I knew I couldn't fight him off forever. Mom had told me not to have sex until I was married, but at that time I knew she was having sex with men she wasn't married to. I decided to give away my virginity as an act of defiance to my stepfather—*you may force me to sleep with you, but I won't let you take my virginity.* I found some guy I didn't know very well. I told him when my parents would not be home, and we had sex. It hurt so bad that I didn't ever want to do it again.

Things finally escalated to a breaking point with my stepfather when I was a freshman in high school. At this point, I had stopped calling him Dad, wouldn't hug him and would barely talk to him for fear of what he might do. The night before, my mother had told me that she was very unhappy with the way I was treating him. I went to bed thinking about that. So the next morning, he wanted to give me a hug before I went to school. I hugged him, and even though my mom was showering in the next room—he wouldn't let me go. He started kissing on my neck. I screamed, pushed and kicked, grabbed my bag and left. Mom came running outside asking what was going on. I threw out some excuse and took off to school. I didn't come home until 10 or 11 at night because I didn't want to be home alone with him.

I went to my mother the next day and told her what happened. I knew it was time to take matters into my own hands. I told her that if she didn't get rid of him, I would run away... *for good.* I gave her a week. A couple of days later my mother came to me and finally acknowledged what had been going on. She was crying and apologizing because the same exact thing had happened to her when she was young (except she hadn't gotten away).

My mom told my stepfather to leave—so it was my mom,

my brother and I. I remember my mom pulling me aside and telling me, "Now that I'm getting rid of him, you have to help me. I can't take care of all of this myself." I was fourteen and my brother was four. I felt like she blamed me for her marriage failing and even for not having a man in her life.

It seemed like everything was out of control. There was nothing I could control but my own actions. So I started smoking and drinking, experimenting with marijuana mixed with opium and who knows what else. I would wear revealing clothes that showed off my big bust line. I would lead guys along, and then refuse to do anything with them. By the time I was in high school, I decided that I hated being a girl. I dressed like a boy, cut my hair really short and wore a big army coat. I shaved the back of my head. I did not own any skirts or dresses. But all I really wanted was for all of my problems to go away.

Then our lives were turned upside down when a stranger invited Mom to church at a bus stop. He kept calling, and my mom thought it was because he liked her. I thought she was stupid. She went to church one Sunday. I was fifteen. She invited me to come with her but I thought, *God hasn't done it for me, doesn't know me, doesn't have any love for me—I'm fine.* She started having women over to study the Bible. I would come home drunk and high—and then would sit and listen as they studied.

In August my mom gave her life to God while I was at my boss's house getting drunk and high. She started changing in ways I couldn't deny, but I would taunt her and try to get her to slip up. My mission was to get her to stop living how God wanted. But, bit by bit, as much as I wasn't showing it, I was touched by my mother's changes. I knew it was real. And I was beginning to see in her life what I had always longed for.

Soon afterwards I started studying the Bible, and six months later I became a Christian. People would say, "It's awesome that you've done this at such a young age"—but I didn't feel young. I was fifteen going on thirty-five. So much had happened, and I had such a big wall of emotional protection built up around me that it was hard for anyone to get close to me.

Two years later, I left God. I decided God wasn't making my bad feelings go away. I still had nightmares. I was still seeking attention. And I still had never had a godly man love me. I began to obsess about hurting my stepfather—wishing I could hunt him down and kill him. I wanted to find my real father and kill him as well. I started having thoughts of suicide.

One particularly difficult night, I walked down to the lake. There I imagined myself walking to the middle, sinking to the bottom and stopping breathing. I stood there for two hours thinking about killing myself. All of the sudden, I felt something brush my shoulder, like God himself had reached out and touched me. I turned around and ran to the apartment where my mom was at a Christmas party. It was the first time I had reached out for help. I told my mother everything, and she took me to the hospital. I ended up in the psychiatric ward on suicide watch for a week.

At first I was mad at God—*You brought me this low*. Then I realized that I had needed to come to my knees. I had been trying to handle things by myself for so long that I just crumbled in on myself. Afterwards, I was in therapy for a long time. It took much counseling to begin to understand why I couldn't make myself better.

Later, I became friends with a guy at church—soon, we started dating. I told him that I did not have good self-esteem, and he said, "Leanne, you are the most beautiful girl in the world to me. I don't care what anybody else thinks." His words helped me understand that it really did not matter. Now Andy and I have been married for a year.

Sometimes I still think, *God, why did you put me in this body?* Honestly, I think that I feel safer this way—overweight. I know that my husband is attracted to me, but I know I won't attract the attention of other men. Now I am changing my diet to become healthier, not just to lose weight. I want to live a long time with my husband. And Andy says he loves me just the way I am.

Although Andy is a godly man showing me attention, it doesn't fix my self-esteem problems. Every other day or so, I still wake up and think, *Now why does he think I'm so beautiful?* I still need daily reassurance from him that he loves me, that he won't abandon me. Yet I am seeing that my husband can't fill me up inside. I see that I have to draw deep from God to get that. Andy can't be my foundation or my security—he can't be my Rock.

My biggest battle right now is seeing God's goodness in every situation. I can see that in the past God has always taken care of me, but I start to worry that it's not going to happen this time. I'm still waiting for the time when God doesn't catch me. I still try to take care of things myself. And after I fall on my face trying to do it myself, God comes through again in a way that takes away any doubt that it was from him and not from me.

Psalm 23 tells me that God leads me beside peaceful waters. I picture him holding out his hand to me, and I understand all that I have to do is put my hand in his and trust that he will lead me to a peaceful place. I thank him for the peace he has put in my heart as my true Rock.

# WHO CAN I COUNT ON? THE ROCK
## *Personal Study Guide & Life Application*

How can we remember God as our Rock and fortress? Here are just a few practical suggestions that can help you in your battle to be secure in heart.

**1) Remember and celebrate God's acts of deliverance in your life**—When you're tempted to take your own path, remember the times in your life when you did see God work. Let those times teach you about God's heart of love for you today.

> *Make a list of ways God has come through for you in the past. Beside each, write how this showed God's heart, his foresight or his power. Write a prayer commemorating those times and share it with someone.*

**2) Lean on God's power to deliver you**—We get ourselves into the pits and then reason that we should be able to pull ourselves out. I think it must be an amusing sight to God to see me repeatedly try to climb a slippery slope and then slide down over and over again, rather than simply reaching up to the hand already outstretched to lift me up.

> *Make a list of all the complaints, anxieties and fears you currently battle, and then bathe each of them in thanksgiving. Thank God for lifting you out of the slimy pit and putting your feet on firm ground.*

**3) Put your roots down deep into God's word**—Instead of grumbling, complaining, despairing and then frantically making our own way, God calls us to trust in his word. In fact, grumbling and complaining quickly turns into rebellion against God's good plans for us.

*Study out every time the word "rock" is used in the book of Psalms. Share what you learn with another woman.*

**4) Surrender to God as your Rock**—In the Psalms, David often cried out to God his Rock for help, security and deliverance. In the same way, prayer is key to carrying us out of our self-reliance into a heart that counts on God.

*Preface your prayers with, "Dear God, my Rock." Find a small rock to carry with you for a week to remind you of God's presence. Afterwards, journal about how having God as your Rock alters your perspective.*

**5) Embrace leaders who urge you to trust God**—Sometimes in our desire to control our own destiny, we discount the voice of godly leaders who urge us to honor God and his word. It helps me to remember that these men and women of faith are gifts given to me by God himself to help keep me from being tossed by my emotions, anxieties and fears.[13]

*Write a thank you note to a leader who has challenged you to have faith in a particularly difficult time in your life. Tell this person how he or she helped you rely on God as your Rock.*

**6) Learn from others' battles**—In her story, Leanne says, "I still try to take care of things myself. And after I fall on my face trying to do it myself, God comes through again in a way that takes away any doubt that it was from him and not from me."

*Come up with three ways you still try to take care of things yourself rather than trusting in God. Read Psalm 23. What arenas in your life is God saying that he wants to take care of for you?*

---

13. Ephesians 4:13–15

"After I had been in a horrible marriage for two years, I started what quickly turned into an emotional affair including numerous lunches, dinners and hours spent on the phone. Since my husband worked nights, he was totally unaware. I really believed this guy loved me in a way my husband never would.

"We were headed towards physical adultery when God intervened. Becoming a Christian meant never talking to my 'boyfriend' again. It didn't save my marriage, but it made me deal with the deeper issues in my heart and find peace with God."

—Learning to trust in God as my husband

# WILL I BE RESCUED?
## *The Anchor*

They confronted me in the day of my disaster,
  but the LORD was my support.
He brought me out into a spacious place;
  he rescued me because he delighted in me.
Psalm 18:18–19

Fairy tales are more than true—not because they tell us dragons exist, but because they tell us dragons can be beaten.
—G. K. Chesterton

AS A LOVE STORY, THE BIBLE IS ALSO THE TALE OF A GRAND RESCUE.
It starts with Adam and Eve reigning over paradise until Satan
viciously attacks, imprisoning them in the shame of spiritual
defeat. The story ends in the book of Revelation with what is yet
to happen—the ultimate rescue of God's saints through Satan's
complete and final destruction. Even the word "rescue" is loaded
with spiritual implications. A rescuer serves as a savior, defender,
deliverer, guardian, liberator, messiah, preserver and protector—all
Biblical images of God and Christ.

Some of the more memorable stories of the Bible are tales of
rescue. Noah and his family were rescued from a corrupt genera-
tion through obedience to God's word and through water (1 Peter
3:19–21). God rescued the Israelites from Egyptian slavery
through Moses (Exodus 3:8). Lot was rescued because of his own
righteous heart and Abraham's intercession before Sodom and
Gomorrah were destroyed (2 Peter 2:7). Joseph was rescued from

his troubles through God's providence and foresight (Acts 7:9–10). Jesus himself appeared to Meshack, Shadrach and Abednego and delivered them unscathed from a fiery furnace (Daniel 3); and angels shut the mouths of lions when Daniel was thrown in the lions' den (Daniel 6).

One of the greatest insults anyone could ever give God would be to say that he can't rescue his people. Sennacherib, a king of Assyria, found that out the hard way. In 2 Chronicles 32, we learn that Sennacherib had Jerusalem surrounded; his forces were poised to attack and destroy Israel. He sent his couriers to intimidate and dishearten those on the wall, insulting and blaspheming God in their own language.

> "Now do not let Hezekiah deceive you and mislead you like this. Do not believe him, for no god of any nation or kingdom has been able to deliver his people from my hand or the hand of my fathers." (2 Chronicles 32:15)

Big mistake! God promptly rescued his people decisively, sending an angel of destruction to kill Sennacherib's fighting men, leaders and officers right in their own camp!

With all this in mind, it's easy to understand why Satan still chooses rescue as a sore point to press on in our psyches: *Just look at your circumstances! Where is this rescue you're supposed to be receiving?* Satan whispers: *After all, he has rescued his other children. Just look around you and you'll see the many others that he is rescuing. Why do you suppose that he hasn't intervened for you? He sees your heartache. Why isn't he responding?* And then, to add insult to injury, he seeks to make us believe that we should expect, even demand, that others come through for us in the ways that we desire. And when they don't, he plants the thought that not only have people failed us, but that God has failed us as well.

**Desperately Seeking Rescue**

By the time I was in my teens, rescue was a theme I was well acquainted with, largely through the pages of the romance novels that my mom would leave lying around the house. As my father's alcoholism accelerated and his accompanying verbal abuse increased, I longed for a rescue—a way out. And in my mind, at least part of the answer was finding someone who would love me unconditionally.

When I got involved in a church at age sixteen, there was a sincere desire for God's rescue. But it was mixed with a desire for human validation and love. Soon after I gave my life to God, I was asked to get involved in the thriving children's outreach ministry at our church. I was assigned to work with Vince, a married man, on a visitation team. Vince and I would go out canvassing for four to six hours on Saturdays visiting children in the housing projects in a nearby city, playing with them and inviting them to church events. Unbeknown to me, Vince was struggling in his marriage.

Vince was a combination of a second father, uncle, role model and even rescuer to me. He would swoop me away from troubles at home and take me to reach out to families. He entertained me with jokes and quips; he had a great sense of humor. I quickly became very fond of him and came to rely on his wife as a mother figure. I would often go over to their house and spend hours talking with her.

As time went on, Vince increased the attention he gave me. We'd be walking away from a house, and he might put his arm around me and give me a little squeeze or grab my elbow to guide me across a busy street. When we went out to lunch, he took me to nice places, and then would playfully kick my feet under the table. He was giving me the kind of human touch my father rarely gave me.

After months of working together, he asked me if I'd like to play tennis one day after our visitation time. I remember asking him, "Don't you need to get home?" He assured me that his wife did not mind and off we went to play tennis. I should have come to my senses when I started having dreams that his wife died. I wish I had seen the inappropriateness of all the attention he was giving me. I wish my church had thought twice about teaming up a man struggling with his marriage with a young, mixed-up teen girl who was just at the bare beginnings of Christianity. Regardless, I was blinded by my own need for affection and approval from a father figure.

Satan was dangling another woman's husband in front of me as a path to emotional security and spiritual rescue. It turned out that Vince's motives were less than pure. His teasing went to a new level when he proposed, joking of course, that he and I take off for Hawaii. I laughed. I felt a little uncomfortable, slightly confused, but also just a little flattered. On the way to take me home one Saturday, he cradled his arm over the seat where I was sitting. "Why don't you scoot over closer?" he teased. When I hesitated, he tried to coax, even reaching over and pulling me next to him in the seat. "Oh, no, no...I don't think so," I managed to blurt out.

I alerted our ministry leader, who advised that I take a break from the ministry while they sorted things out. Sadly, Vince took no responsibility at all for his actions and told his wife that it was all my struggle. She never spoke to me again, making it absolutely clear she blamed me. A while later, Vince was embroiled in an affair with a young Christian in our church and left his pregnant wife and two young boys, shaking our small fellowship to the core. That so easily could have been me.

For the longest time, I blamed Vince for all of it. Certainly, Vince was responsible as an adult pursuing a minor. But now I realize that I was the other side of the equation. After everything had happened, I realized the real loss for me wasn't losing my relationship with Vince; it was losing my much-treasured relationship with his wife.

It wasn't just Vince who picked up on my neediness. Even after my experience with Vince, other women in the church pulled me aside and told me that they were uncomfortable with the way I looked at their husbands. I was bewildered since I did not feel attracted to any of these men. The truth was they represented something that I was seeking, but that I could only find from God—approval, affection and emotional rescue. But it would take much more than my experience with Vince to expose and then break that stronghold of neediness in my heart.

Less than two years later, I was at a Christian college and involved in a bus ministry at a small church off campus. I was working the bus route with my boyfriend. But when we weren't ministering, studying or attending class, we would participate in my boyfriend's favorite spare-time hobby of "getting some sugar" as he would call it. We would go to the woods near campus, build campfires, talk and kiss for hours. If it was too cold we would sneak into unused buildings on campus that were unlocked in the evening. Since we were both trying to live Christian lives, the relationship never went much beyond kissing, although it was full of sensuality.

When I found out he was seeing another girl on the side, I just redoubled my efforts to keep him, despite his attempts to explain to me that he felt crowded and unsure. My "love" was making me blind and deaf! In fact, it took him dropping me for the relationship to end. It took almost a full year afterwards for me to let go of him in my heart.

Ultimately, I took this neediness into my relationship with my husband to be. Although our relationship had been pure, once we were engaged, I soon found myself in the same old pattern. The first time he touched me intimately, I put my head in my hands and wept after he left, devastated at dishonoring God. But the next time I wasn't so devastated. In fact, it wasn't too long before we were spending hours making out, even in the church building where he worked as a youth minister. Although, all this hidden sin was causing me untold guilt, I was hooked—afraid to lose the affection I craved.

Although technically I never lost my virginity, I lost much more. I lost perspective on God and his perfect love for me. I lost the security that comes from standing up for my convictions. In fact, it was years into our marriage before I began to really deal with the idolatry in my heart toward having the affection of a man. And then I finally began to see that the deepest needs of my heart couldn't be filled by a man. My heart would only come to rest through finding security in God, and God alone.

## The False Security of Dependence

One of the most common themes of fairy tales is a damsel in distress waiting to be rescued and a handsome prince who must battle dragons and evil rulers to rescue her. Many of the movies we endearingly call "chick flicks" are fairy tales of sorts, some with the more modern twist of the woman rescuing or redeeming the man through her love. If you search on the internet for *handsome prince to the rescue*, many of the hits will be online personal ads placed by women. In fact, many women will come out and say, "I want the fairy tale." But let's face it; the fairy tale is far bigger than having a man. Even being married doesn't satisfy the desire. Many of us look at our "prince" and realize that on some days he is more into saving his favorite sports team than saving us!

Although I'm very grateful for the strength my husband brings me, I've discovered that my desire for the fairy tale symbolizes something much bigger. Being rescued means having Hallmark movie-like endings to all of my troubles. It means being able to climb mountains in my life—physical, financial, emotional, relational and spiritual—without taking any disabling spills. The fairy tale is a security that gallops in on a white horse and swoops me away from all of my hardships. It's a happy ending that is totally predictable regardless of how many twists and turns there are in the story.

Some of us act out our desire for rescue by living on the other side of the fantasy. We build who we are around trying to rescue. As strange as this may sound, I think we seek to be rescued by rescuing someone else. We act out the true needs of our own heart by showering someone else with the same brand of attention we crave.

Or in our search for security, we take another route: *Maybe if there isn't a handsome prince coming my way, I can take this rougher version and create my own prince. Perhaps who I am will change who he is.* And so we open up the door to living with someone who abuses us or who is even an avoider, who runs from intimacy with us running behind him seeking the romance, love and connection we desire.

The very nature of the word "rescue" should alert us that rescue isn't something one human being can give another. A trip to the thesaurus shows us that "rescue" has far more to it than just having a man in the equation. Being rescued means being delivered, liberated, released, safeguarded, saved, emancipated, redeemed, recovered, ransomed, unleashed, disentangled and set free. Is it any coincidence that most of these terms are Bible words for what God does for us?

| | |
|---|---|
| Delivered | For you have delivered me from death and my feet from stumbling, that I may walk before God in the light of life. (Psalm 56:13) |
| Liberated | ...that the creation itself will be liberated from its bondage to decay and brought into the glorious freedom of the children of God. (Romans 8:21) |
| Released | We have been released from the law so that we serve in the new way of the spirit... (Romans 7:6) |
| Safeguarded | I know whom I have believed, and am convinced that he is able to guard what I have entrusted to him for that day. (2 Timothy 1:12) |
| Saved | ...who has saved us and called us to a holy life—not because of anything we have done but because of his own purpose and grace. (2 Timothy 1:9) |
| Redeemed | You were redeemed from the empty way of life handed down to you from your forefathers... (1 Peter 1:18) |

| Recovered | But God does not take away life; instead, he devises ways so that a banished person may not remain estranged from him. (2 Samuel 14:14) |
| Ransomed | The ransomed of the LORD will return. They will enter Zion with singing; everlasting joy will crown their heads. (Isaiah 35:10) |
| Disentangled | Since we are surrounded by such a great crowd of witnesses, let us throw off everything that hinders and the sin that so easily entangles, and let us run with perseverance the race marked out for us. (Hebrews 12:1) |
| Set free | I run in the path of your commands, for you have set my heart free. (Psalm 119:32) |

Only God can set us free from emotional dungeons reinforced by deeply rooted hurts. The ropes that bind us are satanic strongholds that he has deviously built for his end goal of enslaving us. The dragon that stalks us is the deceiver of the ages. An epic battle is being fought for each of our souls that far exceeds fairy tale dimensions. And this battle hasn't always had a happy beginning, middle or even ending. Eve's temptation was only the beginning of this battle. When she faced off with the serpent and lost, her handsome prince followed along behind.

## Back to the Garden

> Now the serpent was more crafty than any of the wild animals that LORD God had made. He said to the woman, "Did God really say, 'You must not eat from any tree in the garden?'" (Genesis 3:1)

The Bible tells us right from the beginning that Satan was crafty. Go back to the thesaurus and look up "crafty," and you'll find literally hundreds of words that describe his true nature including shady, shifty, slippery, treacherous, double-dealing, counterfeit, lying, underhanded, tricky, scheming, misleading, fraudulent, subtle and sneaky. Satan's brand of craftiness only has to do with one thing—the destruction of our souls. And part of Satan's disguise as an angel of light is to masquerade as a rescuer. His goal? To get us to give up on God's rescue and become needy—dependent on anyone or anything other than God.

To illustrate Satan's craftiness, the scripture tells us how he approached Eve. Satan, showing the fancy footwork he likes to employ when we go out on his dance floor, twists the truth grandly in a single question: *"Did God really say?"* God had spoken his word clearly and irrevocably to Adam and Eve. Satan got Eve to doubt God by first getting her to doubt herself: *"Eve, my dear, perhaps you misunderstood. Because I can assure you, you won't die."* This highlights Satan's number one way to fuel our neediness—getting us to doubt the standards that God has clearly set in place through the Bible: *Maybe that's just my interpretation. Perhaps there is more than one way. Not everybody sees it this way.* Satan's specialty is getting us to choose sources other than God's word to feed our security.

But then, as Satan loves to do, he unloads the second deceit, even bigger than the first: *"Did God really say you must not eat from any tree in the garden?"* God had only prohibited one tree. Satan subtly made it seem like God was trying to prohibit everything! By doing this, Satan got Eve focused on what she didn't have. Instead of seeing all the gifts that God had graciously given her, she was now focused on the one thing she didn't have. And guided by Satan, that forbidden fruit came to represent so much more—the ability to make her own decisions independent of God, completeness in knowledge and wisdom, and even the courage to explore her sensuality by taking what looked pleasing and tasted good for her own.

Satan's ploy was simple:

1) **Deceive Eve**—Convince Eve that she needed what God said she couldn't have by tapping into her questions and her feminine longings.

2) **Discredit God and highlight his lack of rescue**—*"He does not want you to have what you need. And he certainly isn't going to give you what you need. Is it really so bad for you to want something for yourself?"*

**3) Propose another source of rescue**—"*You need to look outside of God to get what you need. Here, let me help you.*" Satan wanted Eve to believe that he could bring her the rescue that God wouldn't bring.

**4) Unravel Eve's trust in God**—Satan knew that if Eve called out to God, he would intervene. So he planted just enough guilt that Eve would be uneasy about asking God. *How will he feel about me since I doubt him?*

The forbidden fruit that Satan dangled represented Eve's neediness. That shiny "apple" and its promise of wisdom and knowledge created fear that God wasn't enough. But although Satan won the battle, he was far from winning the war. God's plan to rescue his treasured creation, represented in Adam and Eve, had only just begun.

## Our Soul's True Anchor

I love to go to the ocean and watch the powerful waves. Recently when we were in Hawaii for our twenty-fifth anniversary, we had the good fortune to witness big surf rolling in. We spent several hours in lawn chairs on the top of a rocky cliff, watching twenty-five-foot waves roll onto shore. As you watch these churning masses of water, pushing, curling and pounding onto shore, you get a small glimpse of the power of nature. I love to watch big waves, but you couldn't pay me enough to go out into those powerful currents. The most terrifying thing I can imagine is to be stuck in deep waters with no rescue in sight. Perhaps that's why the psalmist used the phrase "deep waters" to aptly describe the place where we often find ourselves—hardship and trials so intertwined with emotion and spiritual questions that we have trouble knowing which end is up.

In order to rescue us, Jesus had to paddle into what would be the equivalent of a 1,000-foot wave—the cumulative sin of mankind, reaching back all the way to Adam and Eve and spanning into the future to us and beyond. The only way Jesus could set anchor for us and for our faith, was to let go of his own anchor and paddle out alone, through a cruel and shameful death, through a tomb carved out of the side of a cliff, and even through Hades itself.

> We have this hope as an anchor for the soul, firm and secure. It enters the inner sanctuary behind the curtain, where Jesus, who went before us, has entered on our behalf. (Hebrews 6:19–20)

In this passage, the phrase that the writer uses—"who went before us,"—in the original language comes from the word *prodoumus*, which means "one who rushes on, a frontrunner, one who goes ahead to make sure the way is safe." Jesus had to forgo rescue, in order to make the way safe for us.

Satan knew this and was fully prepared to use this against Christ. The chief priests, teachers of the law and elders—no doubt spurred on by the great accuser himself—taunted Christ while he was on the cross, saying, "He trusts in God. Let God rescue him now *if he wants him...*" (Matthew 27:43, emphasis mine). In fact, Jesus' lack of rescue was a big part of the pain of the cross.

Consider the following passage from the Psalms:

> In you our fathers put their trust;
>     they trusted and you delivered them.
> They cried to you and were saved;
>     in you they trusted and were not disappointed.
> But I am a worm and not a man,
>     scorned by men and despised by the people.
> All who see me mock me;
>     they hurl insults, shaking their heads:
> "He trusts in the LORD;
>     let the LORD rescue him." (Psalm 22:4–8)

Through David's prophetic words, we get a glimpse into the mental turmoil of the cross. As Jesus hung on the cross, Satan was quick to throw before him the fact that God had rescued others, but no deliverance was in sight for him. Was he just a worm, even less than the men God had performed mighty acts of deliverance for? When Jesus, Lord of Lords, and God's only begotten Son, compared himself to others—mere men in fact—by all appearances he was on the losing end. Just like us, Jesus had to wrestle through his feelings and find faith that there would be joy beyond what appeared to be a lack of rescue. Jesus understands what it feels like not to be rescued. He understands your insecurity including the temptation to compare yourself to others. And that understanding means that he can help!

But what makes the story even more amazing is the fact that Jesus could have rescued himself at any moment. In fact, he had many opportunities. One of his first temptations from Satan was to hurl himself off of the pinnacle of the temple to see if angels would rescue him as the Scriptures said they would.[1]

At any point, he could have chosen an earthly kingdom that didn't require a cross, rather than the spiritual one God had sent him to establish. He could have done miracles in a way that overwhelmed and intimidated the people, perhaps by calling down thunder and lightning on the Samaritans as James and John suggested at one point in his ministry.[2]

In the garden, he could have slipped away while the disciples were sleeping. And as he told Peter at his arrest, after Peter cut off the ear of a guard, Jesus could have at any point called down legions of angels to rescue him.[3]

Although he could have rescued himself, doing any of these things would have meant that he could not accomplish his mission—"to rescue us from the present evil age, according to the will of our God" (Galatians 1:4). Can you imagine the love and heart it took to deny himself rescue for our sake? And even more,

1. Matthew 4:6
2. Luke 9:54
3. Matthew 26:53

how much love God showed by not intervening himself to rescue his beloved Son!

Let's just suppose for a minute that you could say the word and be rescued from your present distress whether physical, emotional, financial or relational. All you would have to do is sign on the dotted line, and then all of your problems would be removed and resolved according to your wishes and in your timing. Would you do it? Would that give you a secure heart?

Before you answer with an emphatic *Yes*, let's take just a minute to think about the implications. Doing this would mean putting your trust in your own interpretation of rescue rather than God's. And bypassing God's plan for your life and his timing of your deliverance would cost you all of the promises that God gives which are attached to hardship, suffering, persecution and weakness, including

- Perseverance, character and hope—Romans 5:3–5

- A harvest of righteousness and peace—Hebrews 12:11

- God's comfort and being able to comfort others—
  2 Corinthians 1:5–6

- The crown of life—James 1:12

- Refinement of your faith resulting in praise, glory and honor—
  1 Peter 1:7

- Knowing Jesus—Philippians 3:10–11

- God's wisdom and providence—1 Corinthians 1:25–31

- Knowing God's power in your weakness—2 Corinthians 12:9–10

- Revealing the life of Jesus in your body—2 Corinthians 4:10–11

- Eternal glory—2 Corinthians 4:17

In fact, it's clear from looking at all of these together, that it could even cost you (or those you love) eternal life. As much as I would like some of my heartaches to suddenly disappear, I'm convinced that it's not worth losing even one of these promises of God. Here's what you've got to remember. *It's not that God isn't rescuing you.* He's just not doing it in a way that meshes with your human understanding. He sees your situation through his perfect providence, loving wisdom and commitment to your highest good, including having you with him, next to his heart forever.

For Eve, the forbidden fruit was the quick fix that promised her answers to all her heart's questions and insecurities. But when she chose it, she didn't find the brand of knowledge and wisdom she expected. Instead she only found shame, guilt and heartache. Satan's ploy hasn't changed one bit. He wants us to shortchange the wisdom and providence of God and find rescue in humans, human institutions, or even in our own power and strength.

Satan leads us to embrace the false security of neediness by getting us to

- **Exchange rescue from God for rescue from a man**—Instead of clinging to the anchor God has given us, we go back to our fairy tale idea of rescue by a man. Instead of believing that God will carry out his rescue to perfectly meet the need of our soul, we insist on rescue now—even if it means living independently of God's word.

- **Look for completeness in a person rather than from God**—When we find a person who fits our picture of a rescuer, we begin to trust people more than God. *That's what I prayed for. He or she will make everything right.*

- **Become focused on our own need and forget others**—Why would we depend on a man that is married to someone else to meet our emotional needs? Because we are so determined to get our needs met that everything else fades into the background, including the commitment to his wife that man has made before God.

- **Blame others for our lack of rescue**—Since God's plan is to use others to bring us to him, it's easy to confuse their love and support with the rescue of God. If we think our rescue was from people, then we also expect our Christian brothers and sisters to continue to rescue us in ways that only God can do.

- **Believe rescue has to do with physical circumstances**—In our minds, the rescue we long for has to do with things such as our health, our husband (or lack of), our children, finances, home, job and much more. We forget that Jesus has already rescued us, and that true rescue is a heart issue, rather than a circumstantial one.

- **Compare others' rescue with our own perceived lack of rescue**—Just as Satan attacked Jesus, he comes at us with much the same strategy. Satan wants to make it seem as though others are being rescued, and consequently favored by God, when we are not. We forget that God's plan for each of us is as individual and as perfect as our fingerprint.

## Secure in God's Rescue

How long, O LORD, must I call for help,
    but you do not listen?
Or cry out to you, "Violence!"
    but you do not save?

Though the fig tree does not bud
    and there are no grapes on the vines,
though the olive crop fails
    and the fields produce no food,
though there are no sheep in the pen
    and no cattle in the stalls,
yet I will rejoice in the LORD,
    I will be joyful in God my Savior.
The Sovereign LORD is my strength;
    he makes my feet like the feet of a deer,
he enables me to go on the heights.
(Habakkuk 1:2, 3:17–19)

Perhaps one of the most amazing attitude changes shown in the Bible is that of Habakkuk, the prophet. Habakkuk starts with a complaint and ends in surrendered prayer. At the beginning of his book, Habakkuk is upset with God for not rescuing his people. But by the end of his conversation with God, he is a resolved man. What made the difference? Amidst many other admonitions, God told Habakkuk that "the righteous will live by his faith" (Habakkuk 2:4).

In response, Habakkuk goes back to God's mighty works of the past to find faith for the present. From being in God's presence, he learns a valuable lesson—faith is the only thing that can enable him to go on the heights. So he ends his book with a joy that doesn't depend on outward blessings, but rather on faith in God.

We can learn a lot from Habakkuk. Like him, at times we may feel like lodging a complaint against God. *Where is your rescue? Do you see everything I'm going through?* Satan proposes a self-centered Christianity where we use our own definition of rescue as the measure of our faith. *See, you don't have the real needs of your heart. You have a right to lodge a complaint against God.*

But the Bible makes it clear that as God's daughter, the real rescue is your faith. It is believing that you've been redeemed from the empty way of life handed down by your forefathers, from false treasures that are here today and gone tomorrow, and from a false confidence built on how well you think life is going.

The real rescue is the fruit of the Spirit growing and thriving in some of the most difficult times in your life. Real rescue is not only believing that God exists, but trusting that he will reward your faith. It is a confidence that no matter what you may lack physically, that you have every spiritual blessing in Christ.

How do you know you've been rescued? When you trust God whether there is food in the pantry, a ring on your finger, money in the bank or physical healing for your body. When you continue to call out to God for rescue and then trust that what he gives you (or doesn't give you) is for your highest good. Real rescue is being anchored in your faith by Jesus himself, who went ahead of you without rescue, to give you the true need of your heart—spiritual rescue. Your real rescue is the security of heart that only God can give.

# In Her Own Words
### *Joy's Story*

Once, when I gave a lesson to a group of women, I shared about my insecurities. After the lesson, a woman came to me and said, "There doesn't seem to be an insecure bone in your body." So, I thought about that. Either I cover up with confidence, or I'm not open, or I'm very full of pride. In reality, I must have lots and lots of praise from other people to feel worthwhile.

My dad gave us praise if we brought home straight A's. I had an older sister who was always the delight to Dad. And so the competition started. He was a very domineering man and powerful (the superintendent of schools), and I was very afraid of him. I had to please him or life wouldn't be good. Years went by and I learned that he was an alcoholic. He would come home drunk and beat the dogs, but never us. Until one time he threatened to cut off my thumb (I was a thumb-sucker), and Mom couldn't reassure me that he was joking. So, I had to stay on his good side and the only way I knew to do that was by performance.

Our "rescuer" was Mom—a diagnosed schizophrenic, manic-depressive, psycho-sufferer and financial provider. Where could I get my security? In the neighborhood boy who frequently sexually exploited my sister and me? After my dad, this was my second experience with men. My mom was fine to get along with until she and Dad divorced, and then she stopped taking her medications. We still don't know how to deal with her.

Where could I get my security? My sense of worth? I lived a hidden life. My friends (I had many at school) did not know what was going on at home. I had to cover up constantly, pretending to be happy and never inviting anyone to my house. Again, no one knew me. I was hiding who I was and what I was truly feeling. And showing straight A's to the world.

As I went off to college, I tried to get my sense of security by getting people to like me. My whole life, I've never been beautiful or skinny enough. I've gone from being anorexic to trying to fix everyone's personal lives. *I can, at least, be a rescuer of others, right?*

One afternoon I had a conference with one of my college professors. He wanted me to work on a summer project with him. He was quite a character. He even told the class, particularly the women, not to be offended if he walked up to them and kissed them. Once when I was in his office alone, he scooted me to a corner and put his legs around my legs. I emphatically refused to have any more contact with him. Added to that, there was my drunk organic chemistry professor. This instructor would come to "help" sessions completely intoxicated, reminding me of my dad. Of course, the boys would laugh, but I needed help with this class.

My freshman year of college, I wanted to find a church. I missed my old youth group that I was a part of in high school. So, I visited with one of my dorm friends, who asked me to sing with her at this particular church. That was nice but not fulfilling. Then God led me to a church where the men didn't approach me. The women genuinely wanted to be my friends and listen to all the junk in my heart. What an incredible joy. At just the right time, God rescued me! No one knows all the answers to life's upsets, but Proverbs 17:17 says we have a brother who is there to listen through the hard stuff. Now I appreciate how much I've been rescued from.

God rescued me in another way by giving me an incredible husband. He is well adjusted, has no selfish ambition, no pretense and he loves to share the gospel with people.

He also came from an amazingly serving family who know no strangers. One time Aunt Alice was willing to miss her grandson's birthday party to drive with me for six hours to take my mom out of a mental hospital and drive the second car back home.

They have welcomed me into the family with open arms. And they've taught me a deeper level of love and commitment that family should have. I wasn't raised with that. When God said that he'll do immeasurably more than we could ask or imagine, he wasn't just talking. I've seen that over and over again in my life. And that adds security. Psalm 18 has given me strength.

> You give me your shield of victory,
>     and your right hand sustains me;
> you stoop down to make me great. (Psalm 18:35)

About eight months after I was married, numbness occurred on my face and eventually over my entire right side. I went from doctor to doctor with no answers, but only accusations that my husband was abusing me. They would ask accusingly, "Are you sure your husband didn't hit you?"

After five years of testing, I was diagnosed with multiple sclerosis. I refused interferon drugs because of what my mom went through on her medicines. *I wanted to be in control.* I found a Web site and a doctor who had treated his MS with vitamins. So, I began my own vitamin treatment. With that and exercise, I got by.

Each year I've had new symptoms. About two years ago, I was face-to-face with a decision about taking interferon again. After a severe fall while jogging, I lost my vision. For about a month, I only saw double images. After a stroke was ruled out, my neurologist said that I had to go on an intravenous Solu-Medrol treatment for a week to clear up my sight. I had another MRI, a CAT scan, and blood tests. I just didn't want to take the interferons, again, because of the drugs my mom was on my entire life. My neurologist looked at my test results and said that I could go without drugs. I praised God. That just doesn't happen—it had to be a God thing. By the way, during that time period, I was able to run in two marathons.

I still have insecurity in my heart, but at least I can talk about it now. As far as men go, I still can't talk to my dad. I have butterflies and we mostly talk about nothing. His health is going down fast, and I'm concentrating on letting him know that I love and respect him as my dad. I try to remember the good things, such as how he taught me to play baseball and had a pet name for me. I ran with that name printed on my back during my first marathon.

One of my biggest struggles is still with men. They frighten me. I want them to think I'm pretty or have something about me that's desirable, but if I try to talk to them, I get tongue-tied and look like an oaf. So, insecurity binds me again. But I've learned lots of jokes to make my conversations with them bearable.

My granddad, my mom's dad, died about two weeks ago. (He was ninety-four years old and afraid to die.) Mom has three brothers who are equally as emotionally handicapped as she is. I wonder what happened to them growing up. From what I've pieced together, my grandfather (their dad) was very physically abusive to the boys, and Mom must have witnessed it. So, why did God let him live so long? Why didn't he even want to listen to anyone about God? As many mistakes as he made, I know that God is passionate toward everyone and works to allow them to find him. These are questions I can't answer and remind me to simply trust God for the answers.

We are working so hard with our own children. I want them to be secure and to know that they are loved beyond anything. I limit their exposure to my mom. I don't want them to grow up with that kind of influence. Although we'd had plenty of conversations about having Mom live with us, it's too big a risk for us. We want our boys to love God with all of their hearts, to know the security they can have with him and to develop their own confidence in God.

Tomorrow is Mother's Day. I stood in the card aisle at a store, but then had to leave. I knew I was going to just stand there and cry. My mom has been such a source of pain for me, but I love her so much. One of the hardest times was to have to take my one- and two-year-olds to a mental hospital to pick her up. (This has been a frequent occurrence.)

She would come to visit while I was pregnant and tell me to pray that the baby would be dead because it would not be normal. Psychiatrists have told me that she'll always be delusional. If she won't take any kind of sedative, she'll always lose control, be arrested and sent to a mental hospital. God has to be my emotional security.

My sister and I both wonder if we'll be like her, but I have confidence in the providence of God. He'll never leave me on my own to shrivel up. I love Job 11:18: "You will be secure, because there is hope; you will look about you and take your rest in safety." I feel so loved by God. (That's a victory to be able to say that!)

A few years ago, my mom studied the Bible with a woman who has a mother-in-law in the same "state" as my mom. She accepted the Word and the woman studying with her assured me that she was in the right state of mind to be baptized and follow Jesus. And so I did. That was a great moment. But it seems like she reverts to her dreamland so easily. God knows the heart, and that's all I can hope in.

People are complicated and hearts are even deeper.

I love my mother a lot! I am devoted to her finding the right living situation. My sister and I keep a close watch on her so she won't be a threat to anyone. But she still just needs love.

Life can be mixed with all sorts of complications, but each of us has to find our strength in our personal relationship with God. Most of my prayers are filled with gratitude because I have been rescued. Some days I just sit at the piano and sing to God. We usually cry together—like Jesus, I believe God must have strong emotions. Strong enough to tackle mine for me! And I feel closer to God, and to other people, when I'm vulnerable to let out my emotions.

# WILL I BE RESCUED? THE ANCHOR
## *Personal Study Guide & Life Application*

Here are a few practical suggestions to help you in your battle to be secure in God's rescue.

**1) Thank God that you've already been rescued**—The Bible tells us that we've been rescued from the empty way of life handed down by our forefathers (1 Peter 1:18), this body of death (Romans 7:24–25), the dominion of darkness (Colossians 1:13) and from the coming wrath (1 Thessalonians 1:10).

> *What would your life look like without Christ? What has he rescued you from? Write a prayer of thanksgiving to God for the spiritual rescue that he's given.*

**2) Cling to his anchor in the deep waters**—When everything is going well, it's easy to see God's hand. At other times, we are so tossed with emotion, with heartache, even with despair that we can't seem to get perspective. Trusting in God's anchor means finding hope in God by trusting that he does not lie or change, and that whether we see it or not, he is working for our good.

> *Read Psalm 16 and write down every way that God makes you secure. Write on a note card, "You are my Lord; apart from you I have no good thing...surely I have a delightful inheritance" (vv2, 6), and post it somewhere where you'll see it daily.*

**3) Pray for God's rescue, but trust regardless of the immediate results**—In Psalm 142, David prays fervently for God's rescue:

> Listen to my cry,
>     for I am in desperate need;
> rescue me from those who pursue me,
>     for they are too strong for me. (Psalm 142:6)

*What are your most desperate needs? Make a list of your needs, and then take them to God one by one in prayer for rescue and in surrender. Take them to another believer or group of believers and ask for prayers as well.*

**4) Trust that God's power will be shown in your weakness**—Sometimes the situations we find ourselves in are because of choices we have made in our weakness or even in our sin. Being anchored in God means accepting his forgiveness and believing that his strength is beyond our weakness.

*Take a piece of paper and on one side write your weaknesses and mistakes that you feel hold you back. On the other side, write about who God is in contrast. For example, I make impulsive decisions; God is my perfect guide, who knows exactly where he wants to take me. Journal about how you can lean on God's strength in your areas of weakness.*

**5) Trust God to rescue others**—Sometimes the rescue we long for the most isn't for ourselves, but for someone else. Yet if we intervene, we can circumvent God's work in their life.

*Who is the person you are most tempted to rescue? Every day, when you pray to God, surrender that person to him and his plans, and give up your control over the situation. Pray specifically for their spiritual rescue.*

**6) Learn from others' battles**—In her story, Joy talks about a number of ways insecurity took root in her heart including dealing with mental illness in her family, sexual abuse and health issues. But even in the face of so many trials, she says, "I have confidence in the providence of God. He'll never leave me on my own to shrivel up."

*Read Job 11:18. What are the main areas that have created insecurity in your heart? How has God's providence worked in each of these areas?*

"I have multiple sclerosis, am in the process of earning my master's degree and have a job, so the scriptures that talk about God's strength being shown through weakness encourage me! But when I'm discouraged, I question God's purpose for me. 'God do you really want me here?' It's easier to pin it on God's will, rather than face my fear of failure."

—Single professional

# WILL I BE SUCCESSFUL?
## *The Guide*

Although the Lord gives you the bread of adversity and the
water of affliction, your teachers will be hidden no more;
with your own eyes you will see them. Whether you turn to
the right or to the left, your ears will hear a voice behind you
saying, "This is the way; walk in it."

Isaiah 30:20–21

THERE ARE MANY ANALOGIES FOR THE CHRISTIAN LIFE, BUT
more than anything, I see it as a walk. The Bible starts with God
walking with Adam and Eve in the garden and ends with the
nations walking, guided by the light of the glory of God and the
lamp of the Lamb, Jesus. Enoch walked with God for 300 years
and then walked straight into heaven. Noah set himself apart
from a whole nation by his walk with God, and Abraham was
instructed by God himself to walk blamelessly before him.[1]

When the Israelites were given the law, it was full of practical instruction on how to love God through their walk—*walking
in his ways* and revering him (8:6); *walking in his ways* and loving
him (30:16); *walking in his ways* and keeping his commands (28:9).
Psalms, Proverbs, Ecclesiastes and Isaiah are full of exhortations,
promises and commentary on what it means to walk with the
Lord.

The New Testament is no different. John, the apostle of love,
tells us that if we walk in the light, then we are cleansed with the
blood of Christ (1 John 1:7); that love for God means walking in
obedience (2 John 1:6); and, perhaps most challenging, that

---

1. Adam and Eve—Genesis 3:8; The nations—Revelation 21:24; Enoch—
Genesis 5:24; Noah—Genesis 6:9; Abraham—Genesis 17:1

169

"whoever claims to live in him must walk as he [Jesus] walked" (1 John 2:6). In fact, the Bible tells us that the quality of our walk is the acid test of our Christianity: "If we claim to have fellowship with him, yet walk in the darkness, we lie and do not live by the truth" (1 John 1:6).

*Would you like to have a walk with God that gives you a secure heart?* Here's what I've found: Walking securely before God will only come as you make your walk with God the true measure of your success in life. What causes us to walk insecurely? Using the wrong measures of success.

## My Measure of Success

I learned at a young age that accomplishment was the surest route to success. By the time I was twelve, I was enrolled in baton, jazz, tap and ballet lessons. I swam on the swim team in the summer and took art lessons during the school year. By the time I was sixteen, I had more than a hundred trophies and hundreds of medals for baton twirling. I had won a dance scholarship, been crowned Miss Majorette of my hometown, and had set a pool record in backstroke. But God intervened, shining a light into my fog of accomplishment.

In my senior year of high school, I got a severe case of mono and had to give up nearly every activity. I just couldn't seem to get well. Used to being able to eat whatever I wanted, I gained weight and went from a tightly toned athlete to a quite more curvy physique.

I now know God was preparing me for my true destiny, which wasn't based on worldly measurement of success. Because of a young man evangelizing door to door, I ended up visiting a church and doing a 180-degree turn. I gave up my dream of being a baton teacher/judge and embraced a new one—mission work. My parents, having invested thousands of dollars into my training, were understandably floored.

As I started focusing my talents on serving God, my alcoholic father turned up the pressure on me. When I made a mistake, he would accuse me of not being a "good Christian." When I decided to go to college to meet (and hopefully marry) someone with the same dreams, my father and mother questioned my motives. I sold my car, resigned from my job as a secretary, and took off to a small Christian college in Tennessee.

Accomplishment took on a new seriousness, as now I had something to prove. I had always been an average student in school, so now I was determined to be an exceptional student. I decided I would do whatever it took to earn back my parents' respect. I not only made straight A's, but I had two different professors who wanted to take me on as an understudy in two entirely different fields. I spent countless hours testing myself and memorizing formulas that enabled me to ace tests. I looked forward to the days when my parents would receive my grades. *See, I told you I could do this. I am a success.*

I came through almost all of college with just shy of a 4.0 grade point average. But I also gained a hidden eating disorder, where I redirected my rage at having to be "perfect" and hid the shame of how far from perfect I was. While home on break, I would partake in late night binges where I would eat until literally I could not take another bite. Afterwards I would spend days eating next to nothing to compensate.

Once I married and left this environment for good, the eating disorder seemed to evaporate. But the questions in my heart were still largely unknown and unfaced. In fact, figuring out how to get the world out of my motivation would take years of God's patient guidance.

## The False Security of Worldliness

O LORD, by your hand save me from such men,
    from men of this world whose reward is in this life.
(Psalm 17:14)

What is worldliness anyway? Bottom line, worldliness has to do with a determination to be rewarded in this life by adopting the standards of the world. It's a devotion to what is false and temporary. Why does Satan choose the false security of worldliness to try to take our hearts away from God? Because Satan knows how much God desires our undivided devotion. Remember the very first commandment? *You shall have no other gods before me.* The second was similar: *You shall not make for yourself an idol...for I, the Lord your God am a jealous God.*[2]

God wanted his people to know that they would be breaking their covenant, and his heart, by setting anything or anyone on the altar of their hearts other than him—just as surely as an unfaithful husband or wife would be breaking the marriage covenant. But God didn't want this devotion just for his sake; he wanted it for their sake. He knew the devastating consequences that idolatry would bring.

To protect his beloved nation, God met Moses on the top of Mount Sinai and told him to instruct the Israelites not to make covenants with idolatrous nations, including the covenant of marriage, warning that when "those daughters prostitute themselves to their gods, they will lead your sons to do the same."[3] And true to God's loving warning, he saw his people over and over again intermarry and bring the "world" into the Old Testament equivalent of his church. This caused Israel to go so far away from God that some eventually even offered their own children as sacrifices to idols. Why did Israel do this? They sought security from fitting in to the world around them instead of from trusting God's guidance and instruction.

Based on this pattern, we shouldn't be surprised that God's warning that the world can take us away from him continues and gains a new urgency in the New Testament. Jesus' Sermon on the Mount contrasts the heart of a disciple with the heart of the world. Looking out on his disciples, who had left everything in

2. Exodus 20:2–5
3. Exodus 34:16

the world to cling to him and him alone, Jesus laid out the distinctive nature of what success must become to his followers. In just a few short verses in the Bible—blessed are the poor in spirit, pure in heart, the merciful, those who mourn, those who hunger and thirst after righteousness, the peacemakers, the meek and those who are persecuted—Jesus set a whole new standard for blessedness. This includes renouncing our own personal righteousness, dignity, rights and even our own well being, taking us to the point of rejection by those we once walked in step with.[4]

But Jesus was far from finished with this important message. He went on to tell many parables to help us understand Satan's plot to use the world to take us away from undivided devotion to God (see the following chart).

| Principle | Parables | References |
|---|---|---|
| How the cares of life choke God's word out of our life | Parable of the Sower | Matthew 13:3–23 |
| The enemy using the world to contaminate our faith | The Tares<br>The Leaven | Matthew 13:24–30, 36–43<br>Luke 13:20–21 |
| Trusting in worldly possessions and pursuits | The Prodigal Son<br>Foolish and Wise Builders | Luke 15:11–32<br>Matthew 7:24–27 |
| Storing up things instead of being rich with God | Rich Man and Lazarus<br>The Rich Fool | Luke 16:19–31<br>Luke 12:16–21 |
| Giving up possessions for eternal treasure | Pearl of Great Price<br>Treasure Hidden in a Field | Matthew 13:45–46<br>Matthew 13:44 |

## Spiritual Adultery

Why did Jesus emphasize freeing ourselves from the world in his teachings? Perhaps it is because the world seeps into our faith, into our views of success and into our views of the fundamentals of life: love, marriage, career, possessions, children and more. Satan wants us to water down Jesus' teachings and accept a world-friendlier version that gives us the acceptance we crave. He wants to repackage the sin of idolatry as a simple case of mixed-up priorities that we think we can easily correct somewhere down the line.

---

4. For an in-depth explanation of what this renunciation looks like read chapter 6, "The Beatitudes" in *The Cost of Discipleship* by Dietrich Bonhoeffer, (New York: Simon & Schuster, 1959), 105–114.

How does Satan do all of this? In the book of Revelation, Satan is described as "the great prostitute who corrupted the earth by her adulteries."[5] Satan's goal is to corrupt the truth and lead us into spiritual adultery. Remember Eve? We can clearly identify Satan's messages about success by simply taking what Jesus says in his word and flipping it 180 degrees.

| God's Message | Satan's Message |
|---|---|
| "I have chosen you out of the world. That is why the world hates you." (John 15:19) | You are doing something wrong if the world misunderstands you. |
| "For where your treasure is, there will your heart be also." (Luke 12:34) | Your clothing, home and education define your worth as a woman. |
| "The man who loves his life will lose it." (John 12:25) | You can love your life now and have plenty of time for eternal things later. |
| "Do not be yoked together with unbelievers." (2 Corinthians 6:14) | You can date or marry a worldly man without becoming worldly. |
| "Where the spirit of the Lord is, there is freedom." (2 Corinthians 3:17) | You must be accomplished as a Christian for God to be pleased with you. |
| "Use the things of the world, as if not engrossed in them." (1 Corinthians 7:31) | To be a success—school, career, and home must all come before God. |
| "As aliens and strangers in the world, abstain from sinful desires." (1 Peter 2:11) | Claiming your rightful place in this world as a woman is worth any sacrifice. |

With Satan's messages flashing before us day-in and day-out through the television, radio, Internet and print media, figuring out how to live in the world without becoming what the world dictates is one of the most important parts of a secure heart.

Just recently a commercial came on saying that the HGTV Dream Home Giveaway would be taking place in two days. At the risk of sounding completely crazy, I'll tell you that even though I didn't enter this contest, I was feeling some serious angst every time I saw those commercials. *Why didn't I enter? Maybe this could have been the retreat center that my husband, Dave, has dreamed of for years.* I already knew in my heart that I wasn't going to be happy for whoever won. In fact, I took note of when it

5. Revelation 19:2

would take place and made a mental note *not* to watch. Of course, I understood intellectually that even if I had entered, my chance of winning was one in many millions. Yet, the thought of someone else winning pulled up feelings of shortcoming on my behalf.

The next morning as I sat down to work on this chapter, I mulled over what was going on in my heart. *Why is this question so pressing for me? Why do even simple matters pull up such a competitive spirit in my heart?* Mirroring the words of David, the psalmist, I asked God to guide me and to, *"search me, O God, and know my heart; test me and know my anxious thoughts. See if there is any offensive way in me, and lead me in the way everlasting."*[6]

Just a few days later, as I was driving (and praying) on the way to a business gathering to support a colleague being honored for a project we worked on, the answer came to me in the form of memories, all the way back from my competitive baton twirling days. When I was twirling baton, I originally took lessons with a local baton teacher. Eventually my mother began to feel I had outgrown my teacher in ability, so unbeknown to me, she had a couple of the best teachers in the nation observe me at the next large competition. Soon, we were driving three hours one-way for my lessons once a month and paying $50 an hour (and that was thirty years ago!). This teacher crafted a routine that she was sure would be an award-winning one for me to perform at the state championship. In fact, my teacher was convinced I could be a national champion.

When I actually performed the routine in the state contest, I could see the teacher off to the side of the gymnasium with her arms crossed, evidently displeased. After I was done, she walked off without even speaking to me, shaking her head and sighing.

A few months later, I went on to place ninth at nationals in my age group. But instead of feeling joy, I felt that I had somehow let everyone down. A message had been communicated very

---

6. Psalm 139:23–24

clearly to me—less than best wasn't enough. In fact, I once heard it said about me, "Too bad. She just doesn't have enough drive."

So how did I respond to this early pressure to achieve? Whether in physical or spiritual terms, I went into overdrive, becoming an overachiever to the nth degree. It didn't matter whether it was in school, at work or in the ministry—the venue was immaterial. My heart was still seeking the elusive success that Satan whispered I needed. And for everything I did achieve, Satan was always standing by ready to shine his spotlight on another area where I fell short. He had fed me a masterful lie: *Robin, you have to be successful. In fact, you need to be the best at every-thing you do. If you don't, it will expose the fundamental flaws in your character that let others down. And they'll reject you.*

As I rode in my car on the way to that meeting, I went back to those long-forgotten memories and mourned my losses. Then, I tearfully began to forgive. I forgave my mother for the ways her zeal for me led us both astray. I forgave the teacher who gave me disapproval when I needed encouragement. For perhaps the first time, I acknowledged the worldliness of the competitive culture I grew up in and the ways I had carried that worldliness through-out my life.

When I finally arrived at the event, sitting and truly rejoicing with those being honored, I was humbled. I saw that another's victory didn't mean that I was somehow less than I should be. Instead of looking at other people's victories in comparison to where I was, I sat and learned from their success. And I asked God to continue to root out the worldliness that seeks to steal my security of heart.

## Trusting God As Your Guide

"I am the LORD your God, who brought you out of Egypt so that you would no longer be slaves to the Egyptians; I broke the bars of your yoke and enabled you to walk with heads held high." (Leviticus 26:13–14)

What is success anyway? The dictionary defines it as "the achievement of something desired, planned or attempted; or an event that accomplishes its intended purpose." So, how was it after 500 years of slavery in Egypt that the Israelites could walk out of Egypt with their heads held high? In the eyes of the Egyptians, they were less than human, possessing absolutely no rights of their own. On what grounds could they feel success? The only way the Israelites could walk out, self-esteem intact, was to trust that the ultimate purposes of God were being accomplished in their lives—even through their years of backbreaking slavery. In other words, they had to trust God as their guide. They could walk with their heads held high because the true God of the universe was personally walking them out of captivity.

The beauty of success is that it is only defined in relation to an end purpose. I find this downright liberating! Now, let me explain why. When I became a Christian, I surrendered my life to God's purposes. In other words, I gave up my old definitions of success in exchange for God's. My old purpose (baton twirling, dance and everything related) was given over to my new purpose (following Jesus and glorifying God in my life). In my old life, being successful in my purpose came through things such as looking trim and beautiful, winning awards, gaining new skills and eventually establishing myself in a career teaching baton. My new purpose redefined success. This new definition meant realizing that my body shape was no longer the measure of my success—I'm no longer a teenager in a tiered black-and-white chiffon halter gown in front of a male pageant judge (who would write down on the score sheet "Cute body").

Success is no longer just a perfect routine—I'm not going to be penalized for every baton I drop, until I have no chance of winning. As a Christian, my success doesn't come through the virtues of beauty, skills, competency or recognition. Instead, it's walking with God as my guide through whatever twists and turns my life takes.

But this is also where we can get really mixed up. Satan wants to mix his yeast of worldliness into our Christianity. Just what is the purpose of a woman according to the world? Just take a walk through the magazine stands, and you'll find it shouting out from publication after publication. Satan wants us to try to combine our spirituality with inwardly ranking ourselves by our accomplishments, body size, career, finances, childrearing and so much more. He is more than glad to create hierarchies of worth that give us what appear to be unreachable models to compare ourselves to in whatever scenario we find ourselves, *both inside and outside of the church.*

Whenever we apply the world's standards to our walk as Christians, we're heading toward deep spiritual disappointment and misplaced priorities. And I know I'm personally out of focus when someone else's success becomes a threat—not so much because I don't want them to do well. But rather, because I've given Satan a foothold where he can insert the world's brand of success into my soul-esteem. And that leads only to despair. Let's look at how Jesus said it (with my comments added):

> "Neither do men pour new wine [following Jesus] into old wineskins [worldly measurements of success]. If they do, the skins will burst, the wine will run out and the wineskins will be ruined. No, they pour new wine [following Jesus] into new wineskins [God's eternal purpose for their life], and both are preserved." (Matthew 9:17)

To understand what it means to gauge your success by God's purpose for your life, let's take a look at an example from the Bible. The apostle Paul came to understand that true success has nothing to do with worldly accomplishments. This is all the more remarkable when you consider that by a very young age, Paul had accumulated an impressive spiritual and secular resume.[7]

Paul's take on success was turned upside down by Jesus appearing to him on the road to Damascus, where Paul was headed to persecute and imprison Christians. After Paul surrendered his life to Jesus, he wrote these words:

> For whatever was to my profit I now consider loss for the sake of Christ. What is more, I consider everything a loss compared to the surpassing greatness of knowing Christ Jesus my Lord, for whose sake I have lost all things. I consider them rubbish, that I may gain Christ. (Philippians 3:7–8)

How could Paul, who was penning these words from a prison cell, be so convinced that in losing everything he once claimed, he had found true success before God? The key to this is found a few verses later where Paul tells us, "Not that I have already obtained all this, or have already been made perfect, but I press on to take hold of that for which Christ Jesus took hold of me."[8]

Paul found confidence in God despite a thorn in the flesh, beatings, persecutions, being left for dead in Iconium,[9] and now locked in a prison cell when he longed to be traveling and preaching for Christ. Why? Because he had a new goal. His focus now was simple—to live his life in a way that fulfilled the purpose for which Christ had taken hold of him. Paul said in the letter to the Romans: "And we know that in all things God works for the good of those who love him, who have been called according to his purpose."[10]

Why has God taken hold of your life? Why did he choose you? Where does he want to guide you? If success feels like something that other people receive but that evades you at every turn, I think Paul might suggest that you start as he did—by surrendering to God's purpose for your life.

---

7. Philippians 3:4–6
8. Philippians 3:12
9. Acts 14:1–20
10. Romans 8:28. Paul repeatedly talked about God's purpose in his letters. See Romans 9:11, 17, 21; 2 Corinthians 5:5; Ephesians 1:9–11; Philippians 2:13; 2 Timothy 1:9; 2 Timothy 2:21.

## Surrendering to God As Your Guide

> Who, then, is the man that fears that LORD?
>   He will instruct him in the way chosen for him.
> (Psalm 25:12)

I started my own business as a copywriter three years ago. Although I started seeking God thirty years ago, when it comes to business, in many ways I'm like a brand-new Christian. Learning how to walk securely in business (and not let insecurity, perfectionism and notions of performance start taking over) has been challenging. My first three years of business have brought hardships that have tested where my true security lies.

Shortly after opening my business, I was rear-ended by a careless driver. It took almost two years of treatment with many different practitioners including a chiropractor, physical therapist, naturopath and finally an orthopedic doctor to figure out that I had a slight tear in the rotator cuff of my shoulder. Needless to say, I've spent a lot of time working in pain.

About a year after my accident, another physical problem emerged that was even more baffling. Early one morning I woke up with the room spinning around me at high speed. I was afflicted with what turned out to be six weeks of vertigo. Those who have experienced vertigo know that these spinning sessions are extremely debilitating. For days afterward, you feel disoriented, nauseous and just a little seasick, like the room is slanting slightly.

During this time, I was blessed to land an opportunity to work with one of the world's largest manufacturers of fitness equipment, helping develop new manuals for treadmills, bikes and elliptical trainers. In itself, this was a huge stretch for me, since my specialty isn't technical writing. The job required analyzing their new equipment prototypes, then working with their engineers to iron out the bugs and rewrite the manuals. Since the equipment was almost ready to be produced, these manuals were needed as soon as possible.

One particular morning, I woke up feeling dizzy and nauseous. I knew I could call in sick, but since I already had meetings scheduled and important deadlines, I knew it could throw off the whole project. And I had no assurance when I would feel better. So I packed up my bag and got onto the train to go downtown.

As I was sitting on that train, I began thinking that I had no idea how I was going to do this. I felt as if I would start spinning again at any moment. Old insecurities then took the opportunity to rush in: *See, you're not good enough to work at this level. What makes you think you can do this kind of work? You'll never be successful.* Feeling the despair starting to gather in my throat and anxiety pushing on my chest, I opened my Bible and asked God to give me assistance. I turned to Psalm 25, and my eyes went right to this scripture: *"Who then, is the man that fears the Lord? He will instruct him in the way chosen for him."*

Tears gathered in my eyes as I realized several things. First of all, I knew that I feared God. I also knew that God had made it absolutely obvious that I should go into business for myself. I reminded myself how God had opened the door to working for this company and all the ways he had shown himself already. But what really struck me was the phrase, *"He will instruct him in the way chosen for him."* I said softly to myself, "God will instruct me how to carry out what he's given me to do." I smiled. The dawn was beginning to become visible in my heart. I then went back and read all of Psalm 25 and there found my faithful guide, God:

> Show me your ways, O LORD,
>     teach me your paths;
> guide me in your truth and teach me,
>     for you are God my Savior
> and my hope is in you all day long. (verses 4–5)

> He guides the humble in what is right
>     and teaches them his way.
> All the ways of the LORD are loving and faithful. (verses 9–10)

The LORD confides in those who fear him;
  he makes his covenant known to them.
My eyes are ever on the LORD,
  for only he will release my feet from the snare.
(verses 14–15)

I walked off of the train with my head held high, because I knew God would patiently, lovingly and faithfully guide and instruct me. When I arrived at the job, I went straight to my manager, told him about my vertigo, and expressed my desire to do my best to make it through the day. He graciously gave me permission to leave at my discretion. God walked me through that day with a secure spirit. He also taught me a lesson in security that I'll never forget—that I can rely on God's willingness and desire to take my hand and lead me in every part of my life, including my business.

But for God to be my guide, the only road I can travel is the road *he* has laid out. And to be honest here, I have many plans and dreams in my heart that are clamoring for God's attention. Many are good things I feel pretty confident that God would want me to have as his daughter—a thriving marriage, faithful children, a growing ministry, a productive business. Looking at all this, I can start to feel like Isaiah the prophet when he said, "I have labored to no purpose; I have spent my strength in vain and for nothing" (Isaiah 49:4a). Just like Isaiah, there are times when I interpret the delay of fulfillment of these hopes as a sign that all my efforts in these directions are futile. *God, why does all my labor seem to be for nothing? Have I spent my strength in vain? Do you see the way I expend myself seeking your honor and glory?*

But if the truest desire of my heart is God's glory, then the only way I can continue with God as my guide is to, like Isaiah, fall before him in surrender: "Yet what is due me is in the Lord's hand, and my reward is with my God" (Isaiah 49:4b). Only in surrender will I turn to the Bible to seek out what God's purpose is.

(I can be very stubborn in my desire for a worldly brand of success!)

Trusting God as your guide is the key to holding your head high, no matter what the world thinks of you. It's the key to finding joy, even when you feel misunderstood. It is the key to interpreting whatever happens to you without bitterness or losing heart. It is the key to long-term faithfulness to God, and above all, it is the key to a secure heart.

# In Her Own Words
## *Xin's Story*

I was born and raised in Beijing, China. I grew up in a culture where what you think of yourself means absolutely nothing. What matters is what people think of you. And people measure you by what you have accomplished. If you are a student, you need to be the number one student among your peers. If you are an employee, you need to be the most hard working and competent employee in order to get the praise. In other words, either you are the best or you are nothing, meaning that you have failed.

My dad is a perfectionist and my mom is very ambitious. They taught me at a very early age to never be content with the present, to focus on what you will become in the future, and to always give your best in all situations in everything you do. As a result, I was never allowed to be a child or treated as a child. Comfort was not a necessary part of life; what was more important was to push through all your emotions in order to be the best you can in the present and for the future. They never told me I needed to be the best, but compliments only came along when I was the best. So I figured that was the way to go.

Expressing affection and intimacy is not in the Chinese culture. So I do not blame my parents for never saying "I love you" or "I am proud of you." (I doubt whether they ever said those words to each other.) But that is how I grew up. I was put in a day care after I turned three-months old, and was there for most of my preschool years. I could only see my parents once a week when they picked me up on Saturday nights so that I could spend Sundays with them. I guess they had to work hard during the week to make it themselves.

If I were to pick a color to describe my childhood, it would be grey—dark grey. The image that is stuck in my mind till this day is the dark, empty rooms and the unfriendly faces of the workers in my day care center. I was scared and lonely most of the time—just like an orphan.

After a long six years of emotional torture, I was sent to my grandparents to start grammar school for another six long years, during which I could only see my parents once a week as well. I guess they did what they thought would be the best for my future.

During that time, I thought if I could be the best in everything I do, they would think I was good enough to be brought back home. So I did. I did well in every class: math, Chinese literature, English, music, art, athletics, etc. It did not matter what it was; I was the best. Then I made it to a top-ten middle school in Beijing which held all the number-one students from all the grammar schools. My parents were proud (at least I think they were). And I was brought back home finally because they thought I would need more help with school from that point on in order to make it to the best high school and college in the future. I figured I needed to continue being the best in order for them to keep me. So I did. And I made it to a top-ten high school which held all the number-one students from all the middle schools in Beijing.

By then I had established my "status." My mom bragged about me with all her coworkers, friends and relatives because I was a better student than all of their kids and that was all that mattered. People would often say to their kids, "If you can be half as good as Xin, I would be very happy," or "You are almost as good as Xin." I remember those comments, and I thought the only way for me to be loved and accepted was to always be the best.

After finishing college in Beijing and much hard work to pass the GRE test, I was able to receive a scholarship from a graduate school of a university in Chicago. That was the highest dream I had as a student. It felt good—so far anything I wanted to accomplish in life I did. It confirmed my belief as an atheist that you are the god of yourself; you can be whatever you want to become as long as you work hard enough.

The first year being in the U.S. was hard. It was the first time I had been apart from my family and friends. Loneliness, culture shock and not being able to speak English well made me feel that I had to start life all over again and prove to this brand new world that "I am good and more than good" all over again.

After the first semester, I started to get the hang of the school system in the U.S., and I began to get straight A's again. But something strange happened at that time: I was not motivated to work hard as I was before. I knew I could get my master's degree. I knew I could get a decent job in the future and even a "decent" husband. But then what? Make money and raise children? Buy a big house and a nice car? Prove to people along the way that I am good and more than good?

I felt exhausted—not just in my body but in my heart and my mind. I was tired of always living for the future, feeling the need to compete with people all the time and feeling threatened by people who could do anything better than I could because somehow that meant I had failed. I said to myself, "If this is all there is to life, even though I'm just getting started, I'm already tired."

Another thing I noticed was the decline of my spiritual life. Even though I grew up in an atheistic country, my parents still taught my sister and me a lot of moral values that were good. However, since my goal in life was always to prove to people that I "perform" well in anything I do, "heart" issues had become insignificant. A lot of times I had to even ignore my conscience in order to do things just to "look" good. And because I gave myself so much pressure in life to achieve, sometimes I wanted to do things just for pure pleasure as long as people did not find out. Consequently I did many things that I never thought I would do. I was involved in many immoral relationships. One of them even led to adultery.

I began to be disgusted with who I had become and scared of how far I would go with the wickedness of my heart. However, I also began to realize that I was not the god of myself, rather I was my own biggest enemy. I knew I was powerless in changing myself. Is there a way out of all these struggles? Pleasing people in order to be accepted was not good enough to motivate me any more. I said to myself, "I'm not sad enough to die, but I need a reason to live."

As I was feeling lost, empty and sad about life, some students on the campus where I went to school reached out to me. They invited me to church and Bible studies, which I never even heard of. As I opened the Bible for the first time in my life, I began to see light at the end of the tunnel. However, my conversion was not an easy process. First, believing there is a God, then trusting he is in control and I am to surrender to his control for my life, is the opposite of what I had been taught all my life. Needless to say, this change of mind and heart turned my world upside down. But God is powerful. He humbled me enough to realize that following Jesus is the only hope for my life. I do not need to perform any more to let him accept me—he already showed his acceptance by dying on the cross. I am accepted for who I am, not what I do. God accepted me not because I am the best, but I am his daughter. How liberating! I had never even heard of this concept! I was convinced if there was a way I wanted to live my life, this would be it!

I still remember the morning after I was baptized. I opened up my eyes feeling like a newborn baby. From that point on I knew my life would be different. I couldn't help sharing with many of my friends the good news of Jesus, and I saw many of them become Christians.

Five years later, I went into the full-time ministry. It wasn't an easy decision. According to my father, it was the one "bad decision" I had made in my life. It was hurtful to say the least, knowing that I had failed my parents whom I had been trying all my life to honor. However, I believed it was God's calling for my life, and I went for it, though disappointing my parents has left a huge scar on my heart.

It has been five years since then. I have gone through many battles in life and have fought through them faithfully. Two-and-a-half years ago, I was happily married, and I thought I had really moved on in life. I thought I had learned to put my securities in God and not in people. But what I've been learning lately is that my conversion is a continuous process as I follow Jesus.

About a year ago I went through a stage of depression to the point that I had to seek counseling. Now, you have to understand, somewhere in me there is a prideful soul. If I admitted not only I was depressed, but I needed help with my emotions, that meant I was in really bad shape. I had nightmares every single night. I felt restless. I used to be so healthy, full of energy. Not any more. I was sick a lot and always tired. Emotionally I became very fragile. I never thought I was a very sensitive person, but I was—to every word people said to me. In other words, I was losing my mind.

At first I was resistant to getting counseling. For what? My parents loved me growing up. Now they did not say that, but I knew. I was never abused in any way. I love working in the ministry beside my husband—it's my passion and my life. I have a wonderful marriage…what do I have to talk about? It is embarrassing to even tell people I am depressed. But I went out of desperation. And of course, we talked about my past. I started to feel all kinds of emotions I never thought were even there. Then, I heard a little voice in my head, *They are no big deal; you are stronger than that.* I tried to control my tears, but before I knew it, I began to sob. *Am I that hurt? What's the big deal?* I still asked myself.

Through those tears, my past came back. Then I realized how deeply I was hurt by my past and how much it is still in me—the atheism in me was not just in my mind; it was in my blood. Yes, I have decided to follow Jesus, but it is going to take a while and a continuous effort to flush the atheism out of my body.

Not until a year ago did I realize that my understanding of "God loves me for who I am" was intellectual. Of course, I had lived the opposite way for two-and-a-half decades before I became a Christian. As a Christian, I am grateful for what Jesus did for me; I have no doubt he loves me. However, I am constantly afraid of disappointing him by not doing my best, and sometimes that is even mixed with not being the best, which is the opposite of what I believe about God's love. I know it in my mind, but it is so much harder to know it with my heart.

I also feel the need to be accepted and approved by people. Since I was never trained to evaluate myself, my value as a person only relies on what people think of me. If my fellow Christians or those in leadership do not say anything good about me, I automatically think they do not have anything good to say. As a result, I constantly walk around feeling insecure and desperately waiting for someone's approval or validation so I can be okay with myself and keep going.

The healing process has been painful and has required everything I've got to push through, yet it has allowed me to understand myself on a much deeper level and to know why I struggle in the way I do. As least now I know what my enemy is. I am not in a blind battle anymore or blaming myself for having a bad heart of people-pleasing or being insecure. As a result, I have grown as a person and as a Christian in ways I never imagined. I am so grateful to God that he does not just want me to make it on the last day, but to be healed and feel loved by him with all my heart, mind and soul so that I can love him and his people in the same way.

# WILL I BE SUCCESSFUL? THE GUIDE

*Personal Study Guide & Life Application*

Here are a few suggestions for helping you find security of heart through trusting God as your guide.

**1) Get acquainted with God's purposes**—Sometimes we are so full of our own purposes that we confuse our goals with God's perfect plan for our life.

> *Go to www.biblegateway.com or to a concordance and look up the word "purpose" in the Bible. How do God's purposes differ from your own?*

**2) Ask God to be your guide**—Following a guide always starts with a decision to surrender. The very nature of a guide is that they lead, and you follow. They take the wheel, and you ride along. They explain, and you learn. They model, and you imitate. They advise, and you learn from their experience.

> *Every morning start your day with a prayer of surrender: "Jesus, I give you my marriage, my business, my relationships, my children, my ministry, my money, my heart." Ask him to instruct you in the way chosen for you.*

**3) Open up about your disappointment with success**—Like me, you may battle messages about success that came from your past. You may still carry guilt about arenas in which you haven't been successful or sins that still plague you. Opening up is the first step to finding God's bigger purpose in your heartache.

> *Journal about your experiences with success. Get with a woman you trust, and ask for her listening ear. When you are finished sharing, pray together.*

**4) Commit to God to walk with him**—True success in life isn't about what you've accomplished or what possessions you've amassed. True success lies in who is walking beside you.

> *Take a prayer walk with God, and talk to him about your walk with him. Plan a daily time into your schedule for you and God to walk together.*

**5) Regularly seek guidance from others**—Certainly God didn't mean for us to figure out how to overcome the world all on our own. Oftentimes the deepest healing from the onslaught of the world on our faith can be found by sharing our struggles.

> *Open up to another Christian about the place you feel most vulnerable to the false security of worldliness—whether it's beauty, career, ministry, motherhood, men or other accomplishments. Talk about how you can know and rely on the love God has for you (1 John 4:16).*

**6) Regularly ask God to cleanse you from worldliness**—We're not always aware of how worldliness creeps into our thinking. When you start to feel insecure and anxious, ask God to reveal the roots of those thoughts and feelings.

> *Pray David's prayer found in Psalm 139:*
>
> *"Search me, O God, and know my heart;*
> *  test me and know my anxious thoughts.*
> *See if there is any offensive way in me, and lead me in the*
> *  way everlasting."*
>
> *Watch for God's answer.*

**7) Learn from others' battles**—In her story, Xin talks about her struggle to find her self-esteem outside of performance and others' view of her. Through understanding God's love, she came to the place where she doesn't feel like she's in a blind battle or accuse herself of having a "bad heart" because of her insecurity.

> *How does your performance affect your view of yourself? Read Psalm 103. Journal about how God's love and guidance can help you have a different outlook.*

"After our first child, my husband and I were anxious to add another to the family. But instead of another pregnancy, I had one devastating miscarriage and then another. After that I couldn't get pregnant for years. All the disappointment and pain eventually led my husband and me to consider adoption.

"A full ten years after our first child, we adopted a daughter. (And a couple of months after that adoption I was pregnant again.) Now I understand that we would have never adopted our precious daughter without the years of infertility. I see that God had a much higher purpose in mind for me."

—A grandmother to my
adopted daughter's daughter

# WHO WILL PROTECT ME?
### *The Guard*

"While I was with them, I protected them and kept them safe
by the name you gave me...I have given them your word and
the world has hated them, for they are not of the world any
more than I am of the world. My prayer is not that you take
them out of the world but that you protect them from the
evil one."

John 17:12,14–15

WE CAN LEARN A LOT ABOUT GOD'S HEART OF PROTECTION
through how he reveals himself in the Bible. When God came to
Abraham to make a covenant with him, he said, "Do not be
afraid, Abram. *I am your shield*, your very great reward" (Genesis
15:1, emphasis added). When God commissioned Jeremiah, he
promised, "They will fight against you but will not overcome
you, for I am with you and *will rescue you*" (Jeremiah 1:19, emphasis added).

Even beyond that, have you ever noticed how many of the
names or descriptions of God have to do with his protection of
us? As our *counselor*, God protects us through his word, warning
us about the destructive nature of sin and guiding us in paths that
protect our souls from spiritual onslaught (Psalm 119:24). When
troubles and suffering come, he offers to be our *stronghold*, *hiding
place* and *tower* (Psalm 18:2, 32:7 and 61:3). When our enemies
falsely accuse us, he steps in as our *defender* (Isaiah 19:20). When
we are unaware we are being attacked, God acts as our *rear guard*,
protecting us in ways we can't see or understand (Isaiah 52:12).

For those of us who come to adulthood handicapped by the humanity of those who raised us, or victims of such affronts to the heart of God as rape, abuse and unfaithfulness, he offers to be our *comforter* (2 Corinthians 1:3–4) and to bring healing as our *physician* (Luke 4:23).

When we are weary, he tenderly offers to be our *shade from the heat* (Isaiah 25:4) and a *shelter* for us to rest under (Joel 3:16). As our *Father*, God tells us that he knows the number of hairs on our head (Matthew 10:30). Nothing escapes his notice. Angels are also part of God's plan to protect us. In Psalm 91, God tells us that if we make him our dwelling, "then no harm will befall you, no disaster will come near your tent. For he will command his angels concerning you to guard you in all your ways" (verses 9–11).

I can personally vouch that one of the primary desires of a woman's heart is protection. I can't say how many times during twenty-five years of marriage that I've said to my husband, "I need to feel protected." (And also how many arguments we've had when I've interpreted his actions as a lack of protection!) Paul tells us in 1 Corinthians 13 that love always protects. For God to love us, he must also protect us. Since God's love is perfect, his protection of us must be perfect. But our understanding and human insight into God's protection is often far from perfect. We are tempted to think that protection should mean a lack of hardship, illness or trauma in our lives. And then when we aren't "protected" from these things, we can very easily want to start protecting ourselves instead.

The question is, how do we reconcile the challenging things that happen to us with God's protection? How do we see beyond our battles, large and small, to see God's perfect love for us? And how do we let God's protection move us toward security in heart?

## My Measure of Protection

Earlier, I talked about going off to a small Christian college. My reason for going to college was simple. I wanted what students jokingly called a MRS degree—to come out of college married to a minister. Ironically, a big part of my first two years of college ended up revolving around a new boyfriend, who had no aspirations of being in the ministry.

After our breakup, I decided to move on to another Christian college. By this time, I wasn't sure if or how a man might come into the equation, but I knew I was ready to recommit myself to my original goal of doing mission work. I met Dave almost immediately. He had spied me out at a "Preacher's Club" meeting (where I was the only girl in attendance). Soon after that he came up and introduced himself at church. Dave was organizing a mission team that was going to Chicago for the summer and invited me to join.

It was only a month later that I came to the quiet realization that Dave was the man I wanted to marry. He was a charismatic leader on campus, heading up many spiritual events. His zeal for evangelism and prayer inspired me. He had been raised in a Christian home and had a deep love and respect for the Scriptures. Since I was relatively new to Christianity, Dave's knowledge deeply impressed me. We spent many hours talking about spiritual things and God's heart of love for us.

Although Dave pursued me in the beginning, the tables quickly turned when Dave decided he just wanted to be friends. We quickly became best friends. In fact, we spent that year of college just getting to know each other better without dating. The turning point came right before we left on our mission trip. Dave confided in me that he was going to fast for a week in preparation. Having never fasted before, I asked if I could join him. Together, we burned our meal tickets and embarked on a week-long fast.

By the end of the week, our hearts turned toward each other. We spent our dating relationship on a mission campaign, serving, praying, reaching out and studying the Bible together. God had honored my many prayers for a Christian mate in a powerful way. Although our engagement period was marred by serious struggles with impurity, once we were married I had every reason to hope for a future serving God together.

I know I speak for every woman who sets out to marry a Christian in saying that none of us expect to end up in a relationship that involves addiction. Neither Dave nor I would come to understand the nature of Dave's sexual addiction until well into our marriage. To be fair, Dave also had not realized that he was marrying a codependent and all the implications that would have in his battle to be pure.[1]

I first faced the depth of Dave's struggles when we were at a marriage seminar six years into our marriage. (It wasn't that Dave hadn't tried to be open with me about his struggles with pornography. I just wasn't secure enough to hear about them!) We had just moved from leading a thriving youth ministry of seventy-five teenagers in New Mexico to get more training with a large, evangelistic church in Chicago. At the seminar we attended, one of the speakers talked about the importance of total openness with your mate. He challenged each couple to go back to the room and disclose anything that had never been talked about.[2]

Later that night, I was expecting romance. Instead, my husband came to me with a list of twelve things he had never told me—dark things acted out in adult bookstores and strip clubs. Our world was literally turned upside down as my husband made the courageous decision to go before our church leaders with his sin. We had three small children. I felt more vulnerable at that point than I had at any other point in my life. *What will happen to us? How will I forgive him? How will others view us now? Will we lose everything?*

---

1. According to the National Mental Health Association, codependency is an "emotional and behavioral condition that affects an individual's ability to have a healthy, mutually satisfying relationship. It is also known as 'relationship addiction' because people with codependency often form or maintain relationships that are one-sided, emotionally destructive and/or abusive."

2. This topic is debated, but from my experience, confessing sexual infidelity is best done in the context of Christian counseling, where the offended mate can decide how much information they want to receive.

Through many intense sessions with godly men, Dave came to the realization that his walk down the aisle at the age of twelve didn't equate to Biblical repentance and conversion. On his birthday, he was baptized and emerged a new man. It felt like my protection had returned. I was confident that the old patterns wouldn't return.

Let's fast-forward to about ten years later. By this point, we were out of the ministry and had successfully transitioned to new careers. Dave had experienced two years of purity after his "second conversion," but the old patterns had slowly re-emerged. He might go incident-free for three to six months, but then he would fall again. Dave had often gone to church leaders for help. He was read multiple passages on repentance, and when the pattern didn't cease, he was threatened with church discipline. We went to a counselor in our church who for many months gave his heart and his time to try to help us.

But something else even more disconcerting was happening. Discouragement was turning into defensiveness. Because of the shame he felt, Dave sometimes cloaked his addiction with deceit by leaving out details and supplying only half-truths. His behavior came to a breaking point when he called a dating line and talked to a woman. After a strike of conscience (and after she made it obvious she didn't want to talk about sex), he asked her to throw away our phone number and assured her he would not be calling back. He wanted me to see some kind of victory in the situation. *Couldn't I see how God protected him?*

After a heated discussion, I asked him to leave so I could take some time to think. Dave ended up spending three nights sleeping in his car in the parking lot of our health club before he came home to sleep on the downstairs couch.

When we came back together almost forty days later, it was on the condition that Dave recommit himself to recovery for sexual addiction. But I was also realizing that I needed more serious help as well. Despite all the reading I had done about sexual addiction up to that point, I had been resistant and even angry at the suggestion that I had made *any* contribution. Now I was seeing that although my struggles were different from my husband's, they were just as deeply rooted.

I saw that I was an approval addict who had learned from the time I was a little girl to repress unacceptable emotions. The worse thing I could imagine was being abandoned. And this fear of abandonment kept me from the kind of honest communication and confrontation that Dave needed. Because I couldn't handle Dave being unhappy with me, I was easily manipulated. When he would storm off after conflict, he could be sure that I would eventually come running after him to patch everything up. I simply didn't know how to handle his defensiveness without taking a blow to my own self-esteem.

This pattern was part of what I call our "dance of addiction," and I was as equally well versed in my steps as he was in his. I started attending a Christian codependency group where I worked through the 12-step program. We then entered what would be the start of years of counseling.

In writing this book, the first time I typed out the words, "Who will protect me?" I felt a rush of emotion as memories came flooding back. I remember going often to the park near our house and lying on the park bench weeping as I prayed. I remember going to war for my husband and our marriage, praying fervently for God to remove the stronghold of sexual addiction.

But as I look back over Dave's and my battle, I also see God's strong hand of protection. I see God as my shepherd, guiding me to places where my codependency could come into full view, so I could find healing and help. I see God as my defender, enabling me to let go of the shame of not having a perfect marriage by talking openly about our struggles without fear. Now I understand God as my refuge—the only place where I can express the full range of my emotions, no matter how confusing and painful. I also see God as our guard, moving us into just the right cities, where we would find counseling, healing and hope from others who were also fighting sexual addiction.

Dave and I both have experienced firsthand the comfort and healing of God at some of the most vulnerable moments in our marriage. Dave has come to a better understanding of sexual addiction and has made the brave move of telling his story again and again. Through his courage, he has been able to help many.

If I had chosen my life's path, I'm sure I would have never chosen this one. But I'm convinced that you wouldn't have this book in your hand without it. God's protection in my life has been absolutely perfect, in line with his perfect love and eternal purpose for me. And I'm confident that one day, when I'm in heaven, he'll explain to me the parts I don't understand. But for right now, I'm content to continually recommit myself to trust.

Here's the question we all face at one point or another: *Where is God as our protector when, in our human estimation, our trials are more than we can bear?* This is exactly the question that Satan is more than happy to twist to his advantage. Satan is not just standing by when the big struggles appear. More often than not, it's the little things that can have us running for cover. Satan wants us to run outside of God's protection by seeking our own solutions to our difficulties. I have done this through putting up multiple layers of self-protection.

## The False Security of Self-Protection

We can trace the false security of self-protection all the way back to the Garden of Eden. When Satan offered Eve the forbidden fruit, he told her that she would be like God, "knowing the difference between good and evil *and* blessing and calamity."[3] Really, Satan was suggesting she would receive more than being *like* God; he was suggesting that she could become *equal with God*

---

3. Genesis 3:5, *Amplified Bible*

in knowledge. After all, if Eve knew about evil, or as the *Amplified Bible* says, "blessing and calamity," couldn't she better protect herself? I believe what Satan literally wanted Eve to do was to replace God in her life with her own self-protective devices. After all, isn't that the path that Satan forged for himself? He didn't want to trust in God, so he went after self-glory, self-leadership and self-protection. Satan's goal was to lead Adam and Eve to exactly the same place.

> Then the eyes of both of them were opened, and they realized they were naked; so they sewed fig leaves together and made coverings for themselves.
> Then the man and his wife heard the sound of the LORD God as he was walking in the garden in the cool of the day, and they hid from the LORD God among the trees of the garden. But the LORD God called to the man, "Where are you?"
> He answered, "I heard you in the garden, and I was afraid because I was naked; so I hid." (Genesis 3:7–10)

Once Eve threw off God's protection by doing what he explicitly asked her not to do, she was suddenly left scrambling for any possible way to protect herself. In fact, Eve became a seamstress right on the spot, using her creative nature to design a way for them to clothe themselves with aprons of fig leaves. In doing so, she made a big statement to God: *You're not going to protect me, so I have to protect myself. You didn't think to clothe us, so we're going to have to figure it out on our own.*

For the first time, in the face of fear, Adam and Eve also felt the urge to hide from God. For us looking on now, a few fig leaves and a couple of bushes seem like an incredibly futile way to hide from the God of the universe. Did they really think God wouldn't be able to find them? But that brings up an even bigger question. What were they protecting themselves from exactly? What did they think God would do? I can only imagine how much their distrust and fear hurt God. And I'm guessing that the one thing that didn't occur to Adam and Eve is how their actions might have made God feel.

Self-protection has largely to do with *me* becoming what God has assured me that *he* wants to be in my life. What do I mean? Let's go back again to some of the ways that God promises to be our protector and contrast those with our self-protective devices (see the following list).

| God's Promise to Protect | Our Self-Protective Devices |
| --- | --- |
| "For you have been my refuge, a strong tower against the foe." (Psalm 61:3) | We retreat behind walls of our own strength (I'm strong enough to handle this) and then shut the windows so that no one can see in. |
| "Guard my life and rescue me; let me not be put to shame, for I take refuge in you." (Psalm 25:20) | We retreat into fantasy through books and movies. Or even seek to numb our shame through alcohol or prescription drugs. |
| "As a shepherd looks after his scattered flock... so will I look after my sheep." (Ezekiel 34:12) | We keep our spirituality to ourselves, thinking we can find our own way back if we wander. |
| "When they cry out to the Lord..., he will send them a savior and defender, and he will rescue them." (Isaiah 19:20) | We become defensive, putting up barriers in advance just in case someone else might judge us. |
| "You are my hiding place; you will protect me from trouble." (Psalm 32:7) | We hide our struggles under a veneer of perfection and strength. |
| "It will be a shelter and shade from the heat of the day, and a refuge and hiding place from the storm and rain." (Isaiah 4:6) | We seek to prevent trials before they happen, or we seek to prevent persecution by living in a way that keeps our Christianity undercover. |
| "The angel of the Lord encamps around those who fear him, and he delivers them." (Psalm 34:7) | We stop taking any risks at all so that we can make sure that we don't fall. Or we test God by embracing unsafe situations or relationships. |

The truth is that we can't protect ourselves. A quick scan of the news on any given day makes that glaringly apparent. But Satan, as he does with all of the other false securities, glamorizes self-protection and makes it appear to be something that it's not. As the accuser, he specializes in making us afraid of each other, and most of all, afraid of being vulnerable—emotionally and spiritually naked before God and others. He whispers his judgment in our ears, and then he tries to make us believe that his judgment is actually coming from God and from other people. But when we have the courage to come with humility before God and others, the Bible promises us healing, spiritual protection and hope.

## Praying for God's Protection

Just like us, many women in the Bible struggled with self-protection. Sarah protected her heart from the fear of disappointment by laughing when she overheard an angel announcing to Abraham that she would bear a child in her old age.[4] Rebekah sought to protect her favorite son, Jacob, (and no doubt herself) by teaching him how to deceive his father—ensuring his future, but condemning him to an insecure existence.[5] My favorite story involves a woman who had every reason to protect herself, but who instead turned to God again and again for protection:

> In bitterness of soul, Hannah wept much and prayed to the LORD. And she made a vow, saying, "O LORD Almighty, if you will only look upon your servant's misery and remember me, and not forget your servant but give her a son, then I will give him to the LORD for all the days of his life." (Hannah's prayer in her infertility—1 Samuel 1:10–11)

> "My heart rejoices in the LORD; in the LORD my horn is lifted high. My mouth boasts over my enemies, for I delight in your deliverance.... There is no one beside you; there is no Rock like our God.... He will guard the feet of his saints, but the wicked will be silenced in darkness." (Hannah's prayer after she devoted Samuel—1 Samuel 2:1–2, 9)

Hannah was a Jew, married to Elkanah, a God-fearing man who was devoted to worshipping God and a man who loved her deeply. But the one thing she really wanted, Elkanah couldn't give her. Hannah was infertile. This may have been the reason that Elkanah took a second wife, Peninnah. But above all, Hannah was a woman of prayer. Year after year Hannah took her

---

4. Genesis 18:11–12
5. Genesis 27

infertility to God in prayer, pouring out her heart with great anguish.

In stark contrast to Hannah's infertility, Peninnah had babies year after year. We can only imagine Hannah's struggle to find joy in her heart as year after year Peninnah announced pregnancy after pregnancy. Hannah surely couldn't miss Elkanah's pride and anticipation as Peninnah's belly swelled and then as she bore a child of his seed. She watched as Peninnah nursed a tiny infant, and felt her heart grip with desire. How many children did Peninnah bear? The Bible mentions Peninnah and "all her sons and daughters."[6] In fact, later in the story, Hannah refers to Peninnah's many sons.[7] Because Hannah was a righteous woman, this put her in a difficult position. I'm sure she loved all of the children and even was regarded as a second mother. But there must have been times when they only magnified her heart's desire. *God, why haven't you allowed me even one pregnancy of my own? Is there some sin on my part that I'm not aware of?*

The Bible tells us that Elkanah desired to comfort Hannah. Once a year, when he went to Jerusalem to worship "he would give portions of the meat to his wife Peninnah and to all her sons and daughters. But to Hannah he gave a double portion because he loved her, and the LORD had closed her womb" (1 Samuel 1:4–5). But Hannah's grief went much deeper than her infertility. Peninnah, sensing Elkanah's deep love for Hannah, saw Hannah as her rival and set out to make her life miserable.

> And because the LORD had closed her womb, her rival kept provoking her in order to irritate her. This went on year after year. Whenever Hannah went up to the house of the LORD, her rival provoked her till she wept and would not eat. Elkanah her husband would say to her, "Hannah, why are you weeping? Why don't you eat? Why are you downhearted? Don't I mean more to you than ten sons?" (1 Samuel 1:6–8)

Hannah couldn't even worship in peace. Although the Bible

---

6. 1 Samuel 1:4
7. 1 Samuel 2:5

doesn't tell us the exact words that Peninnah used to torment Hannah, I think we could take a good guess. *Going to pray again, Hannah? Too bad that God has closed your womb. It must be quite a burden to know that your righteousness isn't enough for God to give you children. I'm thankful that I'm not in your shoes.*

Where was God's protection in Hannah's life? Hannah obviously was a worshipper of God. *Why do you allow her to persecute me year after year? Don't you see my sorrow, hear my prayers for protection?* But Hannah kept worshipping God.

Finally one year, during their yearly trip to the temple, Hannah in "bitterness of soul" and weeping (1:10), prayed to God and made a vow, promising that if God would give her a son, she would consecrate the child to a lifetime of service in God's temple. God heard her prayers and gave her a son, Samuel. As soon as he was weaned, Hannah honored her vow and took him to the temple to live and to be raised by Eli, the high priest. Soon afterwards she was pregnant again, and went on to have three sons and two daughters.[8]

Hannah's story highlights an important part of developing a secure heart: understanding that God's protection is always in line with his purpose. Hannah's delayed ability to have children, and even the persecution she received, played an important role in God's eternal purpose for her life. God had chosen her to give birth to Samuel, who would become a prophet that played an important role in God's plan. (In fact, two books of the Bible were named after him!)

Would Hannah have consecrated Samuel without the years of heart preparation that went before? Hannah had many years of silence from God before his purpose would be revealed. Yet she kept taking her sorrow to him and refused to become bitter toward God. Do you think that Hannah would say now that God protected her? Absolutely! Like her, we may not understand the ways that God acts as our guard until further down the road, or

---

8. 1 Samuel 2:21

perhaps even until heaven.

One of the most difficult tests of understanding and surrendering to God as our guard comes when we pray. How can we feel protected when we've prayed about something for months, years or perhaps even decades, and still haven't seen the fruition of those prayers? What if you pray for your husband who doesn't know Christ, and twenty years later, he still seems unmoved in his reluctance to embrace Christianity. How about having children that you've prayed for from the day they were born, yet they aren't Christians? Trusting God as your protector is much like faith in general. There is no faith involved if you already see it with your eyes. Faith comes in when we don't see it and can't understand it.[9]

## Embracing Our Vulnerable Nature

When Dave and I were recently in Maui for our twenty-fifth anniversary, I signed us up for a bike ride down the volcano. The excursion featured a van ride to the top of the island, where you could watch the sunrise and then coast down the side of the mountain on a bike. When I bought our tickets, the activity vendor assured me that it was "perfectly safe." Honestly, I was picturing a leisurely bike ride in the sunshine. My first clue that I had misunderstood came at 2 AM, when they picked us up. I asked the van driver if he could wait a moment while Dave ran to the car for our sunscreen. "Sunscreen?" he said. "Uh, I don't think you'll be needing any sunscreen."

My second clue came when we reached a small café where we were given our gear. There was a newspaper article on the wall about the bike ride, entitled "Bike Ride Down Haleakala — Not for the Fainthearted." When they started fitting us for wind suits, padded gloves and helmets similar to what a racecar driver would wear, I was more than a little concerned.

Riding up the winding mountain roads, I watched out the side window as the cities below us turned into tiny twinkling

9. "Now faith is being sure of what we hope for and certain of what we do not see." (Hebrews 11:1)

lights. I was now having serious doubts as to whether I wanted to
do this. After we unloaded at the top, we watched a spectacular
sunrise high above the clouds. The wind was blowing so hard
and it was so cold that I couldn't stay outdoors for more than five
minutes before I'd head back into the shelter.

Once the sun was up, they brought us back into the van for
our pep talk (at least that's what I was hoping for!). There our
leader let us know that if we had any doubts about whether we
could make it down the hill, that we shouldn't go. (We had the
option of riding down in the van.) He explained in graphic details
the dangers (we were riding on a steep, winding highway with
sheer drop-offs on one side), and then finally reassured us that as
long as we followed directions and our leader, we would make it
down safely.

I'm not a quitter by nature, so I decided to at least give it my
best shot. With my heart pounding in my chest, I set off behind
the two other women who were in our group. Within the first ten
minutes, I started to relax a little. I felt God's presence helping
me overcome my fears and protecting me from harm. The views
were breathtaking, and the wind was actually helping to slow us
down just a bit. The bikes were made especially for coasting
downhill; they were heavy and low to the ground.

I only had two scary moments where I felt slightly out of control. Once I found myself drifting toward the middle when a car
came around a blind curve, a little closer than I would have liked.
The second time, I was so busy watching for big waves as we got
close to the ocean that I didn't notice our leader had pulled over.
I had to make a quick pull over and almost went tumbling. But
thankfully God protected me from harm as we took the thirty-
eight-mile bike ride together. I used the time to sing, pray and
rejoice in the beauty.

When we were finished, we got into the van for the pilgrim-
age back to the other side of the island where we were staying.

Being a journalist at heart, I started asking our guide more questions. He told us that in twenty years, eleven people had died and countless others had been injured making this bike trip. In fact, he said that ambulances come down pretty much every day.

When I asked him how these people got injured, he said that there were two common scenarios. The first was that someone wouldn't pay attention, would drift into the other lane of the highway and get hit by a car coming around the curve. The other was in the lower part of the bike ride. A rider, thinking they were doing the easy part now, would get lost in the view and not notice when everyone else was pulling over. My heart did a quick jump. Those were the exact two scenarios I had experienced up on the mountain. *That could have been me.*

Later that day we did a whale watch and shared with two ladies on the boat about our bike ride. One of them told us that she had flown to Maui sitting next to a lady who was on her way to pick up her sister, who was in a coma after riding her bike right off a cliff. Even though I had come down the hill safely, I was now feeling very frightened, vulnerable and even a little guilty at enjoying something that put someone else into a coma. Even seeing my vulnerability in retrospect was making me question myself—filling me with dread and insecurity.

But there was something else bothering me. After the bike ride, Dave and I had a conversation that concerned me. Something he had said planted a question in my mind about his purity. When I woke up the next morning, we headed to the beach for a walk. I had a heavy heart. I knew I needed to talk with him, but I was scared that Dave would take it all wrong—as casting some kind of black cloud over our anniversary trip. But I had an even greater fear: I was afraid of the truth. *What if he has fallen and didn't want to tell me since it was our anniversary? How will I handle the rest of the trip? We still have a full week together in paradise.* My old insecurities would have meant either avoiding the situation all together or getting myself so worked up that I would handle it most ungraciously, making it hard for my husband to hear. Dave jogged on ahead of me, so I took some time to pray, seeking to surrender my fear to God.

As I prayed I realized something important. Being vulnerable and honest with my husband in this specific circumstance was just as scary to me as riding the bike down the volcano. In fact, in some ways, it took more courage. I so wanted to go back to my old self-protective ways. *Can't I be in denial just this once?* But just as God took me down the side of a mountain, I knew God would guard my heart, no matter what the outcome.

When Dave returned, I had an upfront, and just a little tearful, talk with him. He was completely humble. He asked for my forgiveness for what he had said and gently reassured me that his purity was still intact. Most of all, he told me how proud he was of me for opening up. His response helped me to remember how much he had changed, but also helped me to know that I could not go back to my old life of self-protection and hidden fear.

You may be wondering, "How does this apply to me?" Just like me, you might prefer to ride down the side of a volcano than open up to someone else about your deepest fears, shortcomings and hurts, especially if you've done so in the past and found something less than grace. But you can be sure that since God asks you to open up and be vulnerable (see James 5:16), that he'll be right there with you as you round the hairpin curves. We feel safer when we are protecting ourselves spiritually. But I think you'll also find that most magnificent vistas (spiritually speaking) come through letting go of self-protection and trusting God with your vulnerable side. One thing is for sure, I can't think of anyone better to join me for a ride down the side of a mountain (or to take my hand as I walk straight through my fears) than my personal guard, my God.

## God's Perfect Timing

> Hear me, O LORD, and answer me,
>> for I am poor and needy.
> Guard my life, for I am devoted to you.
>> You are my God; save your servant who trusts in you.
> Have mercy on me, O LORD,
>> for I call to you all day long. (Psalm 86:1–3)

Perhaps the question I've grappled with the most in my life is the issue of God's timing. But here's what I've come to understand: Although God may or may not deliver me from my troubles in the exact manner, or in the time frame, that I hope for, I can be certain that God is doing battle for me. And God engages that battle in the way that best fulfills his eternal purpose for my life.

How about you? What situations in your life highlight your feelings of being unprotected? What are you praying for that has not come in the timing that you desire? Whatever arena you are seeking God's hand of protection in—whether it's financial, emotional or physical trials, or praying for healing from hurts and harm outside of your control—you can be sure of one thing: As God's daughter, God's perfect protection surrounds you. And you can rest assured that his protection is perfectly in sync with his eternal purpose for your life, geared to help you find true security of heart.

# IN HER OWN WORDS
*Camille's Story*

I grew up in a loving home with my mother, father and younger sister. We didn't have much, but we had each other. I never had a close relationship with my dad, and there wasn't much physical affection. I did know that he loved me, but the only way he ever said "I love you" was in a card. My father worked hard, provided for our family and occasionally took me to the movies.

My mother was the same way, except on special occasions such as my birthday, Christmas or my high school graduation, when she would tell me that she loved me and that she was proud of me. But there was still something missing,

Then when I was about twelve years old, my family life began to crumble. My father, our sole provider, began using drugs. I remember watching him get high. Honestly, I never thought that his recreational drug use would turn my life upside down. The reliable man I once knew disappeared before my very eyes.

Recreational drug use quickly became a hard-core drug problem. Then my father began to disappear, at first for a day, then for three to four days at a time. He would come back after he had spent all his money, with promises to change. We all desperately wanted to believe him, especially my mother. I believe she needed to believe him.

I watched my mother grieve the loss of her husband. They had been together since they were teenagers. She would cry, only to later become angry, but each time my father would return broke and with empty promises, she would take him back. This cycle continued for years.

My sister and I endured family counseling with my father when he admitted himself to a residential drug program. It was hard watching the man I had once admired sit with a group of drug addicts and their families, listening to horrible stories of drug life, crime and self-hatred.

My father was admitted to rehab two times; the last time no one attended family therapy. One day when I was around sixteen years old, he was gone for good. My mother had finally told my father to leave. I cried because I wanted my father back, but at the same time I was relieved. For a short period of time we had peace in our house.

The last time I saw him was nine years ago when I found out he was living several blocks from me. At that point I had not seen him in years. I actually went to his home, and I was surprised—he was different. Physically, he was much smaller than I remember. Spiritually, his spirit and soul were vacant; he talked as if he were in a dream. I could not tell if it was the drugs talking or the effects of the drugs. One thing was for sure: the man before me was not the man I grew up with. Not only had he changed physically and spiritually, he now had a new family that included three daughters. I felt rejected and abandoned even though I was now an adult. There was a part of me that felt sorry for him, but there was another part of me that wanted her Daddy.

I cried out to God and prayed for a week to recover. I needed God to comfort me. I needed God to tell me that he still loved me even though I felt like my father had traded me in for new daughters. Even today, I still feel the sting of seeing my father with his new family, but God continues to give me the strength to accept that this is the path my father chose. My God reassures me that he will never leave me and that he will be the Father in my life.

At the age of twenty I began living my mother's life. I met my husband-to-be, Joseph, while hanging out with friends. We moved in together after only dating six months and got married two years later. We were a bad mix from the beginning—my relationship with Joe was an extension of what I was looking for from my father. He was very funny and outgoing, some of the same things I liked about my father. But there were also some downfalls: he was terrible with money, compulsive and didn't think things through. These were the same things that I disliked about my father, but for some strange reason, I was drawn to Joe.

After two years of marriage I became a Christian, partly out of desperation. My marriage was in serious trouble. Joe had engaged in several affairs that almost drove me to insanity. I felt useless as a woman and would even cry when I would see a pretty woman, thinking, *Is this the type of woman my husband wants?* I had nothing, no reason to continue living and, at times, even considered suicide. I just wanted the pain to stop, and that's when God stepped in. The Lord heard my cry and sent a woman to study the Bible with me. Not only did she teach me about God, she and her husband began befriending Joe, who became a Christian seven months later. Not only did God protect me, he began rebuilding my life.

After becoming a Christian I became pregnant with my first child. I felt God was honoring me by blessing me with a child. Words cannot explain our happiness. When shortly afterward Joe became a Christian, this was icing on the cake. I thought to myself, *We are finally going to be a real family*. Unfortunately my dreams were short lived. Joe had another affair two weeks after being baptized.

This was the beginning of the end. Joe's affairs continued even though he regularly attended church. We even led a Bible study group and helped other couples become Christians. God is amazing! My faith was increased by seeing others becoming Christians and by having a child.

As time went on, Joe's sin became more evident—it was as though he made no effort to hide his sin. We lived apart more than we lived together. I wanted us to be a family and was willing to do anything to make the situation right. I had become Joe's biggest enabler. I believe the turning point in our relationship was when he continued to be unfaithful even after we had become pregnant with our second child. He said and did things that to this day cause me to ask God for help to forgive Joe.

Our marriage had become a "thorn in my side." Not only was Joe an unfaithful man but also a financially irresponsible man. My daughters and I lived without lights, gas and a telephone at different times throughout the years. There were times I would sleep with my Bible under my pillow because I had nothing else to hold on to. Joe had left the church and whole-heartedly lived in sin that included telephone dating lines, Internet dating and pornography. I would pray *"Why am I not enough? God loves me. Why doesn't Joe love me?" "How am I going to raise godly children in this situation?"* Then I kept asking myself: *"Am I still going to trust God?"* I searched my Bible day and night for answers. I wrote many, many prayers and listened to music to uplift my soul. I listened to one song so many times that my daughter knew every word, note and melody by heart! I knew God had a plan for my life but I didn't know if I could hold on to see the fruit of his plan!

After eight years in an unfaithful marriage, I finally told Joseph that it was over. After much prayer, I had decided to stop living my mother's life. Like my mother I wanted to save my family at any cost, but the costs had become too high. I did not want my daughters to live the life I had lived.

Rebuilding after Joe left was not easy. I had never lived on my own, and now I was living on my own with two small children. God has protected me in so many ways.

*God protected my sanity.* Even through the worst of times, God not only allowed me to cry through my pain, but also gave me the wisdom to make decisions to strengthen my faith and my family.

*God protected my daughters.* The separation and subsequent divorce were very hard on my older daughter, but God is healing her heart. God has put people in both of the girls' lives to help them through the rough times while at the same time becoming their trusted friends.

*God protected my faith.* God never failed me! Not one single time! He gave me exactly what I needed and the desires of my heart.

*God protected my self-esteem.* There were times when I felt worthless, but God continually reminded me that I am the "apple of his eye." I would tell myself that God thinks I am awesome and he loves me! Today, I am more confident and can honestly say that I love myself.

There are still some things I haven't fully worked through from my marriage. I still struggle with trusting people, and some days are easier than others, but I can look back over the last ten years of my life and see how God protected me and my daughters.

The most important thing I have learned is that God's protection is perfect and that my definition of protection is flawed and worldly. As I look back over my life, it is so evident that in each phase God protected my life, heart and soul perfectly. If he had not, I would not be here to tell this story. I would not have come out of a troubled childhood and a bad marriage being able to embrace my future with open arms and an open heart.

# WHO WILL PROTECT ME? THE GUARD

*Personal Study Guide & Life Application*

How can trusting God as your guard help you walk more securely? Here are a few suggestions.

**1) Look to God for protection**—The fact that God reveals himself to us in so many protective terms shows his desire to protect us. The response that God desires from us is our trust. "Some trust in chariots...but we trust in the name of the LORD our God" (Psalm 20:7).

> *Which part of God's protective nature or name of God speaks most deeply to your heart? Study out that attribute or name of God. Then write down three ways that you can trust that part of God's character.*

**2) Look to past victories to understand present struggles**—When it comes to understanding God's timing, your hindsight will always be much better than your foresight. Perhaps that's why the Bible encourages you to "remember those earlier days after you had received the light, when you stood your ground in a great contest in the face of suffering" (Hebrews 10:32).

> *Read Hebrews 10:32–39. Think of a struggle from the past that caused you heartache, but that you now see had a bigger purpose. How can what you learned in the past help you persevere in present struggles?*

**3) Identify ways that you protect yourself**—Most of us learn self-protective mechanisms in our childhood. When we were little girls, they may have served us well, even protecting us from harm. But most of us keep using these self-protections long after they are really needed.

*Go over the chart contrasting God's protection with our self-protective devices. Circle two that you struggle with the most. Then get with another woman and share how those devices manifest themselves in your life.*

**4) Let others in on your fears**—The reason we protect ourselves usually boils down to fear. And fears that are kept secretly stowed away in our own hearts often have the most power to take away our security. God tells us that he'll send his peace to guard our heart and mind when we lift that fear to him in prayer with thanksgiving.

> *Read Philippians 4:6–7. What fear is currently battling to take away your security? What can you be thankful for? Lift that fear to God with thanksgiving and ask him for his peace as your guard. Then confess your fear to a friend and ask for their prayers.*

**5) Put on the full armor of God**—God doesn't leave us defenseless. In fact, he urges us to put on his full armor—truth, righteousness, readiness, faith, salvation and the word of God—to guard ourselves against Satan's attacks.

> *Go back and read the section on God's armor in Chapter 2. Is there any part of the armor you've been neglecting? What schemes does Satan use when you leave that part of your spiritual life unprotected? Pray through Ephesians 6:10–18 every day for a week.*

**6) Pray for those who judge you**—Sometimes the protection we long for is from others who don't understand our battles and needlessly add pain by their comments. Like Hannah, our biggest test of our security may be knowing that another person judges us harshly.

*Do you have a Peninnah (or even several of them) in your life? What kind of insecurities does their criticism bring up for you? Pray for them, asking God to use them for his purpose in your life.*

**7) Learn from others' battles**—Camille's story highlights how a spiritual viewpoint can change your perspective. She talks about how even through great difficulty and trial, God protected her sanity, faith, daughters and self-esteem.

*Make a list similar to the one Camille made at the end of her story. How has God already shown his protection in your specific circumstances?*

"I know all the scriptures that tell me how God feels about me. I hate it that part of me cares what other people think. I look at that as unspiritual. Perhaps that's why I don't open up about my battles."

—Wife and mother

CHAPTER
TEN

# WHAT DO OTHERS THINK OF ME?
## *The Advocate*

Am I now trying to win the approval of men, or of God? Or am I trying to please men? If I were still trying to please men, I would not be a servant of Christ.

Galatians 1:10

"Even now my witness is in heaven;
my advocate is on high.
My intercessor is my friend
as my eyes pour out tears to God."

Job 16:19–20

DO YOU WANT SPECIAL INSIGHT INTO WHAT ONE PERSON THINKS about another? For starters, try listening to the names of endearment they have for each other. These can be as simple as "Honey" or as sentimental as "Princess." But these endearing names demonstrate much more than our aptitude for words— they are a reflection of the security and safety in a relationship. These words or phrases help us reaffirm our love and affection. As part of a private language, they may not mean anything to the outside world, but they speak a wealth of meaning to those who share them.

Even if you've never had a name of endearment from your parents or from a man, or even if you've had others give you "nicknames" that hurt you, as a daughter of God you can take heart. God has a whole private language that expresses his fondness for you.

For starters, God guards you as the "apple of his eye" (Deuteronomy 32:10–11). In case you've always wanted to feel like a queen, God considers you his "crown of splendor" and "royal diadem" as a part of his church (Isaiah 62:3). Do you ever find yourself feeling disheartened because of circumstances outside your control? No matter what others think of you, picture God singling you out in the heavenly realms and saying, "*She is my Hephzibah— my delight is in her*" (Isaiah 62:4).[1] You are one of the children of the promise and his most treasured possession (Deuteronomy 14:2). Want to feel beautiful in someone else's eyes? As the ransomed of the Lord, everlasting joy crowns your head (Isaiah 35:10), and in his eyes you "sparkle in his land like jewels in a crown" (Zechariah 9:16).

Perhaps some of the most beautiful pictures of the intensity of the love in a relationship with God are all of the terms of endearment in the Song of Songs (or Song of Solomon), regarded by many scholars to be as much about God's love relationship with his children as about human marriage. Imagine God pointing to you and saying, "Like a lily among thorns is my darling among the maidens" (Song of Songs 2:2).

As Christian women who are literally showered by God's affection, why do we spend so much time and energy wondering what others think of us? Why do we give the words and opinions of other people too much weight in our estimation of ourselves? Is it a reflection of childhood losses and hurts that we've experienced at the hands of others? Can we possibly blame it on Satan's plot to steal our security by accusing us in every arena of our lives? Or could our struggles with approval reflect our own struggle with taking our convictions about how God really sees us from our heads to our hearts? For me, I'd have to say all of the above. But although I can't change the losses I have experienced, I can still cling to the one absolutely true and perfect advocate I have in my life—Jesus.

---

1. *Hephzibah* means "my delight is in her."

## My Measure of Approval

I shake a little almost every day.
Because I'm more frightened than the strangers ever know.
And if at times I show my trembling side
(the anxious, fearful part I hide)
I wonder.
Will you be my friend?…
Who, when there's nothing left but me,
stripped of charm and subtlety,
will nonetheless remain?
Will you be my friend?
For no reason that I know.
Except I want you so.[2]

—James Kavanaugh

Like most little girls, I was tuned in to the approval of others from the time I was very young. But I also had an unusually sensitive personality. As what has now become coined as a "highly sensitive person or HSP,"[3] I came equipped with a special kind of radar, deeply in tune with the moods and emotions of others. From the time I was young, I noticed if someone seemed less than pleased with me—even if his or her words said otherwise. Because I was so tuned in to the reactions of others, I worked especially hard to please others. I also noticed the very subtle changes in my environment that would go undetected by other children. And these changes often left me feeling insecure.

But as much as I feared negative attention from others, I longed for positive attention. Along with some of the other little girls living on my street, I often staged elaborate shows using a makeshift stage in my backyard. We danced, sang, tumbled and performed skits for anyone who would watch. We had elaborate dress-up parties, where we would beg our mothers for beautiful clothing to put on so that we could parade our beauty.

The problem was, as a young girl, I had no way to understand why I got my feelings hurt so easily. When I would cry and fret

---

2. James Kavanaugh, *Will You Be My Friend*, (San Francisco: Harper, 1985).

3. For more information on highly sensitive people (or HSPs) see *The Highly Sensitive Person—How to Thrive When the World Overwhelms You* by Elaine N. Aron (New York: Broadway Publishers, 1997).

about what my parents saw as "little things," they would try to get me to lighten up by singing a little jingle: "Nobody loves me, everybody hates me, think I'll eat some worms." So I would retreat to our backyard swing set, where I would swing and sing that little song over and over again.

What turned my sensitivity into a full-fledged clamoring for approval? Perhaps, as a child who was restless and easily distracted, it was the disapproval I remember receiving from teachers. Perhaps it came from the neighborhood boys who were older than I, who took me into bushes and into the woods and asked to me to partially disrobe. Since I didn't understand my own need for approval or possess the kind of self-esteem and boundaries needed to refuse these requests, I was in a very real way defenseless.

I'm also realizing that much of this was not my parents' fault. The speed with which they were adding children to our family makes it easy to see how one very sensitive little girl could fade into the background. And I was equally as good at escaping notice as I was at performing. I could retreat to the woods that surrounded my neighborhood. I spent many happy hours out there close to a quiet creek, building forts, swimming or hanging out under the railroad bridge.

I also retreated into the worlds contained in the pages of books. (In my childhood I read every single science fiction book in our entire small town library.)

The other place I would flee when the world didn't understand me was the world of performance, where I could become an entirely different person. Certainly, entering into baton and dance was a boon for my self-esteem. Suddenly I found something I was naturally talented at, and the approval flowed in. The problem was that I never learned to take this confidence outside of the performance arena. So although I might be a "princess" in a Miss Majorette contest, when I came back to school, I felt like an out-of-place wallflower.

In addition, I was self-conscious about my teeth. I had two serious problems—an inverted upper jaw and too many teeth. I learned from a young age to smile with my hand over my mouth. (Once a little girl ran up to me at church and said very loudly, "Did you know you're a snaggletooth?") The only place I smiled without inhibition was when I was twirling or dancing. Somehow with the beautiful costumes, hair and makeup, it didn't really matter.

Needless to say, my heart's desire from the time I was quite young was braces. My parents wanted to have my teeth fixed, but the procedure at that time required hospitalization and cost thousands of dollars. My dad's insurance didn't cover it. (Finally, when I was a freshman in college, due to a change in insurance and in the procedure, we were able to move forward. I had my upper jaw broken, spent a summer with a metal plate in my mouth and a gap big enough to put a finger through, and then was rewarded with my much-anticipated braces.)

I also learned to use my body to get approval. I remember one dance recital when I was in my teens, where a man in attendance (who I had never met before) came up to me after it was over, leaned over and whispered to me with a telling little smile, "You sure know how to move your body!" I smiled innocently and thanked him, but it wasn't until much later that I had a clue what he was talking about. Around that age, I remember being quite proud of the bikini (which my mother helped me pick out) that featured a cut-out heart on both the top and the bottom. I would proudly show teenage boys around the neighborhood my heart-shaped tans.

Yet, because of my propensity to overreact when taunted, I was an easy target for other children at school. I was teased relentlessly about my name. The boys would call me Robin Red Breast, or would say, "Hey, Robin, where's Batman?" In fact, I have very few memories of junior high school except for the world I had outside of school. My predominant memory of high school was that of a painful awareness of what others were saying about me behind my back and the snickering of the popular girls when I walked by.

By the time I was nearing adulthood—and by the time I first encountered Christianity—I had an approval deficit that ran deep and wide. The real root of it was that I didn't know how to trust myself, my judgment or even my spirituality, so I looked to others for esteem and validation instead. How did this thirst for approval continue throughout my life? Here are a few examples:

- **College**—I carried around a poem called "Will be you be my friend?" (quoted at the beginning of this section). I had friends read it as a way to show them how I felt about myself, but could not express. In fact, before Dave and I started dating, I asked him to read it. The night he asked me to marry him, I had a burning question that he needed to answer before I would say yes. *Do you really accept me for who I am?*

- **Marriage**—When Dave would say or do anything that I would equate with disapproval, I would run after him for reassurance in whatever form I could get. For years, I got a disproportionate amount of my self-esteem from him.

- **Christianity**—After attending a Christian college for a semester, I visited a state college with a student I had a crush on. When some of his Christian friends voiced their reservations about Christian schools, I was swayed. At a devotional, I stood up during the sharing and made an impulsive vow to transfer. When I realized that I couldn't afford the out-of-state tuition, I carried guilt for years.

- **Career changes**—When I worked with a boss who didn't believe in encouragement, I was torn by my desire to please someone who couldn't be pleased. Even though others who worked there were sympathetic, I felt nothing short of panic when I made a mistake that I might get ridiculed for. I started having nightmares that an ocean wave rushed into my office and swept me away.

When did this start to really change for me? Only after pursuing a passionate relationship with God have I found peace and security with who I am. I also believe that God has tenderly and lovingly let me explore my feelings of inadequacy through facing deficits in myself, in my family and in our marriage. These deficits have turned into blessings that have taught me to get my self-esteem from God and God alone.

But like me, you may also be wondering why we are so anxious about what others think of us. Why are we so convinced that we need approval? And does approval deliver the well-being that Satan promises?

## The False Security of Approval

What is approval anyway? Approval has to do with whether we feel accepted, respected and even protected. It has to do with the little things such as being appreciated, and it also has to do with the big things such as whether others respect our right to choose who we want to be. Approval has to do with the unspoken questions that we approach others and God with:

*Do you believe in me enough to hear my deepest needs?*
*Will you uphold my cause?*
*Is it safe for me to show you my vulnerable side?*
*Will you reject me if you see who I really am?*

How then does Satan come into the picture? Satan's expertise is filling us with shame. Shame is different from guilt. Guilt is a God-given protection that alerts us when we're doing something that causes pain to our soul. Guilt lets us know that we've wandered outside of our consciences. (Satan, of course, wants to give us a false guilt that has nothing to do with what God thinks of us!) But even more so, Satan wants to fill us with shame by

- **Filling us with anxiety about what others think**—We worry about our performance, our looks, our weight, our children, our home and our body type. And in all of these areas, Satan is more than happy to offer his standards—giving us ever-higher hurdles to leap over that exhaust and discourage us.

- **Getting us to compare ourselves with each other**—Satan tries to convince us that if we find someone who is "not quite as good as we" then we might feel a little better about all the people we see as being "better than we."

- **Discouraging us from opening up**—For most of us it just takes one bad experience with vulnerability for us to slam the door shut. Satan's goal is to give us that experience. In this way, he can keep us from the truth that if we persevere, we'll endear ourselves to other women by talking about how we really feel.

- **Encouraging us to justify ourselves**—Satan wants us to believe we must defend ourselves in every situation, lest someone think wrongly of us. But if we're always on the defensive, we are even more unlikely to face and then open up about our real battles. Satan's ultimate goal is to make us afraid of God himself.

- **Insinuating that disapproval from others means God isn't with us**—More than anything, Satan wants us to believe that our standing with people is a direct reflection of our standing with God. He whispers that if others don't approve, it is probably because God doesn't.

As Christian women, we need to also remember that Satan doesn't just go after us with what we identify as "worldly" measures of approval. He knows that seeking after approval also transfers neatly into our spirituality. In fact, some of us who never saw ourselves as needing the approval of others before we were Christians may struggle when we come into God's church. We're excited that we've found a place where we'll finally be accepted. And in a sincere and good-hearted way, we care about pleasing our brothers and sisters. Satan's main goal is to get us to desire the approval of others, shame us for wanting it, then fill us with insecurity when we don't get it—his famous one-two-three punch, designed to discourage and dishearten us spiritually.

How does Satan try to get us to embrace the false security of approval? He takes God's message of security and tries to twist it into a totally different message altogether.

| God's Message About Approval | Satan's Twist |
| --- | --- |
| "Accept one another, then, just as Christ accepted you." (Romans 15:7) | You have to help others along in their acceptance of you by only letting them see the parts of your life that are "acceptable." |
| "If I were still trying to please men, I would not be a servant of Christ." (Galatians 1:10) | How well you please others is a good measure of how well you are pleasing Christ. |
| "My grace is sufficient for you, for my power is made perfect in weakness." (2 Corinthians 12:9) | Other people will be inspired by your strength. The best way to help others is to be really strong all of the time. |
| "Who will bring any charge against those whom God has chosen? It is God who justifies." (Romans 8:33) | If other people judge you as unacceptable, it's probably because you need to change. |
| "For the Lord God is a sun and shield; the Lord bestows favor and honor." (Psalm 84:11) | Having favor and honor from people is what enables you to feel good about yourself. |
| "Do not conform any longer to the pattern of this world, but be transformed by the renewing of your mind." (Romans 12:2) | You need to be "worldly" enough that the world will accept you and "spiritual" enough that the church will accept you. |
| "The Lord does not look at the things that man looks at. Man looks at the outward appearance, but the Lord looks at the heart." (1 Samuel 16:7) | You need to use your outward appearance to get approval. |
| "It does not, therefore, depend on man's desire or effort, but on God's mercy." (Romans 9:16) | God's approval of you, just like people's approval, depends on your performance. |

Bottom line, it's easy to think that when we are good, God advocates for us. But when we are bad, he lets us go off on our own until we can figure out how to be good again. But if you think about it, when do we need vindication most? The truth is that we don't handle ourselves perfectly in any situation. If we listen to the accuser of our souls, we'll never think we can expect anything from God. Yet, if we surrender the approval of others at the foot of the cross, God offers a glorious freedom and hope.

## Will I Be Vindicated?

> I care very little if I am judged by you or by any human court;
> indeed, I do not even judge myself. My conscience is clear,
> but that does not make me innocent. It is the Lord who
> judges me. (1 Corinthians 4:3–4)

I just signed off on an out-of-court settlement with an insurance company on a lawsuit I filed eighteen months ago. It all started three-and-a-half years ago when a careless driver rearended our car (as I mentioned in a previous chapter). Two months earlier, I had started my own business and had landed my first big writing assignment. After the accident, I was constantly working in severe pain and making visits to the chiropractor two to three times a week seeking relief. From our very first contact, the other insurance company (representing the woman who hit us) assured me that they wanted to get me whatever treatment I needed. Later when I was referred to a physical therapist and after that a massage therapist, their consistent message was, "We just want you to have any treatment you need." But as much as I wanted to be well, my shoulder kept going through cycles of deep pain.

I'm sure you can guess that as an overly sensitive soul who struggles with trusting myself, I carried some guilt with me this entire process. I sincerely felt bad about not being able to close the case sooner. And Satan was quick to step in with his voice of accusation: *Maybe if you only worked out more or did the exercises more frequently, you would be better. Maybe you're just imagining all this.*

Every three or four months, I would suggest to my chiropractor, "What do you think about wrapping this up?" and she would examine me and tell me I wasn't ready. Finally, a year and a half after the accident, my chiropractor recommended I see an orthopedic surgeon so that I could get a MRI, leading to a diagnosis of a partial tear in my right rotator cuff. Determined not to have surgery (as a writer, I wasn't sure if I wanted to take the risk of something happening to my right arm), I doubled up my exercise to see if that would help.

About that time, the insurance company gave me the first clue that they were thinking about not paying. By now all my treatment added up to many thousands of dollars. They sent an insurance investigator to interview me. He was sympathetic, telling me my case had been grossly mishandled by the insurance company. But even though he made it clear that the insurance company was looking for a way out, I was still in denial. *Surely, they'll come through and at least pay for my medical treatment.*

A week before the time expired when I could sue, the insurance company contacted me and offered me ten percent of the amount of my bills, along with just a small allowance for pain and suffering. The adjuster accused me of getting "over treated" and said that only six weeks of my treatment were valid. It didn't matter that three different representatives of their company had given me verbal approval at three different points in my treatment. Feeling somewhat like I had been kicked in the stomach, and brushing away tears, I told her I would have to think about it.

As I hung up with her, the phone was ringing. It was a downtown Chicago lawyer who had been given my phone number by a lawyer in our church. The timing was unbelievable. He encouraged me and then invited me to his office. He assured me that we wouldn't file a suit unless we were practically assured of a settlement. I reluctantly agreed. The thought of going to court was extremely intimidating. My deeply sensitive nature meant that I had always been quick to pick up on what I interpreted as accusation. I sometimes experienced what I'll call "shame attacks." When someone showed displeasure toward me, it was if I had gone back to my high school days. Shame would wash over me, leaving me with an uneasiness in my chest.

Along with that, I've always had a highly sensitive conscience that could be manipulated by someone who was seeking to instill guilt. Filing a lawsuit for me would have to be something I was convinced that God wanted me to do, or I would never consider it.

I went downtown to at least talk with the lawyer. After meeting with me and reviewing the case, the lawyer announced we were going to sue. The last words out of his mouth were, "We won't lose." I took a deep breath and agreed to proceed. *Hadn't God led him into my life?*

I walked out with my head held a little higher. *God is taking care of me.* Wanting to make sure that I wasn't just entrusting my cause to men, I decided to fast from my three favorite television shows until my lawsuit was resolved.

The process ended up being painfully slow. It was almost a year after we filed suit before they took my deposition. The opposing attorney went straight after me, accusing my motives and testing my memory of every detail. Three months later, my attorney reviewed the case and decided that we no longer had one. In fact, he had moved from his earlier confidence to insisting that a jury would "chew me up and spit me out," adding that "they will be irritated with you for using their time to try this." When the insurance company gave me a settlement offer, he urged me to take it, saying that I was lucky to get it.

I got off the phone with the lawyer in tears. It seemed that my advocate had suddenly turned into my accuser. But there were bigger questions that surfaced: *Why did it seem that God was directing me to file a lawsuit if I was going to come out worse than I had started? What about the year and a half of fasting and prayer? Where was God as my advocate? Would there be any vindication for the years of suffering?*

When I received the settlement papers (leaving me only slightly better off than their first offer), my first response was to stuff them away in anger. To accept their settlement, I had to waive their liability for the rest of my life. *Where is my justice? Is signing these papers like accepting their accusations that my treatment wasn't legitimate?* It all seemed so unjust. But I also sensed that God was speaking to something deeper in my heart. *Does it really matter, Robin, what anyone else in the world thinks of you? Is my approval enough? Will you trust me, even if the results appear totally unfair? Will you surrender your vulnerabilities to me?*

Coming to a place of surrender was far from easy. I desperately wanted to justify myself and every move I had made during the course of treatment. I put the lawyer through a long, painful conversation, talking him back through all the ins and outs of my case. *Surely if he understands, he will rally to my side.* But the truth was, none of that really mattered. By allowing the lawyer to determine how I felt about myself, I was giving him a power in my life that God never intended for him to have. I had a choice: Was I going to let my lawyer's, the opposing lawyer's and the other insurance company's judgments (totally governed by dollars) determine my self-esteem? Or was I going to put my trust in God and his perfect love for me?

As I signed the papers, I realized the statement I was making to the insurance company mattered very little. What really mattered was the statement I was making to God: *I surrender to you, Lord, how others judge me. And I trust you to be my advocate no matter what the world thinks of me.*

## Trusting God As Our Advocate

At the beginning of this chapter, we talked about God's many expressions of endearment for us as his daughters. So the question is, considering God's tremendous affection and protectiveness toward us, why does he allow others to judge us? As a parent, I feel confident that there must be a level on which it angers and pains God to see us treated unfairly. Yet, throughout the Bible, we see people who God loved, people he considered *his* people, being judged, misunderstood and even persecuted by those around them. But it's their response to that judgment that I find most helpful.

David was given one of the most touching terms of endearment of anyone in the Bible when God singled him out as "a man after my own heart."[4] Yet in Psalm 69, David paints a vivid picture of the scorn he received from others:

> Those who hate me without reason
>     outnumber the hairs of my head. (v4)
> For I endure scorn for your sake,
>     and shame covers my face. (v7)
> Those who sit at the gate mock me,
>     and I am the song of the drunkards. (v12)

Yet, David's response isn't one of justifying himself—he doesn't feel compelled to give a long defense. It's not a response of insecurity, such as, "I've got to take how others feel about me into my own hands." He doesn't even look for another person to compare himself to so that he can feel better. Instead his response is one of surrender:

> But I pray to you, O Lord,
>     in the time of your favor;
> in your great love, O God,
>     answer me with your sure salvation. (v13)
> Answer me, O Lord, out of the goodness of your love;
>     in your great mercy turn to me. (v16)

Somehow David learned to let the ill treatment he received from others only magnify the love and approval he received from God. In fact, he looked at a time of persecution as a time of God's favor! How could that be? David had learned an important key to security: he knew that his favor from God had absolutely nothing to do with how others regarded him. In fact, shortly afterwards, David penned one of the most beautiful statements of security in the Bible:

> Yet I am always with you;
>     you hold me by my right hand.
> You guide me with your counsel,

4. Acts 13:21–23

and afterward you will take me into glory.
Whom have I in heaven but you?
    And earth has nothing I desire besides you.
My flesh and my heart may fail,
    but God is the strength of my heart
    and my portion forever. (Psalm 73:23–26)

Any way you look at it, trusting in a human being to be the strength of your heart is futile. I can know this by taking a look inward. The truth is that my flesh and my heart can and will fail. (In fact, having any *one* day where I'm spiritually and emotionally centered; *and* I get everything done that is needed; *and* I meet the needs of my family and friends is a cause for celebration!) When it comes down to it, I am just dust. I love God and try to be a stable, faithful person, but if you traded in your security in God for security in me, you would be making a massive mistake.

Likewise, if you tried to gauge how you should feel about yourself from what I think of you, you'd be at the mercy of my ups and downs (which can be substantial!). If I can't be my own "portion forever," just what makes me think that others can? David says it so beautifully, "My flesh and my heart may fail, but God is the strength of my heart and my portion forever."

Even more importantly, David says that he has only one goal: "And earth has nothing I desire besides you." I think I need to write that scripture on my mirror for when I'm tempted to check and recheck my appearance often. I need to put it on the bulletin board right beside my computer. I need to write it on my scale and secure it on the dashboard of my car for when I'm driving to meetings.

One thing is for sure: as God's treasured daughters, we need to get tougher about not letting what other people think of us influence how we feel about ourselves or our relationship with God. To help us, God wants us to know he has the judgment arena perfectly covered by his perfect nature (see the following chart).

| Attribute | Definition | Our Response |
|---|---|---|
| Advocate | One who pleads another's cause, who helps another by defending or comforting him. | Go to Jesus with our sins and shortcomings. (1 John 2:1) |
| Defender | To make or keep safe from danger, attack or harm; to ward off. | Trust God to take up our case. (Proverbs 23:10–11) |
| Counselor | Someone who gives advice about problems, a lawyer who pleads cases in court. | Make the statutes of God's word our counselors. (Psalm 119:24) |
| Vindicator | One who clears of accusation, blame, suspicion or doubt with supporting arguments or proof. | Trust in the Lord without wavering. (Psalm 26:1) |
| Justifier | To free from the guilt or penalty attached to sin. To demonstrate or prove to be just, right or valid. | Refuse to justify ourselves in the eyes of men. (Luke 16:14–15) Thank God for his perfect justification. (Romans 8:30) |

In God, we have an advocate, defender, counselor, vindicator, justifier and friend. And the truth is that he doesn't gauge his feelings about us by our day-to-day performance, beauty, strengths and weaknesses, or even our spirituality. As his daughter, you can be sure that God is standing up for you *because you are his daughter*. And if we have God on our side, what else could possibly matter?

> If God is for us, who can be against us? He who did not spare his own Son, but gave him up for us all—how will he not also, along with him, graciously give us all things? Who will bring any charge against those whom God has chosen? It is God who justifies. Who is he that condemns? Christ Jesus, who died—more than that, who was raised to life—is at the right hand of God and is also interceding for us. (Romans 8:31–34)

# IN HER OWN WORDS

*Lenora's Story*

Ever since I was a little girl, I dreamed of getting married and having a family. I thought that was one of the main goals in life and would be a kind of anchor in my life. Sometimes I would wonder, *What if my marriage has troubles? What if things don't go as happily as I have dreamed they would?*

I didn't even give those worries a thought later in life when I was actually getting married. Why did I have to worry? After all, I was marrying a good Christian man, a minister even! He was handsome, charming and could quote scripture for every need and situation. I seemed to be marrying the man of my dreams. I could sense that my family didn't feel the same way about my future husband. I just brushed their hesitation off as their not understanding him like I did. Maybe they didn't comprehend his spirituality and his devotion to the ministry. I thought that they would come to accept him more as time went on. I didn't realize that they could see and sense things that I didn't want to see or sense.

Very soon after we were married, I began to feel uneasy about some things in our marriage. My husband would leave for long periods of time and return without any clear explanation of where he had been or what he had been doing. He would give vague answers about, "...doing the work of the ministry...studying the Bible with people...counseling people." I felt lonely and confused about why my new husband would leave after dinner and not come home until the early morning hours several times a week.

We had moved to a new city after we got married, and I did not feel that I could go to anyone to talk these things over. I didn't want to make my new husband look bad or give them the wrong impression about him.

My husband became very upset with me when I did ask him why he had to be out so late so often. He accused me of not being supportive and not trusting him when he was out working so hard in his ministry.

The few times that I did talk to someone else, he became very upset with me. He acted like he was a "victim" of an untrusting and unspiritual wife. I felt guilty and even "sinful" for doubting him and causing others to question his work. I also did not want us to look bad to other people.

My husband and I moved to help in different congregations during our marriage and added three children along the way. In every place we lived, his "work habits" continued. He left the ministry after several years to sell insurance. Even then, he would leave after dinner, or after the children went to bed in the evening, and not come home until well after midnight several nights a week. He still claimed that he was working while he was gone and didn't appreciate me questioning his hours.

My husband also handled all of our finances. I rarely knew anything in any detail about our finances because my husband said it was too "stressful" for me. He would take care of all of it.

During all this time, I felt more isolated and alienated from my friends and family. I felt like a single mom with my husband rarely around to spend time with us. Through all of this, I really tried to hide what was going on and make it look like we had a great marriage and a "together" family. Part of this act was because of my fear of my husband's anger, and part of it was due to feeling guilty for not trusting him. I also didn't want anyone to think less of me and my family. My pride and fear of my husband and of having my life fall apart kept me from asking for help.

I began to realize that my focus was more on how I appeared to other people than on loving God and truly taking care of my family in a healthy way. I did begin asking for help from others in our church congregation. It was difficult for others to comprehend what was going on in our marriage at first because I had done such a good job of making things look like they were going well. I had cared so much about what other people thought of me that it actually worked against me when I really needed help!

When we received counseling from couples in our church, my husband would act like he didn't understand why I was so upset, and he would promise to improve his work hours and be a better husband. He could be so charming and humble during these counseling times, and I would become very upset. Many of these counseling sessions ended up focused on me and how difficult to please I must be. After all, everyone could "see" how eager he was to be a good husband and how humble he was, and I was the angry one!

Many of the people I turned to for help told me to stop complaining and be a good wife—to act like a Christian wife should. Many of them also stopped talking to me altogether. They didn't want to hear of my fears of his possible infidelity and my claims that he was a completely different person behind closed doors.

I turned to God in a much deeper way than I ever had before. God knew my heart, and he knew what was going on. I had tried for several years to get people to listen and to help me. I had gotten more and more upset and panicked for help. I realized that I needed to truly trust God and stop putting my hope in people. A calm actually came over me when I made the decision to put myself in God's hands and ask him to help me in his time. My marriage did not improve, but the peace in my life did.

Soon after this, I found out that I had contracted a sexually transmitted disease. I was shocked, angry and even more deeply hurt. I had been faithful to my husband! I had questioned his fidelity many times and been laughed at, or had been the recipient of his outrage for me even thinking of such a thing! This was, though, a very clear answer to my doubts about my husband.

At first, when I told other Christians, they were literally speechless. Then, they too felt outrage. When my husband was confronted with this, he reverted to his charm and to his being a victim of my misreading him and misunderstanding him. Surely I had gotten the disease from a "dirty toilet seat or a dirty towel," but not from him! (This is not possible with this disease.)

It seemed so obvious to me what was going on; why couldn't anyone else see it? I was shocked to be confronted by people doubting me and giving him the benefit of the doubt because of his smooth talking. Again, I had helped to make him look like such a good guy that it did make it hard to believe what was going on.

As the struggles in my marriage escalated, I turned to God in a deeper way. I came to realize in a more real way that it didn't matter what people thought of me or if I looked like I had it all together. That kind of thinking had led me down a miserable road of loneliness, isolation and a shallow relationship with God. It was tempting, at times, to feel bitter at my husband, at the people who doubted me when I needed help, at God himself. At those times, I read through the book of Psalms and focused on how God's love is faithful, protective and trustworthy.

A couple in the church, who had known us for years, approached me and asked to talk with me. They were concerned for me and could see that I wasn't happy and wanted to hear why. It took me a long time to trust them and open up. They listened to my story and believed me. That was so comforting that I couldn't stop crying. I had bottled up my feelings for so long to protect myself. God had sent me an advocate to take a stand for me!

They actually did research on the disease to prove to others that what my husband had claimed about how I got the disease was not possible. What they did for me opened the door for help for me and my family.

My husband was confronted with the facts, but chose not to take responsibility for the things he had done. For years I had stayed in the marriage for the sake of my children and wanting to be a complete family. I had hoped for things to change. I could see that change was not possible living with such great deceit on my husband's part. His deceit had destroyed the trust in our marriage and any kind of deep relationship. I had lost the real me a long time ago in trying to look like everything was fine. I had also believed that I somehow deserved everything that had happened to me for not being a "good wife."

It took a painfully long time to sort through more deceit on my husband's part, and more questions, some that were never answered. Thankfully, I completely recovered physically. After much prayer and soul searching, I decided to divorce my husband. I could not live with deceit and unfaithfulness with no intent to change.

I have been divorced and raising my children alone for a few years now. God has helped me to get stronger, more secure, more peaceful and more real. It is a huge challenge raising children alone, but I am not truly alone. I have been on my knees more than a few times asking for guidance, and I know that God has a direct hand in helping us and watching over us. I know that I never want to go through those things that happened in my marriage again, but at the same time, those things forced me to decide to turn to God in a deeper and more desperate way than I ever had before.

I still face being misunderstood at times—maybe even judged—for being a "divorced Christian." Some of my former friends have even become distant, maybe because they feel uneasy about divorce in the church; I don't know.

On the other hand, God has given us some great friends and a wonderful family who have been a help, comfort and support to us. I do know that my relationship with God is very close and real; I know he has been with me this entire time. His timing allowed me to go through situations that pushed me to decide who I put my trust in—people (who can make mistakes) or God (who is loving, faithful and protective of his children).

One of my favorite scriptures is Psalm 68:4–5:

Sing to God, sing praise to his name,
    extol him who rides on the clouds—
his name is the LORD—
    and rejoice before him.
A father to the fatherless, a defender of widows,
    is God in his holy dwelling.

# What Do Others Think of Me?
## The Advocate
### *Personal Study Guide & Life Application*

Here are a few suggestions on how to find security of heart by trusting God as your advocate.

**1) Entrust yourself to God's gracious judgment**—It's a liberating thought to know that we no longer have to fear other people's judgment. David, Paul and Jesus all entrusted themselves to the just judgment of God when others accused them falsely.

> *Read 1 Peter 2:21–23. Now take a journey back through time and write down the three most hurtful accusations you've received in your life. Get with another woman to talk about them and then pray together.*

**2) Look to the examples of those before us**—If you are feeling judged, take heart that you aren't alone. Most of the great heroes of the faith, mentioned in Hebrews 11, suffered false judgment at the hands of men.

> *Read Hebrews 11 and then choose several of these examples of faith. Make a list of all the ways they were judged by the world. How did they put their trust in God?*

**3) Thank God for his justification**—Sometimes the pain of what others think can cause us to forget the love of God, which is reflected in his goodness to us.

> *Read Romans 8:32–39. According to this scripture what does it mean to be justified by God? Make a list of all of the things that God has graciously given you directly out of hardship, persecution or being judged by others.*

**4) Give others grace**—What I've learned in codependence recovery is that when another person is insensitive, it overwhelmingly *isn't* because they set out to hurt me. Rather they were trying to comfort themselves (even if they chose a way that was inappropriate or hurtful).[5]

> *Think of a person who's been a thorn in your flesh. Lift that person before God in prayer, and ask God to comfort them in their battles.*

**5) Make it your goal to please God**—Deciding to be more transparent with your battles can cause a backlash. Some might even use your openness as a reason to judge you. Others will be deeply moved by your faith and openness.

> *Read Philippians 3:4–6 and 2 Corinthians 5:6–10. Where did Paul get his confidence before he was a Christian? How did his motivation change? For one day, or even one week, commit to only doing what pleases God. Journal about the results.*

**6) Learn to trust God's heart toward you**—Remember that God's expressions of endearment toward you represent far more than just words. They represent his commitment to you.

> *Review the terms of endearment that God gives us at the beginning of the chapter. Then choose a term of endearment that you would like to give to God (i.e., my bridegroom, my mighty warrior) and write a prayer using it to express your love.*

**7) Learn from others' battles**—In her story, Lenora talks about how painful it was to realize that other people weren't able to see what she saw in her relationship with her husband. Even after God sent an advocate who gave her the courage to finally stand up to her husband's deceit, she still dealt with others not

---

5. Mellody Pia with Andrea W. Miller and J. Keith Miller, *Facing Codependency—What It Is, Where It Comes From, How It Sabotages Our Lives* (San Francisco: Harper, 2003), 50.

understanding. Ultimately all of this has thrust her into a deeper and more fulfilling relationship with God.

> *Being misunderstood has the potential to make us tremendously insecure, but it can also teach us new levels of security. Journal about a situation in which you feel misunderstood. Find a passage in which Jesus was treated poorly because he was misunderstood. What can you learn from how Jesus dealt with those who didn't understand him?*

"When it comes to finding a man, I find myself wanting the end result without the process. It's like I'm searching for some kind of spiritual equation to help me get married. And, I can get so wrapped up in comparing myself to other women and what they've received, that I forget that God has wrapped his goodness around me."

—Still hoping for love and marriage

# WILL I BE ALONE?
*The Comforter*

> We neither suffer alone nor conquer alone nor go off into
> eternity alone. In Him we are inseparable: therefore, we are
> free to be fruitfully alone whenever we please, because wher-
> ever we go, whatever we suffer, whatever happens to us, we
> are united with those we love in Him because we are united
> with Him.
>
> —Thomas Merton, *No Man Is an Island*

> I can see now, God, that your decisions are right;
>     your testing has taught me what's true and right.
> Oh, love me—and right now!—hold me tight!
>     just the way you promised.
> Now comfort me so I can live, really live;
>     your revelation is the tune I dance to.
>
> Psalm 119:75–77, *The Message*

ONE OF THE DEEPEST FEARS OF A WOMAN'S HEART IS TO BE COM-
pletely forsaken—to be abandoned or left utterly alone. Because
our very nature moves us toward relationship, the thought of
being abandoned by those we love can easily fill our hearts with
fear. But if God is on our side, are we ever really alone?

To answer this question, let's think back to all the parts of
God's nature we've already explored. Through God's goodness,
he promises to use every single detail of our lives for our good.
As our Rock, he promises to be the one solid place we can stand,
unafraid of the storms of life. As our Anchor, God promises that
we can rely upon his eternal, unchanging nature, knowing that

his Yes means Yes—forever. As our Guide, God extends his mighty hand of love, grasping us by the hand and helping us navigate the perplexing parts of our journey. As our Guard, he stands protectively beside us, watching over our comings and our goings, while making sure that life never gives us more than we can bear. As our Advocate, he stands up for us against an accusing world (and the great accuser himself!).

Beyond this God gives us many illustrations to help us understand that we are never really alone. Would a mother leave her newborn all alone? God assures us that a mother could more easily forget the baby nursing at her breast than he could forget us. In fact, he says that our names are engraved on the palms of his hands (Isaiah 49:15–16). Would a good shepherd forget his sheep? As our good shepherd, Jesus knows each of us by name, goes ahead of us to make sure the way is safe, and protects us from spiritual wolves that would destroy our faith and steal our joy (John 10:7–10).

As his children, when we come into the darker moments of our lives, God promises to be with us: "I will turn the darkness into light before them and make the rough places smooth" (Isaiah 42:16). When we go through the fire of testing or a literal flood of mishaps, God reassures us that "when you pass through the waters, I will be with you…. When you walk through the fire, you will not be burned; the flames will not set you ablaze" (Isaiah 43:2).

Whenever we are lost, injured by the wayside, or struggling to find our bearings, God looks for a way to find us. In fact, many of the parables Jesus told have to do with God's concern for the one who wanders away and is all alone—a shepherd leaving the ninety-nine sheep to find the one who is lost; a woman sweeping her whole house to find a single gold coin; and a heartsick father, watching over the plains for his prodigal son to return.

In the book of Psalms, David repeatedly asked God not to

forsake him, but then always came to the conclusion that "the LORD loves the just and will not forsake his faithful ones. They will be protected forever..." (Psalm 37:28).

Does God ever leave or desert us? What if you've trusted God for a mate and have ended up single long-term or if you are still hurting from the breakup of a marriage or the death of a spouse? Does God understand the depth of your loneliness? Or what if you make the mistake of grasping after a man and, as a result, have done things you are now deeply ashamed and repentant of? Is God still nearby? And why is being alone an arena that can be so loaded with temptation? Let's go back to Eve for some clarity.

## Back to the Garden

> When the woman saw that the fruit of the tree was good for food and pleasing to the eye, and also desirable for gaining wisdom, she took some and ate it. She also gave some to her husband, *who was with her,* and he ate it. (Genesis 3:6, emphasis added)

When we examine everything that happened in the garden, it all boils down to one single, sinister motivation of Satan. The evil one wanted to separate God from his precious daughter, Eve. Of course, Satan knew that getting God to leave Eve was impossible. God was obviously crazy about her, smitten by everything about her from her tender heart to her infectious joy. Every day, he went down in the garden to walk with her and hear about the longings of her heart. He loved his daughter deeply, and seemed determined to protect her. Satan had only one hope—to lure Eve away from God. So he hatched a devious plan to make that happen. And the intent of his evil plan was that if it worked, Adam would follow right behind her.

Lured by the promise of beauty and wisdom, Eve bit. But Satan was looking to provide much more than a delicious taste experience. Satan was offering Eve the first-ever romance—a romantic vision of life after the forbidden fruit. One of the definitions of romance is "a mysterious or fascinating quality or appeal, as of something adventurous, heroic, or strangely beautiful."[1] Listening to Satan talk, Eve felt an unfamiliar pull in her heart of a fantasy life, where both she and Adam would know everything and have absolutely no limitations on their future together. *If I don't take this chance, I might miss out on something really beautiful. Will I ever have this opportunity again?*

Immediately after Eve bit, no doubt delighted with the captivating taste and texture, she offered it to Adam. In fact, she had been given so much by Adam (his rib for starters), perhaps she was hoping to give something back. Much later, in the New Testament, God chose through Paul to add an important detail:

> And Adam was not the one deceived; it was the woman who
> was deceived and became a sinner. (1 Timothy 2:14)

Eve bit into the fruit because she had been deceived by the devil. But Adam knew what they were doing was an act of disobedience. Why didn't Adam put on the brakes? Perhaps he was enticed by the sensuality of the moment. *Eve looks so beautiful and eager to do this. Her eyes are sparkling with anticipation.* Perhaps, he feared stepping out and leading. *What will Eve think of me if I tell her the truth?* Regardless, he not only disobeyed God, but he sinned against his conscience and against Eve. Adam had the opportunity to take a stand and protect Eve. But sadly, he didn't.

This adds another important clue as to how we can defend ourselves from Satan's craftiness. Satan attacked Eve in her blind spot and then sought to bring Adam along for the ride, through his own desires. What are our blind spots? Although each of us has our own unique struggles, I believe as women we tend to have a blind spot when it comes to romance, just as men tend to have a blind spot when it comes to sex.

---

1. www.dictionary.com

|  | Blind Spot | Satan's Temptation |
|---|---|---|
| Woman | Romance | If you are seductive and sexy, you'll be able to find romance. It's better to have romance along with sex, even if you are stepping outside of your convictions, than no romance at all. |
| Man | Sexuality | You need the thrill of sexuality to feel alive, powerful and competent as a man. Getting this thrill is more pressing than holding to your convictions. |

Of course, Satan wants to take us much further than the initial romantic vision that he holds out. Satan wants us to believe that the only way we can attract a man is through our sexuality—the way we dress, how much of our body we reveal, and how we tease with our words. Even as Christian women, we can be influenced by the constant voice of the media saying, *"This is the way to attract and keep a man. You've got to figure out how to be sexier."* Then Satan whispers in one ear, *"It's not your fault if you fall sexually. It's all the man's fault."* And then after we fall, he shames us, *"Really it is all your fault! You better run and hide from God and others."* Is it any wonder that it's so difficult to open up about our battles with purity?

Likewise, a man's desire for sex can turn into a blind spot. In our desire to be with him, we will sometimes follow him into his sexual temptations, even compromising long-held convictions about purity to try to hold on to him. How does this play out? We may end up participating in our husband's sin with pornography, rationalizing that our marriage somehow legitimizes it. We may even find ourselves in places where we were sure we would never go, like into the darkness of adult bookstores or even into the demoralizing world of multiple-partner sex. Why would we compromise God's word to go into these arenas? Maybe it's because we're afraid of ending up alone.

After all was said and done, Adam and Eve ended up with quite a stomachache. But the pit in their stomach wasn't indigestion. It was loneliness in its purest form. After disobeying God, they learned the loneliness of moving in separate directions—man earning his keep by the sweat of his brow and woman devoting herself to the home front. They gave up their beloved home, the Garden of Eden, and made their way in a more unforgiving environment. Eve learned the loneliness of spending hours on end taking care of small children, while Adam worked the fields. And ultimately her heart broke when Cain killed Abel out of jealousy over an offering to God.

But was God still there for Eve? Did he still love her after she left the garden? Did he comfort her in her new life? Absolutely! When Eve gave birth to Cain, she exclaimed, "With the help of the Lord, I have brought forth a man" (Genesis 4:1). The fact that Cain and Abel both gave offerings to God shows that Eve trained them to worship from the time they were small. God even got personally involved trying to help her boys overcome sin (Genesis 4:6–16). And after Cain's sin and discipline, administered by God himself, one of his main concerns was that he would be hidden from the presence of the Lord (Genesis 4:14), showing that he had learned a thing or two from his mother's experiences in the garden.

Here's what we've got to remember: Satan's ultimate goal wasn't just getting Eve to disobey. What he wanted was to make a separation from God that Eve saw as insurmountable. By continuing to draw near to God even after her sin, Eve frustrated Satan's biggest goal. But from Eve, we can also learn to protect ourselves from what can be the deadliest of the false securities that Satan offers to women—romance.

## The False Security of Romance

I'm convinced that there is a level on which God is a big-time romantic. Just read the Song of Songs if you have any doubt. Certainly, it was God who created all the nuances of romance and the unique dance of attraction, love, marriage and sexuality. In fact, Song of Songs is enough to make the most experienced lover blush in its graphic descriptions of sexual love. But as much as God himself created the magic of a kiss, the thrill of one hand clasped by another, and the mystery of sexual union, he didn't create it to become our security or our god. In a sense, romantic love is supposed to be a faint shadow, a small taste of the heavenly union we'll experience one day when our souls are in perfect harmony with their Creator.

But our desire for romance can also easily lead us into a world where we vicariously live out our dreams, either through our own fantasies or through books, television and movies. It can also bequeath to us a deep loneliness, a feeling that the reason our lives aren't turning out the way we hoped is because we are defective. In fact a romance novel is a book that deals with idealized events remote from everyday life. Perhaps this explains why married women are the primary readers of romantic literature. Having a husband certainly doesn't stop women from dreaming of a life full of idealized events! It is also easy to see why romantic fantasy is an area that Satan sees tremendous potential for. In fact, one of the definitions of romance is "to tell romantic or exaggerated lies."[2] I'm guessing that Satan, the father of lies, may even like to think of himself as a misunderstood romantic!

What is the difference between Satan's false security of romance and God's pure version of intimacy? (See the following chart.)

| Satan's Take on Romance | God's Gift of Intimacy |
| --- | --- |
| Romance depends on everything turning out just the way we imagine. | Intimacy thrives in real life problems, heartaches and trials. |
| Romance insists that the only way to true happiness is having our unfulfilled desires met. | Intimacy enables us to connect on a heart level with God and others, whether or not our desires are fulfilled. |
| Romance depends on an almost magical turn of events, whether we've been "kissed by the stars." Astrology can help you find it. | Intimacy springs out of friendship, openness, vulnerability and courage. It blossoms in prayer and is accessible to every person. |

2. www.dictionary.com.

| | |
|---|---|
| The highest expression of romance is a passion that sweeps us off our feet and leaves us defenseless. | Intimacy cares about the best good of the other and is controlled by a conscious decision to love sacrificially. |
| Romance demands that we end up with the object of our desire—living happily ever after. | Intimacy is willing to let go if the relationship doesn't honor God. |
| Romance implies a rescue of epic proportions. It's a security that gallops in on a white horse. | Intimacy realizes its own inadequacies and embraces them. |
| Romance whispers that its gifts are so great, that giving ourselves sexually is a small price to pay to receive those gifts. | Intimacy treasures and honors the sexual relationship by putting sexuality in its God-ordained place in a relationship. |
| Romance insists that the worst thing that can happen is to be alone. | Intimacy with God offers a security that thrives even in lonely times. |

Godly romance is a pure gift from God that acts as a stepping-stone to deeper levels of intimacy. And pretty much every married woman I know would like a little more romance from time to time. But, here's where we each have to guard our hearts carefully. The romantic, idealized world we see portrayed on television, in movies, through love songs, and even in the pages of Christian romance books may not only make us smile and shed a tear—it may make us susceptible to disappointment and insecurity. How does Satan seek to lead our hearts astray through his false security of romance? He looks for ways to

- **Give us false expectations**—Satan wants us think that *his* depiction of life and romance is the standard, setting us up for disappointment. He wants us to romanticize others' victories and downplay their disappointments, so that we'll compare our experience to theirs and feel that we are being shortchanged.

- **Addict us to romance**—Satan wants to convince us that if we hold on tighter and grasp after romance harder, somehow we'll find it. He offers romance as our drug of choice, whispering that it is the only thing that will comfort us and make us happy.

- **Make us afraid of being alone**—Satan knows that God can work powerfully through lonely times. He wants to convince us that loneliness is a rejection from God himself, and that it's our fault if we feel all alone.

- **Take down our guard in our lonely times**—Satan knows that we are most vulnerable when we are lonely, and he would like nothing better than to lead us away from others where he can attack our faith. His tagline? *Nobody will understand.*

- **Get us to give up on love and intimacy altogether**—Satan loves extremes. He'll gladly push us to the opposite extreme of giving up on intimacy all together. We avoid having any relationships with men at all, pretending that we don't care or that we're just "more spiritual than that."

Ultimately, Satan's goal is to rob you of the beautiful intimacy that God offers you, an intimacy that is grounded in real life and real struggles, and that thrives when relationships take second place in your priorities behind your relationship with God. But more than that, just as he did with Eve, Satan wants to drive a wedge between you and God—causing you to miss the strength and security of having God's strong arms of comfort around you.

Most of all, I've got to believe that Satan wants you and me to spend hours every week being tutored in romance by him (through movies, books, magazines and videos) and spend relatively little time in God's word in comparison. Why? He knows that if we constantly whet our appetite for romance, we won't have the strength or perspective to make spiritual decisions in the heat of the moment.

Because most of us learn best from example, let's take a moment here to consider the examples of two women in the Bible: Ruth and Bathsheba.

### The Story of Ruth

We know little about Ruth's childhood, except that she grew up in a pagan culture devoted to the worship of idols. But although we don't know much about her upbringing, we do know that Ruth's heart was seeking something more. So when a struggling Jewish family—Elimelech, his wife, Naomi, and their two sons—made the decision to flee Bethlehem in a time of famine, God's providence brought them close to Ruth, who ended up marrying one of the sons. Ruth might have sensed Naomi's immediate apprehension—God had made it clear that the Jews were not to marry outside of their faith. Yet, during the first ten years of Ruth's marriage, Ruth and Naomi built a great relationship—one in which Naomi told Ruth much about her God.

When tragedy struck, causing all of the men of the household to die in a year's time, the three women found themselves alone in the world—Naomi, Ruth and Orpah, who was married to Naomi's other son. Naomi quickly determined that she needed to return to Bethlehem and receive the support of her people. She encouraged Ruth and Orpah to stay and find husbands from their own people, knowing that their chances of remarriage in Jewish circles were not the best.

As a young woman, these words must have pulled at Ruth's heart: *Will I spend the rest of my life alone?* But she felt a deeper calling. She was intensely devoted to her mother-in-law and was determined not to leave her or to give up her newfound faith in God, even if it meant never remarrying:

> "Don't urge me to leave you or to turn back from you. Where you go I will go, and where you stay I will stay. Your people will be my people and your God my God. Where you die, I will die, and there I will be buried. May the Lord deal with me, be it ever so severely, if anything but death separates you and me." (Ruth 1:16–17)

Although Orpah turned back to find a husband from her own people, Ruth made the long hard journey to Bethlehem with her mother-in-law. When she and Naomi arrived, they had no means of support. Jewish law required landowners to let the poor glean behind the harvesters in their fields. To provide food for them to eat, Ruth humbly volunteered to go out into the fields to glean with the poor. God honored her conviction by guiding her into the fields of Boaz—a faithful follower of God who had never married. He was immediately drawn to her godly character—having been told by others of her sacrificial love for her mother-in-law and her faith in God.

When Boaz showed kindness to Ruth, having her eat with the harvesters and instructing others to leave plenty of grain for her, Naomi began to think he just might be "interested." Since Ruth had been married to a Jew, she had the right for a close relative to become a kinsman-redeemer. This close relative would carry on the legacy of the man who died by purchasing his field and taking his wife, therefore allowing his lineage to continue.

It turned out, in God's perfect providence, that Boaz was a kinsman who could fulfill that role. Following Naomi's advice, Ruth offered the opportunity to Boaz, who was eager to fulfill it. By surrendering her destiny to God, Ruth was rewarded with love, marriage and even a quick pregnancy resulting in a son. God not only comforted Ruth, but also used Ruth to comfort Naomi in her loss of a husband and two sons. Because of Ruth's faithfulness, God honored her with a place in the lineage of Christ.[3]

## The Story of Bathsheba

Unlike Ruth, Bathsheba came from a God-fearing family. She was the daughter of Eliam, one of David's gallant officers (2 Samuel 11). In fact the name Eliam means "God is gracious." Undoubtedly, she was raised from the time she was a child to fear God. It is even conceivable that she might have nurtured a childhood crush on David. Her father probably told her amazing stories of God's conquests through David and his mighty men. He was certainly the dashing hero that women would be drawn to.

When she came of age, she married Uriah—an honorable

---

3. See Ruth 4:13–22. Ruth was the great grandmother of David and, therefore, in the direct genealogy of Christ.

man who feared God and who was a brave and devoted soldier. But although Bathsheba had been blessed by God to have a heritage of faith and a faithful husband, it is quite possible that her heart had an empty spot that dreamed of something more. While her husband was away at war, she was restless and lonely. Had she seen David out walking on his rooftop every evening? Regardless, she turned to her own beauty as a solution for her loneliness, deciding to bathe in the nude in the courtyard behind her home. Her thoughts could have been something like this: *I miss having a man around the house. What could it hurt to be seen and have my beauty appreciated?* And sure enough, when David saw her, he was captivated and sent for her to be brought to him.

Where was Bathsheba's walk with God when she was thrust into temptation's way? Why didn't she refuse to come to the king? And even if she didn't know his intentions, where was her commitment to the vow of marriage she had made to Uriah? She could have refused. Remember Joseph's reaction when he was approached by Potiphar's wife? He fled and as a result ended up being falsely accused and thrown into prison for years. As a result, God remembered him and raised him up to save an entire nation. Since the Jews handed down their history verbally, there's a decent chance Bathsheba knew of Joseph and his integrity.

Whatever her knowledge of Jewish history, as a Jew, we can be confident that Bathsheba knew that sleeping with David, while her husband Uriah was away at war, meant betraying God's marriage covenant. Sadly, Bathsheba engaged in adultery while her husband was risking his life in the service of the man who seduced her.[4]

When she became pregnant with David's child, Bathsheba followed David's path of deception, participating in his plan to bring her husband back from war and lure him into having sex with her so that she could convince him that the baby was his.

---

4. Thanks to Herbert Lockyer for his exposition of Bathsheba in *All the Women of the Bible*, (Grand Rapids: Zondervan Publishing House, 1997), 35.

Uriah, in his integrity, couldn't fathom sleeping with his wife while his fellow soldiers were fighting. Bathsheba sent word to David that Uriah wasn't cooperating. So when Uriah returned to the battlefield, David ordered him to be put at the front line of battle and then withdrawn from so that he would die. I find it hard to believe that Bathsheba didn't have some idea of what David was going to do. One thing's for sure—the further Bathsheba walked out onto the world's path, the more darkness entered her life.

After Uriah died, David brought Bathsheba to him and married her. But none of this had escaped the knowledge of God. Eventually, as punishment for David's and her sin, their son became sick and died, breaking her heart.

Ruth and Bathsheba were two different women with two different upbringings; yet, they both shared a common faith in God—Bathsheba's being handed down from her parents and Ruth's faith in the one true God coming much later in life. Although I hesitate to compare, I'm thinking that Ruth and Bathsheba might not mind (since we are instructed to use the Old Testament stories to help us in our faith) if we gain some clarity on their choices by considering them side-by-side.

| Bathsheba | Ruth |
| --- | --- |
| Was raised in a God-fearing family and blessed with a godly marriage. | Grew up in idolatry but found God through her marriage into a Jewish family. |
| Displayed her beauty by bathing nude in a courtyard. | Displayed her beauty through her loyalty, commitment to Naomi and faith in God. |
| Wanted to be linked with the most powerful man in the nation. | Was willing to walk among the poor, gathering grain behind the slave girls. |
| Let loneliness and her thirst for romance lead her into an affair. | Let loneliness and the loss of her husband turn her toward God. |
| After her fling, participated in covering up her sin to hide her vulnerable position. | Made herself vulnerable by asking Boaz to be her kinsman redeemer, covering his feet with her blanket. |

| Bathsheba | Ruth |
| --- | --- |
| Took satisfying her craving for romance into her own hands. | Took a longer, harder road, with no guarantee of remarrying. |
| Tried to force her life into the mold she desired and ended up losing her first son because of her sin. | Was willing to wait to do all things honorably—showed her interest in Boaz in a way that was discrete and godly. |
| Had to live with her part in her first husband's death. | Lived in good conscience with God and became part of the lineage of Christ. |
| Took for granted her legacy of faith by choosing romance over God's law. | Appreciated her new legacy of faith and was willing to sacrifice to hold on to it. |

Did God love Bathsheba just as much as he loved Ruth? Undoubtedly. But as much as God loved Bathsheba, he didn't shelter her from the natural consequences of her decisions. And like Bathsheba, when we let romantic fantasies take us away from our convictions, our commitment and our obedience to God, we start walking down a path that will only lead to despair.

But if we make a mistake like Bathsheba did, does that mean we can't receive God's comfort? Absolutely not! With time, God restored Bathsheba and comforted her as his beloved daughter. In fact, when she and David bore another son, they named him Solomon. The Bible tells us that God loved Solomon so much that he told David and Bathsheba, through the very same prophet who had brought the news that their son would die earlier, to also name him Jedidiah, which means "loved by the Lord."[5]

*What can we learn from Bathsheba?* From Bathsheba we can learn that in lonely times, or in times of change, we are especially vulnerable to spiritual attack. I learned this in a vivid way when Dave and I got out of the ministry. I started working as an executive assistant to a communications director in a firm. During that time, Dave was struggling to make a transition into a secular career and was doing everything from throwing papers to killing bugs. My income was carrying the family, which was hard on my husband. It was a lonely time for us.

5. 2 Samuel 12:25

About that time, a nice-looking man at work starting showing me a lot of attention. He would stop by my cubicle often and sit and talk with me. His presence was comforting and made me feel attractive and alive. I started looking forward to his visits and even guiltily thinking of him when I chose what to wear. I finally went to a friend, confessed everything I was feeling, repented and asked for her help.

Shortly afterwards, I was fired from that job in a very hurtful, pride-wounding way (which I now understand to be God's discipline and mercy). What was going on here? Just as he did with Bathsheba, Satan wanted to step in during a lonely time in my life and make me think that if I wasn't getting my needs met by my husband, I could find attention elsewhere.

*What can we learn from Ruth?* When Ruth hit up against loneliness, she turned to another woman, her mother-in-law, for comfort, companionship and intimacy. But most importantly, in Ruth's mind, her priorities were clear. God was her goal. He was her reward. He was her comfort. Eventually, what Boaz did for her was only a shadow of what God had done for her. God was the one who redeemed her from "the empty way of life handed down...from her forefathers" (1 Peter 1:18). Ruth was grounded in God's comfort.

When I think of Ruth, I think of several other faithful women I know who have made difficult decisions because of their commitment to keeping God first in their hearts and affections. I think of Nicole, who just made a courageous decision, along with her fiancé to break off their engagement. It wasn't because these two aren't deeply in love. But because of his deep-rooted struggles with purity and her struggles originating in her childhood with self-esteem, the intensity of their relationship wasn't helping them—in fact, it was hurting them spiritually. They were over-entwined emotionally and fought constantly. Although they had been absolutely pure in their relationship with each other, they both needed time to build their relationships with God individually before they could hope to build one together.

As you can imagine, this has been an excruciating decision for Nicole. *Now he's free to go find someone else. I'll be all alone.* She fears lonely Saturday nights (the night she could go on a date). She fears losing her best friend. She's had to deal with telling family and friends (who at one time were anticipating a wedding right around the time they broke off their engagement.) Yet because of her faith in God, she is putting her loneliness on God's altar and trusting him not to forsake her. She's pouring her heart into building intimacy with other women (which has never been her strong suit) and into building a security that comes from God alone. She's seeing a counselor and healing broken parts from her childhood. Like Ruth, she's learning to let God be her reward.

I also think of Mava, a woman I helped bring to Christ while she was studying in the U.S., who eventually moved back to her home country of Barbados. Last summer my sister and I went to visit her, some ten years after we had first met. Nearing forty, she has established quite a career in medical sales, traveling all over the country visiting physicians and hospitals.

Although she is still single with no boyfriend or husband in sight, Mava touched me deeply with her heart. When I visited church with her, it was obvious to me that Mava loves securely and with abandon. She went from person to person encouraging, serving and offering her heart. Has Mava had heartaches along the way? Certainly. Yet she has faith that God will reward her at just the right time with love and marriage. Somehow she has found the difficult balance of yearning for a husband without becoming bitter, while still building intimate relationships with those God puts in her life.

## Trusting God to Be Our Comforter

"Who among you fears the LORD and obeys the word of his servant? Let him who walks in the dark, who has no light, trust in the name of the LORD and rely on his God.... The LORD will surely comfort Zion and will look with compassion on all her ruins; he will make her deserts like Eden, her wastelands like the garden of the LORD." (Isaiah 50:10, 51:3)

Sometimes the Christian life involves times when we are literally in the dark about our future. For a single woman, part of the darkness may be when or how you'll find a mate. If you are divorced, the darkness may be finding your way through the heartache, learning to forgive and rekindling hope for the future. For another woman, it could be the devastating loss of a mate or child, and the deep loneliness that follows. In fact, there are many situations that can throw you into lonely times, including losing a friend or member of your extended family, moving to a new city, changes in your church, changes in your finances, marital unfaithfulness, a child or a spouse leaving God, illness or injury and more.

But God's plan is never for us to walk alone. In fact, he pleads with us to walk with him in times of darkness and rely on him when we have no light. And when we do, he promises that he will make our deserts like Eden and our wastelands like a garden of the Lord. In other words, some of the loneliest times in our lives can be the times of the deepest growth if we'll only turn to God as our source of comfort.

Like Abraham and Sarah, we can learn faith from the times when we're uprooted from a comfortable lifestyle to follow God's calling. Like Moses, we can trust that our exile in the desert is for a bigger purpose in our life, training us for something ahead that God sees in his perfect providence, but that we aren't aware of. Like Esther, we can believe that when our husband isn't as emotionally accessible as we desire, that God has a bigger plan for our lives. Like Paul, we can know that the rejection of others does not equal the rejection of God—in fact it's an opportunity to know Christ better by sharing in the fellowship of his sufferings. Like the saints of old, we can anticipate lonely times as strangers and aliens in this life, yet hope for glory as we wait for the blessed appearing of Jesus and our true rescue as children of God.

# IN HER OWN WORDS

*Patrice's Story*

I remember the day that I was baptized. I remember thinking to myself that I will always be married to my husband and we will have a super marriage; any issues that we had would dissipate. I recall thinking that now that I am a "real" Christian, God will protect me, and I will not have to worry about life again. I believed that my daughter would grow up to follow God, and she would avoid all the bad decisions, hurts and betrayals that I endured.

My dreams and visions were quickly squashed when a year later, I was ready to deal with the molestation that had come from the hands of my father. Coming to terms with what had happened, and then telling it to my sister first, enabled me to seek the counseling I needed, and eventually confront my father. In addition to individual and group counseling, I read a book for adult victims of childhood sexual abuse. One passage stood out to me:

> Do I believe that God is a loving Father who is committed to my deepest well-being, that He has the right to use everything that is me for whatever purposes He deems best, and that surrendering my will and life entirely to Him will bring me the deepest joy and fulfillment I know this side of heaven?[6]

I needed to believe that no matter what happens to me, God desperately loves me. I also believed that it was God who gave me a husband who loved me and supported me unconditionally.

Returning from Ohio where I confronted my father in the presence of my mother (they were divorced by then) and my sister, I felt as if a huge burden was lifted and I was

---

6. Dan B. Allender, *The Wounded Heart* (Colorado Springs: NavPress, 1995), 191.

finally free. Being back home in California, I noticed a tension with my husband. He told me that the pressures of what I had been through had taken a toll on him, and he needed a break from it all. Immediately, I felt guilty that I was molested. (Yes, I do now realize that I am an enabler and that I am codependent.) As a result of this conversation, I agreed to a separation. But, I also agreed to take my five-year old daughter and sleep on my friend's floor so my husband could have the house to himself. Of course, he agreed.

After five months of being separated and spending no time with my husband, and with friends convincing me that my husband was being unfaithful, I went to our home early Saturday morning and realized that he hadn't spent the night there. After I left many voicemails on his cell phone, he came home. I accused him of cheating, and he condescendingly retorted that I was crazy and neurotic. I was emotional and pushed him and told him to get out. He then threw me on the ground, grabbed a golf club and struck me on the leg, shouting some obscenities. After I had lain there for a few minutes, he noticed I was bleeding heavily, and he rushed me to the hospital. The amazing thing is that even while I was in the emergency room, all I cared about was not getting him in trouble.

My leg was broken, and I was in a full leg cast up to my hip for eight weeks. My husband refused to come home and help me, and he also thought it was best if our daughter stayed with me. He said it was because I had some issues; I believed him. Believe it or not, as a result of my husband breaking my leg, I was the one who attended "anger management" classes.

At this point, I really wanted to work on my relationship with God because I clearly wasn't having one. I was striving hard to obtain my security from my husband. I called the leader of the church, asking for someone to come over and help me spend time with God. I was told that I needed to work harder on my own relationship with God. In addition, it seemed as if many of my friends in the church had abandoned me. I believe it was because my situation was too emotional, and no one felt equipped to handle it. I was at the lowest point in my life. I was all alone. I couldn't even think that God was with me. However, I never blamed God; I just believed that I wasn't good enough for anyone's love—especially God's.

As the next few months went on, I finally discovered conclusively that my husband was having an affair. At this point, I immediately filed for divorce. I was out of control whenever I saw my husband; I would throw myself in front of his car; I made many harassing phone calls; nothing loving or godly ever came out of my mouth when I spoke to him. The situation was just ugly. I still went to work and took care of my daughter, but whenever I was around my husband, I reacted with pure evil.

At this time, I became involved immorally with a man from work. Ironically enough, there was a part of me that didn't want to close the door on God; I still believed intellectually that my security would only come from him, but I was weak.

Being a divorced woman certainly was appealing to many married men at work. I taught in a male juvenile prison in which the majority of the employees were men. I flirted ferociously but played it off with a hint of innocence. I definitely soaked up all of this attention. But when it was all said and done, I was still lonely.

As the months progressed, I just made a decision to love God as he commanded me to. I was getting stronger. I bought my first new house on my own. My daughter was doing well. I absolutely loved being her mom. We had a lot of fun together. It is strange because during my divorce, there were times when I believed that I wanted to die, but looking at her cute face reminded me of how selfish that would be. I truly wanted to do what was right.

Life was getting better. I was divorced; I formed a great relationship with another single mom; I was on the right track with God; I was away from my ex; and I was content. Then unexpectedly I was informed at work that I was under investigation for inappropriate sexual behavior with two inmates, for bringing in a controlled substance and for receiving personal items in the mail from inmates' families. My first reaction was not to worry because these false accusations couldn't be proven. Two months later, the investigators believed the word of two convicted juvenile felons over my word, and I was fired. I remember clearly the humiliation the day I was walked off the grounds by the sergeant.

I went home, called the union, and then got ready for a woman's night our church was sponsoring. Yes, I was distracted by the events of the day, but I had two friends coming with me. The turning point had come. I finally realized that it wasn't about me anymore. For the first time in my life, I completely and wholeheartedly gave my life over to God. I clung to the scripture, "If you do not stand firm in your faith, you will not stand at all" (Isaiah 7:9).

For the next three months until my hearing for appeal, I prayed, read my Bible, stayed faithful and realized that God is in control. My sister and friends were quite astounded at how strong I had become. I finally believed that God would work through me and that he so deeply loves me. I now understood that God is my security, not man.

When I went to my hearing, the judge reinstated me because he realized there was no evidence. I took a month off to have a time of serenity with my daughter.

I returned to work, holding my head high. Why did this happen? It didn't even matter. Life happens and I will have more trials and struggles, but God must be in the driver's seat, not me or any other person.

I wish that I could say that everything was great after that. The foundation of a prison is rumors. I was the talk of the institution. The wards had their own misguided versions of why I was gone for awhile, which led to many uncomfortable and demeaning situations for me. Yet, I pressed on every day.

In addition, to complicate my life even more, my former husband had broken up with his girlfriend. Since I was still totally codependent with him, I was there to pick up the pieces. We were hanging out. I liked that he needed me. (Let's call it what it is...in reality he *used* me.) I bailed him out of jail twice. When I knew he was lonely, my daughter and I would invite him over and cook dinner for him. I needed confirmation from him that I was worth something. Yet, even when we hung out, I felt very lonely inside. Being with him depressed me. Then, the light bulb finally came on in my head—I don't need him to feel worth. God has already confirmed my worth.

At one point, I was toying with the idea of moving out of state to be close to my family. I really needed to get away from my ex-husband. In addition, I wanted to be in an area in which I would thrive spiritually. After praying, thinking and talking about it, I mentioned it to my daughter who was then ten. On the way to church one Sunday, she bent her head as if to pray. I asked her what she was praying about. She said that if God wants us to move, that there will be a fight in my classroom this week. (At this point, I had started teaching in a public school setting rather than in the correction facility.)

Because I have little faith at times, I reminded her that there were few fights in the twelve years I taught there.

Well, early Monday, I was standing in front of my classroom prepared to deliver the lesson, when a planned attack on a student broke out. I came home and shared the fight with my daughter, and her first words were, "Now we have to move." I had forgotten all about her prayer.

I called my sister and told her what had happened, and I asked her if she thought God was answering my daughter's prayer. She practically shrieked, "What is wrong with you; what do you think?" By the end of the week, I put my house on the market and gave notice at my job.

We packed up and headed to our new city. I bought a house on the same street as my sister and got a teaching job at a middle school. It was a great year. I made friends; I was close to my sister, and my daughter was happy. I was doing great spiritually, and I was free. I like to tease my sister that she spoiled it for me because she introduced me to the nicest man I had ever met. He was a single dad of three children, having lost his wife to suicide. Several months later, I married this incredible man and went from being a mother of one to a mother of four children.

My life is good, but it comes with daily challenges. One thing that I have learned is that what God has given me is a pure testimony of his love for me. God has always been there comforting me, even when I didn't take the effort or time to acknowledge his presence. Now I know that whatever happens, I am never alone.

# WILL I BE ALONE? THE COMFORTER
*Personal Study Guide & Life Application*

How can you develop a security of heart that comes from knowing God as your comforter? Here are a few suggestions.

**1) Rely on God for comfort**—When you are feeling lonely, instead of looking to others right away, offer your feelings up to God. Surrender your circumstances to him in prayer and lean on his comfort as you wait patiently for his response.

> *Write down three times you've felt particularly lonely in the last couple of years. What kind of temptations did you face? Prepare for the next time you feel lonely by picking three scriptures that speak to lonely times. Write a prayer to God for lonely times and keep it in a special place.*

**2) Allow others to comfort you**—If you are distressed, God first tells us to look for his comfort. But he also uses our distress to prepare us to comfort another person.

> *Read 2 Corinthians 1:3–11. What would you say is your number one heartache? Set up a time to talk with another woman who has had a similar difficulty. Ask her what gives her the most comfort, and then share a scripture that comforts you.*

**3) Turn to God, not romance, in the deserts of your life**— When we hit lonely times, our first response is to end them by any means possible—"We will ride off on swift horses!" (Isaiah 30:16). God tells us instead to trust in repentance, rest, quietness and trust, believing that he longs to be gracious to us. In fact, he rises to show compassion.

> *Read Isaiah 30:15–21. On one side of your paper write different phrases that describe spiritual deserts. On the other*

*side write ways that God rises to show compassion. Get with*
*someone you know who needs encouragement and share.*

**4) Look to God's word for comfort**—One of the primary purposes of God's word is to give us comfort in our trials, in persecution, in times of struggle and when we face deep loneliness.

> *Read Psalm 119:81–88 and Psalm 130. Why is it so diffi-*
> *cult to wait for God's comfort? When you're feeling lonely,*
> *pray for God to comfort you through his word, and then open*
> *the Bible expecting his comfort.*

**5) Look for ways to develop intimacy instead of
romance**—Satan wants us to continually chase after romantic
dreams instead of learning to build intimacy with our husbands,
brothers, sisters and family members.

> *Read the whole book of Ruth. How did Ruth build emotion-*
> *al intimacy with Naomi? How did that intimacy benefit her*
> *and Naomi? What do you think Ruth would tell you about*
> *intimacy? What woman could you build a closer relationship*
> *with?*

**6) Say "No" to ungodly passions**—When it seems that true
romance is far away, it is easy to look to worldly passions such as
romance novels or ungodly relationships for temporary comfort.
By saying "No" to ungodly passions, you will demonstrate to
God that you trust in him as your true comforter.

> *Read Titus 2:11–13. What worldly and/or ungodly passion*
> *does God's grace teach you to say "No" to? Ask another*
> *women what she thinks it means to live a self-controlled,*
> *upright and godly life in the present age. Put "Just say No!"*
> *on your mirror and look for ways to live it out.*

**7) Learn from others' battles**—In her story, Patrice shares about all the ways she tried to get her security from her husband even after his affair, his physical abuse and their subsequent divorce. The turning point for her was when she realized that she didn't need to get worth from her ex-husband—"God has already confirmed my worth."

*In what places do you seek security other than God? Look up all the times the word "comfort" is used in the Psalms and make a list of all the ways God seeks to comfort you. How can you better accept God's comfort?*

# PART THREE

## *Walking Securely*

"Let the beloved of the L ORD rest secure in him,

for he shields him all day long,

and the one the L ORD loves

rests between his shoulders."

Deuteronomy 33:12

"Some of the things that I'm most afraid of are the things that haven't even happened yet. When something bad happens to me, I wonder why God let this happen to me and not to someone else. I forget that the point isn't what goes on here on earth. I'm finally beginning to understand that God has a greater purpose for what happens in my life."

— Learning to trust God's unfailing love

# SECURE LOVE
## *The One True Treasure*

"Though the mountains be shaken
　　and the hills be removed,
yet my unfailing love for you will not be shaken
　　nor my covenant of peace removed,"
　　says the LORD, who has compassion on you.

Isaiah 54:10

And the night shall be filled with music,
　　And the cares that infest the day
Shall fold their tents, like the Arabs,
　　And as silently steal away.

—Henry Wadsworth Longfellow

NEAR THE BEGINNING OF THE BOOK I ASKED YOU A SIMPLE QUES-
tion: *Are you ready to go to battle for a secure heart?* I'd venture to say
that you now have a lot better idea of what that battle will entail.
Does security mean so much to you that you are willing to pay
any price for it? Are you ready to defend yourself from Satan's
onslaughts on your self-esteem by letting the word of God define
who God really is and how he feels about you?

Are you ready, like Jesus, to come before God with loud cries
and tears in your struggle to understand your calling as his
daughter and to surrender to his will? The truth is that whether
or not you choose to engage the battle, Satan has declared war on
your heart. In human arguments if one person refuses to continue the discussion, the battle may die down. However, on spiritual fronts the exact opposite is true. Satan is a ruthless opportunist,

a spiritual terrorist, always looking for an undefended spot where he can attack.

His goal is to build seemingly impenetrable fortresses in our hearts. To deceive us, he disguises himself as an angel of light, the romancer of the ages, and in many other masks that seem to fulfill the desires of our feminine hearts. He is delighted if we shrink back, hide in shame or simply try to survive in our Christianity. When we do engage the battle, Satan suggests that we're strong enough or spiritual enough to do it on our own, without the help of other believers.

Thankfully, we've been perfectly equipped by God to fight this battle and demolish strongholds by his divine power (2 Corinthians 10:4). We've come to better understand the battlefield by unmasking and exposing Satan's false securities. Going back to the very beginning, we've looked to Eve to understand the glistening fruit that Satan wants to hand us in exchange for our security. We've felt our hearts tug as we've heard the stories of real women, like us, who want nothing more than to shed the insecurity that challenges them at every corner.

Most of all, we've looked at God himself and his determination to give us everything we need to be secure. Over and over again, we've seen God's vulnerability, accessibility and his personal and loving revelation of himself. We've seen his desire to walk with us reflected through every part of his divine nature, and we've felt his nudging to entrust to him the parts of our hearts that we usually keep tucked away in a safe place.

So where do we go from here? How do we apply what we've learned to our individual circumstances, including where we live, what we do and whom we live with? How do we overcome insecurity despite our upbringing, suffering we've faced or even physical, emotional, spiritual deficits we may bring to the table? And if you're a young woman, where can you find a model for secure womanhood? How do you figure out exactly what it is you're shooting for? Is there a universal starting point for our security of heart that expresses the deepest felt needs of our hearts?

The answer is simple, yet so revolutionary that we can pursue it for a lifetime and still have plenty of room to grow. Practically every story of the Bible somehow comes back to it. And certainly every one of our stories as women revolves around it. *The universal starting point for having a secure heart is God's perfect, unfailing love.*

## Unfailing Love

> But the eyes of the LORD are on those who fear him,
>     on those whose hope is in his unfailing love. (Psalm 33:18)

Throughout the Scriptures, people who were writing from different walks of life all found hope, peace and even comfort in God's unfailing love. Why is unfailing love so worthy of celebration? The word "unfailing" is rich with hope, expressing a love that is always able to supply more; inexhaustible; constant and unflagging; nonretractable; incapable of error; unceasing. What do these words mean to us?

- **God's love is inexhaustible.** We never wear out God's love or our welcome in his heart. God doesn't fall "out of love" with us, and we can be sure that we'll never come home at night to find that he's packed up and moved out.

- **God's love is constant.** His love doesn't come rushing in on our good days and then disappear on our bad days. God's love is not fickle. He doesn't get our hopes up and then crush us with his unpredictability.

- **God's love is incapable of error.** God doesn't choose us and then declare he made a mistake. He doesn't go to court to reverse our adoption as his daughters. When God called

you, you can be sure that there was no mistake—he wanted you, exactly as you are, with all your faults, weaknesses
and even with your sin.

- **God's love is nonretractable.** We don't have to live in
  fear that God will withdraw his favor and his heart from us
  as his daughters. We don't float in and out of his love,
  depending on our spiritual performance. His love never
  fails.

- **God's love is unceasing.** God's love is not just for this
  life, but rather transcends it. His love tethers us to him so
  that when we slip out of this life we can leave with confidence and hope, knowing that we're going straight to him.
  God's love conquers death.

I am convinced that God's unfailing love is the only path to
true security of heart. In fact, *God's unfailing love is the only thing
worth being the first love of your heart. It is the one true treasure.*

*Paul knew this.* In 1 Corinthians 13, Paul declared that every
noble act of the human heart, every gift of knowledge, every sacrifice, every bit of all faith are absolutely worthless unless they
are built on love. Paul was speaking from hard-won personal
experience. Paul thought he knew love before Jesus; he thought
he loved the law and that persecuting Christians was the only
way to preserve it. He had spent years perfecting the gifts of
knowledge, making the sacrifices that the law demanded and living out his faith through a faultless adherence to legalistic righteousness. All of this was motivated by what Paul wholeheartedly believed to be the foundation of his faith—love for God.

Yet Paul's motives were impure, polluted with selfish ambition, legalism and pride.[1] Jesus' words in his personal appearance
to Paul on the road to Damascus, "Paul, why are you persecuting
me?" and then his offer of unconditional forgiveness, converted
Paul's head knowledge of the law to a heart knowledge of the

---

1. Philippians 3:4–10

cross of Christ. Secure love enabled Paul to stop seeking to force others into his mold of following God and to start ministering to others from a tender heart of love.[2] Unfailing love taught Paul how to securely minister to others.

*Abraham knew this.* With his much-anticipated son by his side (born through Sarah, who at ninety was long past the age of child-bearing), Abraham thought he had fulfilled his most important purpose on this earth. As he watched Isaac grow, his heart must have swelled with joy and pride. Evidently, God saw insecure love creeping into Abraham's heart—it seems that Isaac had come to abide in a place in Abraham's heart reserved for God and God alone. Why else would God have asked the unthinkable—for Abraham to literally sacrifice Isaac? Abraham's love for his son, and his God, was perfected on a lonely mountain where Abraham stood ready to sacrifice Isaac on the very altar he had just helped his father build. God taught Abraham a precious lesson in priorities, giving Abraham his son and his first love back.[3]

Abraham, no doubt, walked off that mountain with a new humility and renewed convictions. Abraham learned secure love for his son through God's unfailing love.

*Mary Magdalene knew this.* Mary was tormented by a severe case of demonic possession. In fact, the Scriptures tell us that Jesus cast seven demons out of her.[4] Since seven represents completeness in the Bible, we can feel sure that Mary was completely possessed.[5] She understood the darkest depths of insecurity, the anguish of mental instability and the terror of the terrible visions that would dance through her head at the setting of the sun each night. No doubt, she was a marked and much-avoided woman, considering that the Pharisees tended to believe that demon possession was an outward sign of inward sin. Before Jesus, Mary heard the shriek of demons in her ears, but with

---

2. "Like a mother caring for her small children and as a father encouraging his small children." (1 Thessalonians 2:4–12)

3. See Genesis 17:16–18, 18:2–15, 21:1–6 and Hebrews 11:17–19.

4. Luke 8:2

5. Thanks to Herbert Lockyer for his exposition of Mary Magdelene in *All the Women of the Bible*, (Grand Rapids: Zondervan Publishing House, 1977), 100.

Jesus' gentle voice came complete healing and freedom.

Mary knew she could never really repay Jesus. Unfailing love delivered her from a life of horrific insecurity and mental instability, transforming her into a leading woman in the ministry of Jesus. Instead of using her wholeness to pursue romantic love, she found that only one pursuit mattered to her. She followed Jesus from place to place, supporting him out of her own means. Eventually, forsaking any fear for her own life, she pursued him all the way to the foot of the cross.[6]

As Mary watched her Lord's torment through false trials, mockery, beatings and a torturous death, she understood, perhaps more deeply than the other disciples, because of the suffering she had endured. Possibly as a testimony to her devotion and her courage, Jesus appeared to her first after his resurrection,[7] entrusting her with the honor of telling the other disciples. Mary Magdalene learned security of heart as a single woman from God's unfailing love.

*Stephen knew this.* If anyone felt called to serve God in this life, it was Stephen. Stephen was not only a man of faith and the Holy Spirit, but was also known for the miraculous signs and great wonders that God accomplished through him. His humble heart led to his selection as one of seven servants in the church who made sure that the widows weren't overlooked in the daily distribution of food.[8]

When member of a Jewish clique accused him of blasphemy, his face was "like that of an angel." With the crowd quickly turning against him, he saw the opportunity to serve as God's ambassador. With secure love, he told the story of God's movement through time and boldly called out the sins of pride, spiritual resistance and disobedience. As the crowd surged on him, pronounced his death sentence and ultimately stoned him, he looked up to heaven for his security; and although he was taken violently out of this life, he was brought gently into the next—

---

6. Luke 8:1–3; Matthew 27:56, 61; Mark 15:40–41; John 19:25
7. John 20:10–18
8. Acts 6:1–7

the Bible saying simply that Stephen fell asleep.[9]

Unfailing love gave Stephen the security of heart needed to forgive as Jesus had forgiven him; he used his last words to plead on behalf of the very ones who murdered him.

*Above all, Jesus knew it.* When asked by a teacher of the law what was the greatest commandment, he didn't hesitate. He replied, "Love the Lord your God with all your heart, and all your soul and with all your mind. This is the first and greatest commandment" (Matthew 22:34–38). Jesus demonstrated God's unfailing love through protecting the outcasts of society, forgiving those who had been deemed unforgivable, and setting his focus on his most important mission—demonstrating the undying love of God for each and every one of us. Unfailing love allowed Jesus to scorn the shame of the cross and reach out through the ages with open arms to all who would embrace him.

Jesus gave us the foundation to overcome insecurity. He taught us to be secure in the face of persecution and even death by his vulnerability ("My God, my God why have you forsaken me?"); forgiveness ("Father, forgive them for they know not what they do."); love ("Dear woman, here is you son." "John, here is your mother."); mercy ("I tell you today that you shall be with me in paradise."); and most of all through his security in death ("Father, into your hands I commit my spirit.").

With this in mind, I'd like to suggest that if we can learn to love securely, then we'll also have a better idea of how to live securely, and even how to die securely. In fact, according to Paul, the older women in the faith are supposed to teach the younger women how to love. But as I think we've learned to expect, Satan also has a plan for this all-important arena in the life of a woman. In fact, I'm convinced that the frontier of love is where Satan most wants to deceive us as women. How does he do this? He wants to tutor us in his own brand of "love"—an insecure love that tends to lead us away from God rather than toward him.

---

9. Acts 7:54–60

We've seen this insecure love in each of Satan's false securities: perfectionism, self-reliance, dependence, worldliness, self-protection, approval and romantic highs.

What are the practical applications of loving securely? From here we could talk about so many things. *We could talk about how insecure love gives our love strings.* How Satan whispers that we should use our own needs, or our understanding of the Bible, as the definition of how the one who loves us should respond. Insecure love encourages us to put pressure on others. And then we could look at God's love, and the way he lets us choose to give him our love as a gift.

*We could talk about the desperate love that drives us into unhealthy compromises of our convictions, all in the name of "love."* Then we could counter that with God's love—how he never compromises who he is in order to love us.

*We could look at performance-based love, which demands that others perform "correctly" in order to stay in our good favor.* And we could contrast that with the unconditional love of God that is based on who he is, instead of who we are.

But instead, I think we need to go to the ultimate test of the security of our love and perhaps the place that we most fear—death itself. In my experience, death is the great revealer and the greatest test of our security of heart. Earlier we talked about how my sister's death launched me on my journey to find a secure heart. In fact, I've found that death can transcend our fears and actually become an instructor in surrender, guiding us to new levels of security of heart:

> And so we know and rely on the love God have for us....
> There is no fear in love. But perfect love drives out fear,
> because fear has to do with punishment. The one who fears
> is not made perfect in love. (1 John 4:16, 18)

## Terri's Story

> His love is so much stronger than death that the death of a
> Christian is a kind of triumph. And although we rightly sor-
> row at the sensible separation from those we love (since we
> are also meant to love their human presence); yet we rejoice
> in their death because it proves to us the strength of our
> mutual love. The conviction in our hearts, the unshakeable
> hope of communion with our dead in Christ, is always
> telling us that they live and that He lives and that we live.[10]

I first met Terri some twenty years ago. She and her husband,
John, were interested in studying the Bible and getting to know
God better, and through God's intervention, we became a part of
their lives. Terri and John's marriage was in serious trouble due
to years of focus on the worldly priorities such as career and accu-
mulating possessions.

Through many long talks and Bible studies, Terri went from
being in denial about the severity of her sin to humbling herself
before God and finding his forgiveness and acceptance through
the cross. John, too, began to seek God's will, and through surrendering their lives to Christ, Terri and John found a new marriage and a new life.

Over time, their friendship became priceless to Dave and
me. Eventually, as happens with friendships, we parted as God
called them to a new ministry in a city across the country. A few
years later, we had the opportunity to go visit them, and we spent
a great afternoon and evening, rejoicing in God's grace and hearing about all the ways God had blessed their move and their two
children.

Several years later, Terri was diagnosed with ovarian cancer.
She so easily could have chosen an insecure response to her cancer. She could have questioned whether this was God's punishment for her affair. She could have wondered why God took her all
the way across the country, away from family and friends, and then
allowed her to get cancer. She could have become self-focused

10. Thomas Merton, *No Man Is an Island* ( New York: Barnes and Noble
Books, 2003), 87.

and withdrawn. But she didn't. Throughout Terri's ordeal with cancer, I talked with her at different intervals on the phone. I was always moved by her security of heart—her cheerfulness, faith and upbeat heart were always inspiring. In our conversations, more often than not, she ended up ministering to me. In fact, throughout her battle Terri continued using every opportunity in her walk as a Christian—her career and position in the community, and even her cancer—to reach out to those around her.

The last time I talked to her, Terri was upbeat and hopeful. Her cancer had been in remission, but had just recently come back. However, she shared her confidence in God and her trust that this was just another twist in her story. She was disappointed that the cancer had returned, but determined to fight. Honestly, she was more interested in hearing about how I was doing.

Just a few months later, I was called out of church with an important message. Terri had taken an unexpected turn for the worse, and in a few short days she had gone into a coma. When they proclaimed her brain dead, John had to make a difficult decision whether to have her life support system cut off. Although it was incredibly hard to let go, John knew what Terri would want him to do. After taking the time to talk at length with their son and daughter, in love, he let his wife go to Jesus.

Terri's death disturbed me deeply. She left behind two teenage children, and with teens myself, I found myself rehearsing their pain. It was if my own fear about my daughter getting married without me, my boys having children that I never would meet, was being fleshed out before me. I found myself quite depressed, feeling a deep loss in my heart.

The next day John called us to talk. After Dave talked with him, he motioned for me to take the phone. I knew I should be comforting John, but I was at a total loss for words. I started weeping on the phone. When I apologized to John for my tears, an amazing thing happened—John started comforting me.

"Robin," he said, "I want to thank you with all of my heart. You prepared Terri for this moment. Thanks to you, I know Terri is with God. I could ask for nothing more than that."

But as much as I wanted to hear what John was saying, there was still a stubborn fear in my heart that wouldn't let go. Terri's death was highlighting my own fear of death. The next day, as I sat thinking about Terri, I picked up my Bible. I knew there was something God wanted to say to me. My Bible flipped open to 1 Corinthians 15. Here is what I read:

> But if it is preached that Christ has been raised from the dead, how can some of you say that there is no resurrection of the dead? If there is no resurrection of the dead, then not even Christ has been raised. And if Christ has not been raised, our preaching is useless and so is your faith. (1 Corinthians 15:12–14)

I sat back and closed my eyes, and a clear picture came into my mind. I saw Terri hanging between heaven and earth by just a thread. I saw her look lovingly at John, but then turn her gaze longingly toward Jesus, wanting to be with him. When John reached over and snipped the cord that held her, she was filled with joy and gratitude. She was now free to embrace the unfailing love that had captured her heart years earlier. She went straight into the arms of Jesus.

But God wasn't done with me. *Robin, what is your faith all about?* God gently prodded. *Is your faith just for this life, or is your faith for something much better?* It occurred to me then, that if I stubbornly refused to accept death as the victory, that I might as well stop living for God now. My faith was totally useless. On that afternoon, I realized that God's unfailing love was not just for this life, but that his love would take me safely into the next life as well. I read on in 1 Corinthians:

> For as in Adam all die, so in Christ all will be made alive. But each in his own turn: Christ, the firstfruits; then, when he

comes, those who belong to him. Then the end will come,
when he hands over the kingdom to God the Father after he
has destroyed all dominion, authority and power. For he must
reign until he has put all his enemies under his feet. That last
enemy to be destroyed is death. (1 Corinthians 15:22–26)

The truth is that the moment when we pass from life to
death is when Satan's head is truly crushed by the cross of Jesus.
At that moment, unfailing love has conquered our great enemy
and our greatest fear—death. That's why Paul could say with
such assurance,

"Where O death, is your victory?
Where, O death is your sting?"...

But thanks be to God! He gives us the victory through our
Lord Jesus Christ.
　　Therefore, my dear brothers, stand firm. Let nothing move
you. Always give yourselves fully to the word of the Lord,
because you know that your labor in the Lord is not in vain.
(1 Corinthians 15:55, 57–58)

Terri's death gave me a precious gift. Through Terri, I
learned that death wasn't the worst thing that could happen to
me. Rather it is the ultimate victory of my faith. And that victory gives me the courage to stand firm. It gives me the heart to
continue to love. It gives me the faith to be vulnerable. It gives
me the perseverance to keep laboring in the Lord and to know
that no matter what happens, my work is not in vain. And it
allows me to walk through the valley of death and see God's presence all around me.

But Terri's death didn't just bear fruit in my life. She had
often said that if it took her passing for their oldest son Brad to
become a Christian, that would be her desire. Just three months
after Terri's death on Father's Day 2003, Brad, twenty years old,
was baptized into Christ.

John generously passed along words from the last letter Terri wrote (expressing gratitude to their church for all the ways they had been served, as well as giving her perspective on death) not knowing that it would be only a few months before she would unexpectedly pass into the next life:

> Cancer has given our family the gift of perspective...knowing what is important in life; having a relationship with God, being able to share it with others, helping each other reaching the goal of our faith and building relationships that will truly last an eternity. When John and I turned 30, we realized that the things that we were pursuing in life were nice but that there was a void in our lives. We tried to fill that void with possessions, accomplishments and selfish desires. Our eyes were opened by the Bible and we saw that we were trying to fill a round hole with a square peg. God was waiting to fill that round hole and we were added to his Kingdom on October 28, 1990, being baptized into his Kingdom for the forgiveness of our sins, receiving the gift of his Holy Spirit (filling that round hole).

> Our lives have definitely changed from that day forward as we committed to putting him first in our lives. That day has helped us endure the challenges that have come our way since then, including my cancer in August 2001 and most recently the cancer recurrence beginning in December 2002. I know that my troubles are light and momentary in comparison to the joy that awaits me in heaven.

> I've been comforted by the words of a poem that a friend of my mom wrote back in 1972 when I was 11 and my brother Ricky drowned. He was 7 years old. It goes like this:

> *Today, a little, red-headed boy—fresh from the sand piles and ice cream stands of earth—is looking with wonder at all the splendors surrounding the Throne of God. He plays by the river of life. He finds companionship with children of bygone years. He watches the saints as they prepare to glorify the Father with shouts of praise and in song.*

> *And, then he muses about that Day in God's tomorrow when families whose souls are hid in Christ, shall find grand reunions in*

*that Eternal City, and when he thinks of God's calendar—he smiles—for he knows it will not be long—safe forever in the arms of Jesus. (Joyce Nordhielm—July 4, 1972)*

I look forward to the day that I will be with Ricky again.

Terri Pillatsch

## God's Inexhaustible Love

Little did I know in dealing with Terri's death that God was preparing me for a personal crisis still ahead. Not even a full year after her death, I received the phone call from my sister in Virginia that Mom had been diagnosed with stage-four lung cancer. Through my mother's short-lived battle with cancer, I learned firsthand about God's unending love in the face of death. And perhaps I came to understand just a little better where John found his strength when his best friend left him for a better world:

> For men are not cast off
> by the LORD forever.
> Though he brings grief, he will show compassion,
> so great is his unfailing love.
> For he does willingly bring affliction
> or grief to the children of men. (Lamentations 3:31–33)

My mom's battle with lung cancer was over practically right after it began. We had counted on six months, hoped for six years, but were given just over six weeks. Since I had the most flexible career of the five remaining children, I committed myself to being with my mother as much as possible to help out my two sisters who lived there, and who both worked full-time jobs.

As a result, when I was in there (I ended up spending thirty days total, spread over four different trips), I spent a lot of time by myself sitting with Mom in hospitals. As she began to cycle downward, the time got progressively harder, and I had to dig deep spiritually to find my bearings.

But the real story of God's intervention begins just a little over a week before Mom died. I had flown in to Virginia where she had been transferred to a new hospital in a city forty-five minutes away from her home. Dave and I had made a difficult decision to ask Mom to come to live with us as soon as she was well enough.

Dave was home converting a small area that was part of our family room into a temporary bedroom for my mother until we could find a house better suited to her recovery. We were amazed when another couple, hearing of our plight, offered to switch houses with us indefinitely, feeling their house might be better for Mom's recovery.

## Homes, Mothers, Daughters

When I arrived, I booked a hotel room. By the second night, I realized that coming back to this tiny room after being at my mom's bedside all day was depressing. Needing fellowship, I decided to try to find the couple who had first introduced the Bible to me when I was a teenager—Michael and Karyn. The last time I was back home I had heard that they were now leading a small church in the same city where my mother was in the hospital. Remarkably, that church turned out to be five minutes from my hotel.

The next Sunday I attended the church, and when I was ushered to a seat right beside Karyn, she was both stunned and overjoyed. We hadn't seen each other for twenty-six years! After the service, she urgently pleaded with me to stay at her house (Acts 16:15). It turned out that she was now a trained counselor (God's gracious provision) who would become my ear during the tough week ahead.

My sudden appearance also had made a big statement to her faith. On that very Sunday, she had awakened mourning the rift she was currently having with her adopted daughter. And without any notice, another woman she had studied the Bible with long ago and I showed up and sat on each side of her. Suddenly she realized she had many daughters. She later told me that this was one of the most powerful moments of her life, testifying to God's love for her in a very personal way.

Staying at her house was incredible—they gave me a guest suite in their gorgeous Colonial home. Every night I came back, Karyn and I took long walks, catching up, talking about my mom, our mutual faith, and the turns each of our lives had taken. She was the healing balm I needed. I was the statement of God's love she needed. We discovered we were kindred souls reunited. The truth of Jesus' statement made more than 2000 years ago came alive in a new and real way to both of us:

> "I tell you the truth," Jesus said to them, "no one who has left home or wife or brothers or parents or children for the sake of the kingdom of God will fail to receive many times as much in this age and, in the age to come, eternal life." (Luke 18:29–30)

## Send in the Angels

At the hospital my mom was taking a distressing turn for the worse. Most of her time was spent either having radiation treatments or sleeping, since she was on morphine. When she was awake, she was often queasy, in pain or incoherent. When she was asleep, I took the opportunity to pray and sing over her often, asking God to send his angels to surround us in the hospital. My first sign of angels came in the form of gracious social workers and nurses who literally wrapped their arms around me.

When my sister had died years earlier, I hadn't been able to share my grief with anyone. I was embarrassed and afraid to let anyone in. This time, by God's grace, he allowed me to let others, even kind strangers, in on the roller coaster of emotions I was riding. Likewise, my friends seemed to be able to decipher the moments I would steal away, go outside and turn on my cell phone, and would call me with encouragement right when I needed it most.

Thankfully, a simple medication change brought Mom back to her right mind and what turned out to be her last good day. It was on this day that the doctor explained to my mother that she wasn't going to get better, and that if anything at all went wrong with her health, her body wouldn't be strong enough to combat it, and that she could end up on life support. She made it clear that wasn't what she wanted. She also made the final decision to move to Chicago to fight the cancer. After weeping into my shoulder, she turned to the doctor and said, "You know, there is one bright spot for me. I'll be back with my daughter Jennifer again."

The doctor later told me I should get my mom back to Chicago as soon as possible. Much to her delight, the doctor said she could go home to prepare. I took her home, got her extensive list of medications and caught a flight back to Chicago to prepare for her. She was happy to be home and fell into a deep sleep on the couch. My brother flew in from Indiana to help pack her and fly with her to our house.

I had only been home for a little over twenty-four hours when I started getting calls. Mom was back in pain and crying for help. The next day my sister called in a panic. She had come over to find Mom in a total state of decline. Soon, Mom was in an ambulance on the way to the hospital. When they got her there, they discovered that the radiation on her hip had punctured her colon. The doctor said the surgery required to repair her colon would kill her (and would be a violation of his Hippocratic Oath), but he would do it if we insisted.

My youngest sister, a nurse, called me weeping. She had to tell the doctor what to do. I told her of Mom's desire not to be put on life support. All of the children agreed that the answer was obvious, but devastating. I made plans to fly back that night. My brother from Philadelphia drove in so we could all be there.

## Ministering Servants

The next day, the watching and waiting began. Someone called and talked with my sister. Struggling with her own grief, this person questioned our decision to, in so many words "sit back and let Mom die." My sister was devastated. We went to a waiting room to talk. I was trying to reassure my sister that we had done the only thing we could. I wanted to comfort her, but I sensed she needed something that I couldn't give her.

It was about that time that we noticed a TV high up in the corner. A radiant woman came on the screen and started talking. She said, "There are some of you out there tonight who are struggling, who are facing difficult decisions. You are full of pain and you don't know where to turn. This song is for you." Then she started singing an amazing song about Jesus being the answer and how God cares about everything in our lives. My sister later said it was the most beautiful thing she had ever heard.

At the end we sat for a moment in stunned awe. We noticed that an extra-large, dark-skinned black man in a bright red shirt was trying to get our attention from the other side of the room. "Excuse me," he said in a kind voice. We hadn't even noticed that we had company in the room. He turned to my sister, "Excuse me, but I couldn't help but overhear what you were saying." He went on to tell her, "That song was a gift for this very moment, given to you by God. He wants you to know that he's taking care of everything. That he loves you. That everything is going to be okay. He wants you to give it to him. To trust him."

It didn't occur to me until much later, that I might have witnessed a message from an angel (Hebrews 1:14).

## Singing Mom Out

We had some blood tests done, confirming the doctor's warning that Mom would have never survived the surgery. All they could do was keep her unconscious so that she wasn't in pain. We settled in to wait. Every day I prayed for a little time alone with my mother. And every day, God granted my wish. I had my quiet times with her, prayed over her, sang songs to her, and even confessed her sins as I knew them.

Weeks after she had discovered that she had cancer, she asked me how to get things right with God. She had been baptized years ago, but had fallen away. She wanted to be restored. We read from a beautiful book explaining the way God seeks out a personal relationship with us. She was moved and told me that she had never seen God that way before.

Now, I was realizing that there would be no more opportunities. The doctor said that although Mom was unconscious, she could most likely hear everything we said, so I talked to her more about preparing to meet God. My heart's desire was to sing her out of this life, but the doctors had no idea when it would happen. I spent the night with my mother that Saturday night, and again worshipped over her in the watches of the night.

The next morning I headed to Mom's house to get ready for church. At church, I asked if I could take a songbook with me. I had planned on waiting until the evening to head back to the hospital, but I felt an urgency to get back to my mother.

When I arrived there, my brother and dad were there. My brother saw the songbook and asked if I'd like to sing for a while. We sat and sang for about an hour. Then I looked at Mom and noticed her breaths were getting further apart. The nurse came in and said it was her time. A few breaths later she was gone. God had granted my one parting wish, and my mother was sung out of this life, leaving with a little sigh and a smile.

My mom had been a nanny for many years to a little boy named David, or "little David" as she called him. Little David was in fifth grade now, and was devastated about my mother dying. He came to see her at the hospital, and his mom brought food for us. When my mom died on Sunday, his mother made the decision to wait until Monday afternoon to tell him, after he had a big test at school. On Monday morning, before he knew she had died, he woke up and told his mother he had dreamed about "Nana." He said that Nana had been talking to him when Jesus walked up and held out his hand. Nana took Jesus' hand and they walked away together.

Likewise, my teenage son Caleb was lying in bed on Sunday afternoon thinking about his grandma, when a feeling of peace washed over him. A couple of minutes later, my husband Dave walked in and told him his grandmother had died.

## Music in the Night

Because of the time frame, we decided to move quickly to have Mom's funeral. So we had to make a lot of decisions quickly. God graciously moved the hearts of two of my best friends to make the decision to fly in to support me. Although they independently decided to come from two different cities, they arrived within an hour of each other and were delivered to my doorstep together like a giant kiss from God.

Another dear friend, who we had supported through his own battle with cancer, volunteered to drive Dave and the kids all the way from Chicago to Virginia for the funeral. These friends and servants of God protected me, pulled me away when I needed it, helped me laugh a little and encouraged me to take time to grieve (1 John 3:16–20).

The morning of the funeral, I still had no music for the ceremony. It was on my heart to find the Natalie Grant song my sister and I had heard at the hospital. I ran to a Christian bookstore just four hours before the funeral. Although I couldn't find that particular song, I found four others by Natalie Grant that I knew were perfect.

When I was ready to check out, I told the cashier that the CD was for my mother's funeral. She looked me in the eye and without hesitation asked if she could pray with me. I was surprised, but quickly agreed. She then lightly touched my shoulder saying a prayer that amazed me—talking about how God was sending me a message that my mom was fine, that he had her, and that I shouldn't worry. Another ministering angel.

A couple of days after Mom's funeral, we were going through her things when we found her journal. One of the last entries was this quote:

> And the night shall be filled with music,
>    and the cares that infest the day
> shall fold their tents, like the Arabs,
>    and as silently steal away.
>                               —Henry Wadsworth Longfellow

It struck me that Mom had undoubtedly written this down after she found out she had cancer. Undoubtedly, although she reached the night of her life fraught with pain, that night was also filled with sweet music. God was singing over her and me. Leaving that experience, I knew my faith would never be the same—God had showed himself and his unfailing love to me and my family in a way that would stand forever as part of our family heritage.

## Secure in Heart

> The LORD, the King of Israel is with you;
>    never again will you fear any harm.
> On that day they will say to Jerusalem,
>    "Do not fear, O Zion;
>    do not let your hands hang limp,
> The LORD your God is with you,
>    he is mighty to save.
> He will take great delight in you,
>    he will quiet you with his love,
>    he will rejoice over you with singing."
> (Zephaniah 3:15b–17)

Before we finish this journey, I want to thank you for walking with me. Certainly, as God has led me through the questions that insecurity poses, my battles have only intensified. I've seen firsthand new depths of my insecurity that I hadn't come to grips with. Along with every chapter have come new tests—tests that have left me perplexed at times. There have been times when I've sat down to the computer screen only to be greeted by questions that I thought I had answered, but now knew with certainty that I hadn't.

At times, I had to look up to heaven and ask God, "You think this is amusing, don't you?" I've had to make a decision over and over again to trust, to share my heart and to be vulnerable before the group of women who convened in my home every Sunday for "Soup and Security."

Every other week, I've made that decision again as I ventured on the hour drive to the group I lead for women who are battling and overcoming codependency. Would I be able to lead in humility, or would I revert to old habits of trying to lead in strength rather than through weakness? With God's help, I was able to keep opening up and laying my struggles before them.

Bottom line, the more I delved into writing the book, the more tests and struggles seemed to come my way. Now I think I can tell you with great conviction why there are so few books on insecurity!

But I also hope you understand that we haven't walked alone. The God of comfort has been with us, teaching us to trust him through his divine nature and his promises. He has gently nudged you and me to look at the yet unplowed ground in our hearts, and let him come in and begin breaking up the soil so that it can receive seeds of faith planted through his word.

This isn't a gift that is meant for us alone. Security of heart is something that we can help each other with. It's a gift that we are meant to pass on to others.

The first step is refusing to be ashamed of our insecurities. It's not only admitting them to ourselves and to God, but then taking the brave step of letting other women in on our battles. As you do just that, I think you'll find what I've found—hope, encouragement, faith and the sure knowledge that you're never alone in your battles. But most of all, as a woman, you'll learn how to carry out your calling of loving others through life, and even through death, equipped by your knowledge of God's unfailing love:

> Sow for yourselves righteousness,
>     reap the fruit of unfailing love,
> and break up your unplowed ground;
>     for it is time to seek the LORD,
> until he comes
>     and showers righteousness on you. (Hosea 10:12)

## SECURE LOVE: THE ONE TRUE TREASURE
### *Personal Study Guide & Life Application*

The starting point for true security is understanding God's unfailing love and the ways that his love transcends life and death. Paul, Abraham, Stephen, Mary Magdalene and Jesus himself all knew that God's unfailing love was the one true treasure.

*Choose the Bible character whose story reminded you the most of yourself. Then, using his or her story for inspiration, write the story of your journey to find security through God's unfailing love. Talk about the false securities you've renounced, what you've come to know about God, and where you are in the journey.*

# A Note from Dave

It has been my privilege to walk alongside Robin for the past twenty-seven years. I have watched in wonder as God has molded her character and given her the breadth of life experience she needed to write *Secure in Heart.*

Robin has graciously endured test after test without becoming cynical or hardened in spirit. Her reliance on God has deepened as she has constantly cried out to him, leaving a trail of tears along every nearby bike path and a puddle of tears underneath our elliptical trainer. Unfortunately, many of Robin's tears have come as the result of my sin. The devastation of addiction has darkened our path and at times has threatened to destroy all the good gifts that God has given us.

I have given Robin my full permission to share whatever she felt necessary to communicate clearly our struggles and victories. My prayer is that her openness will give others hope and possibly lead others to seek help earlier than we did. I am so proud of Robin and the way she has persevered to make *Secure in Heart* become a reality in life and in print. I have been blessed as a result, and I am convinced that thousands of women (and men) will also be blessed by God through this book.

—David Weidner
September 2006

# Starting a Soup and Security Group

A Soup and Security group is a place where this book really comes alive. By gathering once a week with other women to share a meal and share in each other's battles, you can work together to fight for a secure life, while building lasting relationships.

The concept is simple. The facilitator should start the group with a prayer, then allow ten or fifteen minutes for everyone to fill their bowl (or plate) with food. After everyone has a seat, starting with the facilitator, each participant takes a turn reading out loud through part of the book. At the end of each section, pause for discussion. Then the person to the left picks up the reading. Reading out loud from the book is powerful because it helps you focus together on the same concepts. Then as you hear each other's responses, you find yourself applying what you are reading to your own life. Allow around ninety minutes from start to finish.

These five S's are key to a successful Soup and Security Group: Spirit, Soup, Safe Haven, Sharing and Support.

## Spirit
Soup and Security provides a time for God's Holy Spirit to work. Before starting, pray specifically for each of your hearts and your response to the Spirit's prompting.

## Soup
Having a meal together bonds women. In our group our mainstay was soup, but as the weather warmed up, we substituted with Salad and Security. Our final party at the end was a Steak and Security meeting. It makes the meetings memorable and catchy.

**Safe Haven**

It is important to create an environment where women feel safe to open up and share their battles. What matters is that when you meet together, you are building each other up and helping each other fight the battle against insecurity. You can do this by encouraging everyone to keep anything that is discussed within the group confidential.

**Sharing**

This is an important part of the process. Make sure that everyone gets a chance to share what's on their heart as they are ready. By opening up and talking about what you read and how it affects your life, you'll begin to engage with one another in the battle for a secure life. After a person shares, the facilitator simply says, "Thank you for sharing." This is not a time for members to try to fix one another's problems. It is simply a time to be able to share openly, without fear of what someone else might think or say.

**Support**

As you go through the book together, look for ways to offer support to one another beyond your time in Soup and Security. You can keep fighting battles together long after the group study of the book is finished.

A Soup and Security group is a great opportunity to invite your friends, family members or other women you know to share your lives with them. Here are what some of the first participants in Soup and Security had to say about their experience:

> *"It was a safe haven; I looked forward to it, and the group setting helped me to persevere and apply the truths of the book to my life. Up to that point I had usually quit reading a book somewhere in the middle."*

> *"It was amazing and encouraging to discover that insecurity is not just my battle. There were women here going through*

*the exact same things that I was. It was useful to take the book and apply it. Now I have been able to go through some of the same kind of circumstances that made me insecure in the past and come out in a better place."*

*"It's taught me to recognize there is an enemy, Satan's voice, and what he is saying and how can I train my mind against it."*

*"Every week I looked forward to Soup and Security. It was by far my favorite time of the week. I came away encouraged, inspired and convicted."*